St. Louis 365
by Joe Sonderman

ISBN   0-9708422-3-6

Printed in the United States of America

Published and distributed by:

Stellar Press
634 N. Grand Boulevard, Suite 10 C
St. Louis, Missouri 63103
877-572-8835 (toll-free)
www.BooksOnStLouis.com
e-mail: info@BooksOnStLouis.com

Dedication

For Lorraine, Cathy and Kim

Acknowledgements

Thanks to Kimberly Powell, for her hard work and for putting up with me every day. To "Uncle Bob" Fulstone and Tori Lyons, for believing in me when few others did. To Bo Sanders and Chris Teague for helping with the editing and for being damn great people to work with. Randi Naughton, for giving me courage to stand up and convincing me to keep trying. And to John Pertzborn, when he said it was good, I believed it for the first time. To Mike McCann, who gave me the idea to put things in a database and Kevin McCarthy, who got it started. To Ken Christian, for helping a dream come true. To Colleen Carlton for her creativity. To Michael Wallis, whose brilliant prose led me to Route 66. To Bob Waldmire, Ted Drewes, Lillian Redman, Lucille Hammons and all of those along all 2,448 miles of the "Mother Road." They showed me that there is more to life than radio. To Shellee Graham, who inspired me to try to get it published. And thanks to Miss Lowe at Russell School and Miss Richey at West.

St. Louis 365
Intriguing Events from Each Day of the Year

Table of Contents

Introduction 1

January 3

February 25

March 45

April 67

May 89

June 111

July 131

August 153

September 175

October 197

November 219

December 241

Bibliography 263

Introduction

Hazelwood West, Class of 1980. That should answer your first question.

This book started as a collection of dates. While at KLOU, I found myself drawn to all things '50s and '60s. I wanted to know more about St. Louis during the rock and roll era. I found some of those old "Through the Years" clippings from the old *Globe-Democrat*, and began using some of them on the air. The more I dug, the more interesting it became. I spent hours at the City Library, pouring over microfilm, looking at those old *Globe-Democrat* columns. I thought I was a hopeless nerd. My dear morning show partner, Randi Naughton convinced me I had something worthwhile.

When I came to work for Metro Networks, we began sending out the "Day in St. Louis History" to the affiliate stations daily. Occasionally, I would hear an item or two used on the air. Randi took them over to John Pertzborn at Channel Two and they began using them. I was thrilled. Maybe this was interesting! I half-heartedly shopped it to a couple of local publishers, but they showed no interest. Randi wrote a book of her own, and she encouraged me to contact Ken Christian at Stellar Press. So here we are.

This is not a scholarly work. (No footnotes!) It is intended as a handy reference to start or settle arguments, or drive your co-workers crazy. I don't claim to be anything other than a St. Louisan with an interest in his hometown. I could never measure up to true historians like Robert Archibald, Father William Faherty or James Neal Primm.

I have just collected the dates. I tend to write in broadcast style, because that's how this whole thing started. I also tend to write as someone who only had a little college after leaving West, and spent most of that time hanging around the Flo Valley radio station. My higher education consisted of Culture Club and Stray Cats records. So English majors may find something to quibble about.

In the interest of brevity, I had to condense, and leave some things out that a true historian might find critical. I did the best I could to sum it up. Some sources give more than one date for events and much local history comes from personal recollections, which can be hazy. When possible, I tried to sort it out by going to the newspaper morgue. Any errors are probably my fault.

Inside, you won't find lengthy treatises, but you will find things you didn't know about the sports teams, streets, politicians, landmarks and events that make St. Louis such a special city. I leave the dry stuff to the academics; I want you to have fun and be proud to be from St. Louis! By the way, where did you go to high school?

- Joe Sonderman, 2002

JANUARY

January 1

1861 The last slave auction in St. Louis took place on the steps of the Old Courthouse. A crowd of about 2,000 abolitionists showed up to thwart the auctioneer. They refused to bid any higher than eight dollars over two hours for a "boy" valued at $800 to $1,000. The auctioneer gave up and went home.

1914 St. Louisans Tom Benoist and Tony Janus began the world's first passenger airline service. The St. Petersburg-Tampa Airboat Line, Passenger and Express Service flew across Tampa Bay between the two cities. Benoist founded the first aeronautical supply company in the United States in St. Louis in 1908. He was the first St. Louisan to pilot an airplane.

1922 One of the most famous hotels in St. Louis closed forever. The first Planter's Hotel opened at Fourth and Pine in 1841. It hosted the great names of the day, including Charles Dickens. A new ten-story building was built in 1894. The building gave way to offices and shops after 1922, becoming known as the Cotton Belt Building. That building was torn down in 1976 to make room for the Boatmen's Tower.

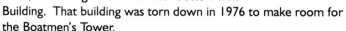

1924 Gussie Busch joined the Anheuser-Busch Brewery. Legend has it that he started by sweeping floors. Within four months, he was named general superintendent. Gussie became one of the most beloved figures in St. Louis. He saw the brewery through prohibition, mainly by selling yeast, glucose corn sugar and other products.

1933 The new Watson Road was finished from the St. Louis city limits west to Gray Summit. The new road was designated to carry City Route 66 traffic to Lindbergh and Route 66 between Lindbergh and Gray Summit. Prior to that date, Manchester Road had carried Route 66 traffic west of the city.

2000 The millennium arrived without a hitch, as police, emergency agencies and businesses that rely on computers stood by in case any Y2K bugs materialized. Connor Rogers was the first local baby born in the new millennium, arriving ten seconds after midnight at St. John's Mercy Medical Center in Creve Couer.

January 2

1901 Joseph Folk took office as the new St. Louis Circuit Attorney. Elected with the help of city "Boss" Ed Butler, Folk showed his gratitude by bringing down Butler and the "boodlers" who ran the city through bribery and fraud. Folk's crusade won him the admiration of the entire state. In 1904, he was elected as the youngest governor in state history.

1930 Colonel Charles Lindbergh said a new airport should be built closer to downtown. He said it was essential if St. Louis was to retain its position as a leader in commercial aviation. Lindbergh said a new airport should be planned "before it is too late."

1948 The largest crowd to see a Billikens game to that date saw the Bills win their seventh straight. A crowd of 11,216 packed Kiel as the Bills, led by "Easy Ed" McCauley defeated defending NCAA champions, Holy Cross.

1951 The St. Louis County Council met for the first time. Prior that date, the County Court had been the governing body of the county. It had been in place since November, 1804.

1986 Bill Veeck died at the age of 71. The colorful owner of three major league teams, he is best remembered for his stunts as owner of the St. Louis Browns. The greatest came in 1944, when he sent a midget up to bat. Eddie Gaedel walked on four straight. The major leagues promptly banned midgets.

1836 Anthony Edward Faust was born in Prussia. In 1862, he opened a small restaurant at Broadway and Chouteau. It became so famous, he was forced to open a larger one at Broadway and Elm. "Faust's," also known as "Tony's," became the gathering place for the elite. In 1878, it became the first building in St. Louis to be lit by electricity. Faust's closed in 1916.

1902 Plans by the Police Board to confine "The Social Evil Element" to one part of town during the World's Fair were under fire by residents of the near south side neighborhood chosen for the district. The residents said it was the duty of the police to rid the city of such women, not to move them in among respectable people.

1909 The city excise commissioner was ordering that all paintings in saloons be taken down or covered up. State law prohibited saloons from featuring works of art, music, entertainment or any other special feature that might inspire patrons to linger.

1923 A mass meeting was planned by Judge Henry Priest to gather public input on the the New Years raid by federal prohibition agents at the Chase Hotel. The raid ended in a riot, with two men shot and the agents fleeing for their lives as the fashionable diners hurled chairs and dinnerware. The judge said blanket search warrants carried by the agents may have been illegal.

1957 TWA became the first airline to offer passengers freshly-brewed coffee in flight. Western Air Express, which later became TWA, was the first airline with flight attendants and in-flight meal service. In 1961, TWA would also become the first airline to offer in-flight movies.

1967 St. Louis basketball fans were stunned to learn that Ben Kerner, the owner of the Hawks, was putting the team up for sale. Kerner cited his failing health, and said he hoped to find a St. Louis buyer to keep the team here.

January 4

1884 The mercury plunged to -26°, the lowest official reading ever recorded here. That terrible night, 26 Sisters of Notre Dame died in a fire at their convent in Belleville. The Old St. Nicholas Hotel, at Fourth and Morgan (now Delmar) burned in a spectacular fire. It had recently been converted to a warehouse, so no lives were lost.

1926 KMOX began regular programming, ending experimental and practice broadcasts. The station signed on at 9:40 each morning, with grain reports every one-half hour. The "popular noontime organ recitals" by Arthur L. Utt would continue. Between 4 and 5 p.m., the station would present short talks on "problems peculiar to the housewife."

1926 Thousands of people, including Mayor Victor Miller, greeted the "Jack Daniels Special" as it made a stop at Union Station. The train was carrying eleven prominent St. Louisans from their trials in Indiana to prison in Leavenworth. They were convicted in a scheme to siphon thousands of gallons of whisky from the Jack Daniels Distillery here. Those convicted included a former circuit clerk, a deputy sheriff and the St. Louis Democratic Ward Leader. Convictions against several other politicians, including a State Senator, had been thrown out.

1942 Cardinal great Rogers Hornsby was elected to the Baseball Hall of Fame. Hornsby played for the Cardinals from 1915 to 1926 and again in 1933. Hornsby batted over .400 three times and set a record by batting .424 in 1924. His lifetime batting average ranks second behind Ty Cobb.

1960 The last Grand Avenue street car made its run, just prior to demolition of the landmark old Grand viaduct over the Mill Creek railyards. That left just four street car lines still in operation. The Public Service Company was still running street cars on the Wellston, Hodiamont, Delmar and University City lines.

January 5

1818 Bishop Louis DuBourg arrived in St. Louis, to take over the newly-created diocese of Louisiana and the Floridas. Within days, DuBourg put plans in motion to replace the old log church with a new cathedral.

1905 The *Globe-Democrat* reported that Louisiana Purchase Exposition Employees had discovered a new use for the hill in front of the Palace of Fine Arts. Now cleared of trees, "Art Hill" made a perfect toboggan slope.

1928 The Board of Aldermen approved a bill providing for the city to acquire the flying field developed by Albert Bond Lambert at his own cost. The bill called for the city to lease the field for $1 a year, and eventually purchase it. A million dollar bond issue would be submitted to the voters for improvements.

1931 The most prominent structure opened in the "Hooverville" shanty town that sprang up on the riverfront beneath the Free Bridge. The "Welcome Inn" at the foot of Chouteau Street served as the main distribution point for charity. More than 2,200 meals per day were served there.

1994 The new Clark Bridge between Alton and St. Charles County was opened. The $118-million structure replaced the treacherous, narrow old span, considered one of the worst on a U.S. highway.

January 6

1877 Joe Battin was one of the first contract holdouts in St. Louis baseball history. J. Battin would not sign with the Browns because of a new National League policy charging the players $30 for their uniforms and deducting 50¢ per day from their salaries for meals.

1912 The magnificent new Main Library on Olive opened. Andrew Carnegie had donated $1 million for the library, with the stipulation that the city provide $150,000 annually for maintenance.

1957 The Land Clearance for Redevelopment Authority unveiled plans for the redevelopment of the Mill Creek Valley. The plans called for levelling 460 acres, bounded by Grand, 20th, Olive and the railyards. Industrial and residential projects would rise on the site, to be joined by an expanded St. Louis University Campus.

1972 Blues coach Al Arbour, along with players John Arbour, Phil Roberto and Floyd Thompson, were hauled off to jail after a riot at the Spectrum in Philadelphia. Bob Plager and other players climbed into the stands to brawl with fans who had dumped a beer on the coach. Four fans were hurt. Al Arbour required 12 stitches, John Arbour ended up with 40.

1994 The Los Angeles Rams announced they planned to terminate their lease in Los Angeles and were searching for a new home.

January 7

1913 Cardinal great Johnny Mize was born in Demerest, Georgia. He held the all-time single season Cardinal record for home runs until Mark McGwire came along. "The Big Cat" was a ten time All Star. He was elected to the Hall of Fame in 1981.

1931 Mayor R.C. Miller ordered construction of a new Municipal Auditorium to provide work for unemployment relief. The Municipal Auditorium opened in 1932. It would later be renamed for former Mayor Henry Kiel. The convention hall was torn down to make room for the new Kiel Center in 1992. The adjacent opera house still stands.

1959 The *Globe-Democrat* reported on a post-war trend. Eleven shopping centers were under construction or on the drawing board in the St. Louis area. Construction was underway on Ballwin Plaza. Preparations were underway to break ground on Grandview Plaza, at 66 and Washington in Florissant. A $12-million shopping center was being planned at 66 and Lindbergh in Hazelwood.

1970 A cold snap caused the Arch to shrink by three inches. Workers adjusting interior cables noticed the difference. Engineers reassured everyone that the summer heat would restore the missing three inches.

1985 Cards great Lou Brock was elected to the Baseball Hall of Fame. Brock led the Cardinals to three pennants, and stole a record 118 bases in 1974. He finished his career with over 3,000 hits and a record lifetime 938 steals. (Both of his stolen base records have since been eclipsed) Pitcher Hoyt Wilhelm was also named to the hall that day. He spent some time with the Cardinals in the late 1950's.

January 8

1815 The British were defeated at the Battle of New Orleans, which gave St. Louis its first millionaire. John Mullanphy learned of the peace treaty and arrived in New Orleans two days before the news got there. He bought up all the cotton that couldn't be shipped because of the war, and re-sold it at a huge profit. Mullanphy became a great philanthropist.

1894 The birthday of Ralston Purina. William H. Danforth incorporated the Robinson-Danforth Commission Company. The 1896 tornado wiped out his building. But Danforth borrowed $10,000 to build a new plant at Eighth and Gratiot. The name was changed to Ralston Purina in 1902. Nestle bought the firm in 2001.

1952 Frankie Baker died in a Portland, Oregon mental institution. She claimed to be the "Frankie" who shot her lover "Johnny" at 22 Targee Street on October 15, 1899. The shooting was immortalized in the song "Frankie and Johnny." The Savvis Center stands on the Targee Street site today.

1993 Carl Icahn resigned as chairman of TWA, relinquishing all control and interest in the airline. The direction of the bankrupt airline was placed in the hands of a two-man management committee, appointed by employees, the unions and TWA's creditors. Icahn had taken the airline private in 1988. The move put $469 million in his pocket, but left the airline saddled with $539 million in debt.

2002 Cardinal great Ozzie Smith was elected to the baseball Hall of Fame. That night, he carried the Olympic Torch into Keiner Plaza. Smith won 13 consecutive Gold Gloves at shortstop. He will be best remembered for his home run that won Game Five of the National League Championship Series in 1985.

January 9

1849 The first death from cholera in 1849 was reported here. Six people died in January, 22 died in February, 78 in March and 126 in April. By June, 86 people were dying every day. By Mid-August, 7,000 people, or about 1/10 of the population of the city, had died.

1931 The St. Louis Police Board was selling 20 of the last 30 horses from the Mounted Patrol District in Forest Park. The board said horses were too slow to fight modern crime. The few remaining horses would patrol Commerce Row, where they could easily thread their way through the truck traffic.

1974 An aldermanic committee approved a proposal to breathe new life into the bankrupt and vacant Spanish Pavilion downtown. They okayed a plan by developer Donald Breckenridge to build a high-rise luxury hotel atop the pavilion. The hotel is now the Marriott. Mayor A.J. Cervantes brought the pavilion here from the New York World's Fair in 1965.

1975 The *Globe-Democrat* profiled the young voice of the St. Louis Spirits basketball team. Twenty-two-year-old Bob Costas was broadcasting the games on KMOX Radio and KPLR-TV. Costas says he began doing play-by-play for his own basement basketball games at the age of six.

1978 It snowed in St. Louis. That's not a big deal, except that it marked the start of 71 days in a row with snow on the ground here. That's the local record.

1984 Disaster was narrowly averted when a DC-3 cargo plane crashed on an embankment in Bridgeton, just yards from the St. James Subdivision and only a few feet from I-70. The pilot died a few days later. A worker at the airport had put jet fuel in the propeller-driven aircraft.

January 10

1899 Ninety delegates from the states of the Louisiana Purchase met here to discuss an exhibition to mark the anniversary of the purchase. They voted in favor of holding the Louisiana Purchase Exposition in St. Louis in 1903. (The date was later pushed back a year)

1928 A jury returned a verdict in favor of the Cardinals in a lawsuit by a fan whose nose was broken by a homerun off the bat of "Sunny" Jim Bottomley. In his deposition, the Cardinals first-baseman admitted that he was  trying to hit a home run, but denied selecting which fan it would hit.

1945 Ozark Airlines began service, flying five-seater planes on a triangular route between St. Louis, Springfield, and Kansas City. H.D. Hamilton, who ran a bus line in the Ozarks, founded the airline. The green and white planes were a familiar sight to St. Louisans until TWA bought out Ozark in 1986.

1962 A dust fire led to an explosion and a huge blaze at the landmark Purina Chow plant at Checkerboard Square. The fire burned out of control for over 20 hours. Two workers died, 41 were hurt, and a fire captain died of a heart attack. It was seven below zero that day. That same day, off-duty firefighters had to be called in to fight a five-alarm fire at the historic Music and Arts Building in Gaslight Square. and a three-alarm fire at the "absolutely fireproof" Ambassador Hotel.

2001 After 75 years, TWA was about to fly into history. CEO William Compton announced that TWA had filed for bankruptcy and reached an agreement with American Airlines. American would acquire substantially all of TWA's assets for $500 million in cash. Compton said the deal would allow the legacy of TWA to continue, while protecting the jobs of TWA employees.

January 11

1903 A St. Louis man, who was seriously injured when the horse pulling his carriage was startled by a car and bolted, was suing the driver for $1,500 in damages. He said the "diabolical" machine made "unearthly noises that would have knocked an equestrian statue off its pedestal."

1944 James H. Howard of St. Louis became the first ace in both theatres. He first flew with the Flying Tigers in China, designing the famous shark's nose logo on their planes. On this date, he single-handedly fought off 30 German fighters headed for a formation of B-17's. He shot down six. Only only one other pilot in

World War II, Butch O'Hare, also of St. Louis, matched the record of six kills in one day.

1963 The first stainless steel section to be used in the construction of the Arch arrived in St. Louis. Each sheet was 12-feet high, three-feet wide and 54-feet long. When three sheets were welded together, they would form a triangular section. One steel section on each leg was expected to go up each week.

1981 Eleven children were killed in a house fire in the 1700 block of Cottage Avenue in East St. Louis. Police said the mother left the kids alone to go for a ride with her boyfriend. It was the deadliest fire in the St. Louis area since 18 residents were killed at a nursing home in Hillsboro in October, 1952.

1991 St. Louis County Police Officer Joanne Liscombe was fatally shot in North County while answering a domestic call. She was the first county officer to be murdered in the line of duty. Dennis Blackman, who lived near the scene, was convicted of the crime and sentenced to life in prison.

January 12

1789 Bishop Joseph Rosati was born in Naples, Italy. He was the first bishop of the Diocese of St. Louis, created in 1826. Rosati opened the first hospital west of the Mississippi in 1828. He started St. Louis College, the foundation of Washington University, and began the work on a "new" cathedral.

1945 Health Commissioner Doctor Joseph Bredeck endorsed a federal government order to limit building temperatures to 68 degrees to save energy for the war effort. He recommended wearing warmer clothes, especially for girls. The doctor said, they "don't wear clothes enough to dust a fiddle with anyway."

1957 Dick Miller, head of an Indianapolis promotional firm, announced plans for a 48-lane bowling alley next the the Arena. He said the "Arena Bowl" would be the largest ever built in St. Louis. Twenty-four more lanes were added after the 1959 tornado destroyed the Arena Roller Rink.

1960 Highway officials unveiled the route for a new expressway, to connect U.S. Highway 66 at Sylvan Beach with downtown St. Louis. The planners chose a controversial route through Webster Groves and "The Hill" neighborhood for what would become I-44.

1997 Steve Fossett took off from Busch Stadium aboard his balloon "Solo Spirit." Fossett was attempting to make the world's first solo around-the-world flight in a balloon. Denied permission to fly over Libya, he ran short on fuel and had to ditch in India. The flight set a distance record. Fossett would finally make it on his 6th attempt in July, 2002.

January 13

1927 Airmail pilot Charles Lindbergh made the first night flight over the newly-lighted St. Louis-to-Chicago Airway. The government had spent $80,000 to install 24 beacons ten miles apart. Aviation experts said the flight proved the practicality of night flying.

1951 The $11 million "Veteran's Bridge" across the Mississippi opened. At the time, the bridge was the sixth largest cantilever-type bridge in the country. It carried Route 66 traffic from 1955 until 1967. It was re-named to honor Doctor Martin Luther King Junior in 1972.

1958 A spokesman for KWK said calls to the station were running five-to-one in favor of the station's "Record Breaking Week." Most of the complaints were coming from teenagers. Deejays gave each rock and roll record a farewell spin before smashing it to bits on the air. The move was attracting national attention, inspiring Danny and the Juniors to record "Rock and Roll is Here to Stay."

1959 McDonnell Aircraft celebrated good news from NASA. The government had awarded McDonnell a $15 million contract to build the Mercury space capsules. A Mercury capsule would carry America's first man in space, Alan Shepard, on May 5, 1961.

1967 The McDonnell Aircraft Corporation announced a merger with Douglas Aircraft. James S. McDonnell started his firm in 1939 in a rented office at Lambert Field. It grew to become the largest producer of military aircraft in the world before the firm merged with Boeing in 1997.

January 14

1898 The birthday of International Shoe. Five Tennessee and Mississippi businessmen opened a wholesale house that would develop into the largest shoe manufacturing company in the world. The firm helped make St. Louis "First in Beer, First in Shoes and last in the American League." The old headquarters is now known as "Windows on Washington." The warehouse now houses the City Museum.

1928 The city of St. Louis formally acquired an airport. Mayor Miller signed a bill allowing for the leasing of Albert Bond Lambert's flying field for 18 months and its eventual purchase. The mayor said work would begin at once to transform the field into "one of the finest airdomes in the world." Lambert developed the field with his own money, then offered it to the city at cost.

1932 The Cardinals signed 19-year-old Jerome Hanna "Dizzy" Dean. "Dizzy" was regarded as the top pitching prospect in the country. He had compiled a record of 26 wins and 10 losses in the minors. Diz said he would win 20 games in 1933 and lead the Cardinals to a third straight pennant.

1959 The controversial Village of Champ was incorporated. Promoter Bill Bangert said incorporation was necessary to move forward with his grandiose plans for the village at the Mark Twain expressway (now 70) and the proposed Circumferential Expressway. (270). Bangert wanted to build a 100,000 seat stadium to host the 1964 Olympics.

1980 A car bomb killed Sophie Marie Barrera of South St. Louis. Dr. Glennon Englemann emerged as the chief suspect. The "South Side Dentist" would eventually be convicted of seven murders. He claimed to have committed 23 dating back to 1958. Englemann would marry off his ex-lovers, then conspire with them to kill the new husbands and collect the insurance money.

January 15

1902 A St. Louis woman was asking Mayor Rolla Wells for a permit that would allow her to wear trousers. She was a house painter, who claimed the skirts hindered her work. A writer said she was unlikely to win, because "only modesty, tradition and the law against wearing trousers prevented women from competing with men in all fields."

1904 Democratic leaders announced that St. Louis had been chosen as the site for the national convention in the summer. Almost immediately, hotel owners who already expected to be filled during the fair found themselves swamped with requests for rooms.

1970 St. Louis was preparing to host the NHL All-Star game. Canadiens coach Claude Ruel was upset with Arena organist Norm Kramer. Ruell said Kramer stirred up the crowd, resulting in a one goal advantage for the Blues. Complaints from other coaches would result in the NHL allowing music only during stoppages in play.

1981 Bob Gibson became only the 11th player in Major League history to be elected to the Hall of Fame in his first year of eligibility. Gibson won 251 games for the Cardinals, leading them to three pennants and two World Series titles.

1988 Big Red owner Bill Bidwell formally announced that the team was moving to Phoenix. Quarterback Neil Lomax said he was pleased. Lomax griped that Fredbird, the baseball Cardinals mascot, had more endorsement deals than the Big Red Quarterback.

January 16

1911 Cardinal great, Jerome Hannah "Dizzy" Dean was born. He pitched for the Cards from 1930 to 1937. He won 120 games in his first five seasons, before his career was cut short by injury. After he retired in 1941, Ol' Diz became a sportscaster here, admired by fans and loathed by English teachers for his colorful language.

1920 The Lemp Brewery closed its doors, a victim of prohibition. At least 20 breweries were operating in St. Louis in 1919. Only 8 reopened after the repeal of prohibition. The Lemp complex would later be sold for just eight cents on the dollar.

1970 Curt Flood filed suit in New York Federal Court to have baseball's reserve clause overturned. The Cardinals had traded him to the Phillies, but Flood refused to report. Flood sat out the entire 1970 season and lost his case in the Supreme Court. But his case is seen as a turning point in baseball labor relations and the start of free-agency, clearing the way for today's salaries.

1991 Ike and Tina Turner were inducted into the Rock and Roll Hall of Fame. Ike Turner arrived in St. Louis in 1954, and his Kings of Rhythm soon ruled the local R&B scene. Tina Turner met Ike in 1959, and the 18-year-old backup singer soon became the star of the show. Ike and Tina placed 25 records on the R&B charts from 1960 to 1975, including the St. Louis wedding reception staple, "Proud Mary."

2000 The Rams played their first playoff game in St. Louis. Kurt Warner threw five touchdown passes and Tony Horne returned the second half opening kickoff for a touchdown, as the Rams beat the Vikings, 49-37.

January 17

1894 A St. Louis County mob lynched John Buckner, a black man accused of raping a white farmer's daughter. The next day, a mob attacked the County Jail. They planned to lynch a black man accused of assaulting two elderly women in Ballwin and two blacks accused of murder. The sheriff got wind of the plans and moved the prisoners to the St. Louis Jail.

1927 Tom Dooley was born in St. Louis. Dooley supervised the evacuation and treatment of hundreds of thousands of refugees from North Vietnam in 1954. Books of his experiences as a missionary became best sellers. In 1957, he founded MEDICO to bring a network of hospitals and medical care to Southeast Asia. His broadcasts over KMOX brought more fame. Dooley died of cancer in January, 1961.

1977 Peter Busch pleaded guilty of manslaughter in the shooting of David Leeker. Leeker was the son of the owner of the So-

Good Potato Chip Company. He was shot under mysterious circumstances while spending the night at the Busch mansion in February, 1976. Peter was placed on probation for five years.

1978 Big Red Coach Don Coryell came to work to find all the locks had been changed. The coach with the most wins in Cardinal history had been involved in a feud with owner Bill Bidwell. Coryell resigned three weeks later, and went on to great success as coach of the San Diego Chargers.

January 18

1900 It was announced that construction would begin soon on a hospital funded by the will of businessman Robert Barnes. When he died in 1892, he left most of his estate as an endowment for his dream of a hospital that would treat people of all races. Barnes Hospital would open in 1914.

1902 The city was buzzing with rumors that the World's Fair would be postponed from the planned opening in April, 1903. The President of the fair, David Francis and Adolphus Busch, the chairman of the foreign relations committee, had left for Washington. Federal officials and foreign governments wanted the fair to open in 1904 so they would have more time to prepare their exhibits.

1904 A grand jury here began an investigation into the biggest scandal in city history, the alleged "boodle" deals by members of city government. Circuit Attorney Joseph Folk exposed the corrupt alliance between city officials and big business in the granting of street railway franchises. His crusade won him nationwide attention and got him elected governor in 1904.

1929 The *Globe* reported that R. Marlin Perkins, the reptile curator of the St. Louis Zoo, was out of danger and recovering nicely after being bitten by one of the most deadly snakes in the world. He was struck by a Gabon Viper back on December 26th.

1970 Alderwoman Doris Bass was pushing an ordinance to prohibit performances of plays featuring nudity. The bill was aimed at preventing the opening of "Hair" at the American Theatre. It was introduced on behalf of the Missouri Women's Federation.

January 19

1809 Robert E. Lee was born in Stratford, Virginia. St. Louis owes a great debt to Lee. As a young colonel in the Army Corps of Engineers, Lee devised a system of dikes that kept the Mississippi River channel from shifting and leaving the St. Louis riverfront high and dry.

1871 Hiram Leffingwell was presenting his plans for a huge city park to the St. Louis delegation to the state legislature. Leffingwell was a developer who owned much of the land in the area around the proposed park west of Kingshighway. Lawmakers approved his plan for Forest Park in 1872, but residents who didn't share his dream challenged it successfully in court. Forest Park finally won approval in 1874.

1899 The first organized hockey game recorded here drew a large and enthusiastic crowd to the newly opened indoor rink, the "Ice Palace." The All-Canadiens beat a team of Washington University students 2-1. The students had never played the game before.

1940 A fire ravaged the Casa Loma Ballroom and seven businesses at Cherokee and Iowa. Damage was put at $250,000. Six firefighters were injured when a wall collapsed. Freezing temperatures hampered efforts to fight the fire. The entire scene was covered in ice.

1983 The Cardinals signed Ozzie Smith to a three-year-deal that made him baseball's first million dollar shortstop.

1983 The St. Louis Museum of Science and Natural History announced it was negotiating to buy the old Falstaff Building at 5050 Oakland Avenue. The museum, then located in Oak Knoll Park in Clayton, was planning a multi-million dollar science center on the site.

January 20

1917 The long-awaited Municipal or "Free" Bridge opened to traffic. For the first time, St. Louisans could cross the Mississippi for free. Before Mayor Henry Kiel's car could start toward East St. Louis following the ceremony, a crowd of 30,000 persons and 3,000 cars poured onto the bridge. The bridge was re-named in honor of General Douglas MacArthur in 1942 and closed to vehicle traffic in August, 1981.

1970 St. Louis became the first expansion city to host the NHL All-Star Game. The East team, made up of players from the original six teams, beat the expansion players from the west, 4-1. 16,587 people saw it. Blues goalie Jacques Plante was spectacular in the last half of the game.

1981 The 52 American hostages in Iran were freed, moments after Ronald Reagan was sworn in as president. In Krakow, Missouri, the parents of Marine Sergeant Rocky Sickmann rejoiced at the news. At 11:57 am, church bells rang out as the plane carrying the hostages cleared Iranian air space.

1997 Former Cardinal outfielder Curt Flood died at the age of 59. Flood was the first player to defy baseball's reserve system. He refused to report to the Phillies when the Cardinals traded him in 1969. His case went all the way to the U.S. Supreme Court.

Flood lost, but he paved the way for today's high-dollar free agents.

1998 CBS News reported that a pilot from Florissant could be resting in the Tomb of the Unknowns at Arlington National Cemetery. The family of Lieutenant Michael Blassie wanted the remains exhumed for DNA testing. The tests would prove that Blassie was buried in the tomb, and the remains were brought home for burial.

January 21

1826 The Missouri General Assembly adjourned for the last time at the state capitol in St. Charles. The following spring, all the state property was loaded onto a keelboat, and the capitol was moved to Jefferson City.

1845 Edward Mallinkrodt was born on his family farm in north St. Louis. He studied chemistry in Germany with his brother, Otto. In 1867, the brothers returned to the United States and opened G. Mallinkrodt and Company with their brother Gustav in a small building on the farm.

1948 An escaped German prisoner of war was captured here. George Rudolph Hye Von Hyeburg had escaped from a camp in Massachusetts in 1943, was recaptured and escaped again a few years later. This time, he was spotted by an alert ex G.I. at the Toddle House Restaurant.

1960 Stan Musial asked for and received a pay cut from $100,000 to $80,000 per year. Stan said he had been overpaid in 1957 and '58, and his salary should be cut back because of his performance in 1959! On this date in 1969, Stan was named to the Baseball Hall of Fame.

1997 The Rams named former Philadelphia Eagles coach Dick Vermeil as their new head coach. Vermiel coached the Eagles from 1976 until 1982. He led them to four playoff berths and to the Super Bowl in 1981. In his third season in St. Louis, Vermeil led the Rams to a win in Super Bowl XXXIV.

January 22

1850 Robert Brookings was born in Maryland. He came to St. Louis in 1867 as a $25-a-month receiving clerk at the Cupples Woodware Plant. Ten years later, he was running the company. He designed the depot and track system at the Cupples Complex downtown. He gave his own money and campaigned for donations to help Washington University move to a new campus west of Forest Park.

1931 Hampton Avenue opened to traffic from Oakland Avenue to a point near Gravois. The long-awaited roadway was built to relieve congestion on Kingshighway. Hampton Avenue was originally the western border street of the Southampton Subdivision. It was extended over parts of Billon, West Park, Cheltenham and Sulphur to create a continuous avenue.

1962 The National Park Service opened bids to build the Arch. The McDonald Construction Company of St. Louis submitted the $12,139,918 low bid. That was 50% higher than the park service expected. The bid was later reduced by one-half-million dollars.

1968 Joe Medwick was named to the Baseball Hall of Fame. He batted .324 during a 17-year career. He may be best remembered for being taken out of the last game of the 1934 world series. He slid hard into a Tiger player, and Detroit fans pelted him with debris.

1972 At least 230 people were hurt, and 100 were left homeless, after a tanker car hauling 30,000 gallons of propylene exploded in the Alton and Southern Railyard in East St. Louis. Damage was estimated at $7.5 million. The explosion damaged 868 buildings.

January 23

1896 A tragedy took place that led to the founding of Webster Groves. Thieves murdered a visitor from Chicago, Bertram

Atwater. Residents of villages that grew up around stops on the Frisco Railroad blamed the crime on the lack of organized municipal government. Old Orchard, Webster Park, Tuxedo Park and Selma merged into the city of Webster Groves.

1975 The 35-story Mercantile Tower was topped out downtown. At the time, it was the tallest building in the city. The Metropolitan Square and the Southwestern Bell Buildings have since eclipsed it.

1986 Chuck Berry was among the first group of performers to be inducted into the Rock and Roll Hall of Fame. Berry was born on October 18, 1926 at 2520 Goode Avenue, now Annie Malone Drive. He worked at the Fisher Body plant and trained as a hairdresser at Poro Beauty School before scoring his first hit with "Maybelline" in 1955.

2000 The Rams won the NFC Championship, with a heart-stopping 11-6 win over the Tampa Bay Buccaneers. Ricky Proehl made a spectacular catch late in the game to give the Rams the win. As a light snow dusted the city, St. Louis celebrated its first trip to the Super Bowl.

January 24

1874 O'Fallon, Illinois was incorporated as a village. The town is named after John O'Fallon, an Ohio and Mississippi Railroad official. O'Fallon, Missouri is also named after the same man.

1896 A constable thwarted a would-be lynch mob near Maddenville in St. Louis County. He was transporting the two men accused of killing Bertram Atwater to Clayton. He drove through a hail of gunfire, abandoned his carriage and hailed a St. Louis-bound train. (Atwater's murder inspired the incorporation of Webster Groves to bring an end to lawlessness)

1967 A January heat-wave was shattered by a tornado that tore across ten communities from Chesterfield to Spanish Lake. Three people were killed, 220 injured and 200 homes were destroyed. Damage was estimated at $15 million.

1968 The St. Louis Symphony Orchestra played its first concert at its new home, Powell Hall. Powell Hall was originally the St. Louis Theatre, which opened in 1925. It's appropriate that the "Sound of Music" was the last film shown at the theater.

1978 Three glass doors at the Checkerdome were shattered and 60 policemen were called in to control a crowd of 17,000 surging to get into a Ted Nugent concert. It was the first and last concert in St. Louis with no reserved seats.

1995 Fifteen-year old Christine Smetzer was beaten, raped and drowned in a rest room at McCluer North High school. Michael

Taylor was convicted of the murder. He had behavior problems, and had been transferred to North one day before the murder. The case led to changes in the law to make it easier for school officials to gain access to the records of troubled kids.

January 25

1959 Bird lovers across the country were upset by the St. Louis Health and Hospital Director's plan to eliminate pigeons. Dr. Earl Smith proposed getting the pigeons soused on alcohol soaked bread. The drunken birds would then be trucked off to the dog pound gas chamber.

1978 The temperature dipped below 32°, which is not normally worth noting in January. But this time, the mercury would not rise above the freezing mark until February 23rd. That's a string of 30 consecutive freezing days, the longest recorded in St. Louis history.

1991 Brett Hull of the St. Louis Blues became the fifth player in NHL history to score 50 goals in 50 or fewer games. Hull scored his 50th in the Blues 49th game of the year, a 9-4 rout of the Detroit Red Wings.

2002 The Trans World Dome was re-named the Edward Jones Dome. The home town brokerage firm agreed to pay about

$2.65 million each year for the naming rights.

2002 A loss to the Blackhawks in Chicago brought an end to the longest winning streak in Blues history. The Blues had won ten games in a row.

January 26

1937 The Daniel Boone Expressway was dedicated from Wentzville to Ballas. Later U.S. 40 and I-64, the highway made it to Lindbergh in 1938. But it dead-ended at Brentwood Boulevard until the 50's. Drivers had to take Brentwood north to Clayton Road, and pick up the "Express Highway," which only took you as far as Market Street.

1940 Governor Lloyd Stark, St. Louis Mayor Bernard F. Dickmann, and the Veiled Prophet Queen attended the gala Missouri premiere of "Gone With the Wind" at the Leow's State Theatre here.

1945 The original McDonnell "Phantom" made its first flight. The "FH-1 Phantom" would become the Navy's first jet fighter. It would become the first Navy plane to fly at 500 miles per hour. On July 21, 1946, an FH-1 Phantom, operating from the U.S.S. Franklin D. Roosevelt, became the first jet combat plane to take off from an American carrier.

1995 The Blues played their first game at the new Kiel Center, a 3-1 win over the Los Angeles Kings. A crowd of 20,282 saw it.

1999 Pope John Paul II arrived in St. Louis President Clinton met the Pope at Lambert Field. Predictions of gridlock never materialized. Downtown parking lot owners were grumbling over the number of empty spaces. 22,000 youths cheered the Pope at a service at Kiel Center. Backstage, John Paul II met Mark McGwire. It was 54 degrees that day, which added to the legend of the "Pink Sisters." The nuns had prayed for good weather for the visit.

January 27

1810 The town trustees of St. Louis passed an ordinance organizing citizens into fire companies. All able-bodied males were required to serve. The ordinance also required all residents to keep two stout buckets on hand.

1933 Mayor Bernard Dickmann first publicly proposed that a memorial to the Louisiana Purchase be built on the St. Louis riverfront. He urged the area's representatives in Congress to back a request for federal funds.

1963 Zoo officials announced plans for a $300,000 miniature railroad to shuttle visitors between four stations on the grounds. A private corporation would build the railroad, with part of the profits going to the zoo.

1999 A crowd of 104,000 attended a Mass by Pope John Paul II at the Trans World Dome. The Pope also led the faithful in worship at the Cathedral Basilica. The high that day reached 68 degrees, and the legend of the "Pink Sisters" was growing. The visit was not without controversy. Missouri Governor Mel Carnahan commuted the death sentence of convicted killer Daryl Mease at the Pope's request.

2002 The Rams clinched their second NFC Championship in three years, with an exhausting 29-24 win over the Philadelphia Eagles at the newly-named Edward Jones Dome. A dramatic interception by Aeneas Williams in the last two minutes helped preserve the win.

January 28

1932 The St. Louis Board of Aldermen named a committee to look into the possible purchase of the financially troubled Arena. Only two years old, it was in danger of being demolished. The owners said the Arena was not generating enough revenue to pay off the construction loans.

1933 Poet Sara Teasdale died at the age of 48. In 1918, her book "Love Songs" won the Columbia University Poetry Society Prize, the forerunner of the Pulitzer Prize for poetry. Her death was ruled an accident, but she had taken a heavy dose of sleeping pills.

1948 Dignitaries watched the opening of a time capsule, placed in the cornerstone of the county courthouse when it was built in 1878. Over the years, the box had ruptured, rendering the contents a soggy mess. All was unrecognizable, except for a few coins. The old courthouse in Clayton was being demolished.

1953 St. Louis Baseball Cardinals owner Fred Saigh pleaded guilty of income tax evasion. He would be forced to sell the club. Offers came in from several cities. On February 20th, Anheuser-Busch bought the club and pledged to keep it here in St. Louis.

1981 Former Iranian hostage Marine Sergeant Rocky Sickmann arrived to a tumultuous welcome at Lambert Field. Crowds lined the highway overpasses as a motorcade took him home to Krakow, Missouri.

January 29

1944 The battleship "Missouri" was launched at the Brooklyn Navy Yard. The Japanese signed the surrender papers at the end of World War II aboard the "Mighty Mo" in Tokyo Bay.

1953 The city building commissioner declared the old Coliseum at Jefferson and Washington to be unsafe. Built in 1908, it was intended to be the equal of Madison Square Garden. It served as the site for the 1916 Democratic National Convention. The building would be torn down later in 1953.

1958 The Cardinals made Stan Musial baseball's first $100,000 player. In 1957, Stan had won his seventh straight batting title. He hit .351 with 29 home runs. Stan said he would have settled for less money.

1959 Harry Fender broadcast live over KMOX from the lobby of Leow's Orpheum for the premiere of "The Great St. Louis Bank Robbery," starring Steve McQueen. The movie told the story of the April, 1953 hold-up at Southwest Bank. Twenty-four St. Louis police officers were featured in the film.

1991 St. Louis radio listeners were stunned to hear a fake nuclear alert during a morning show broadcast on KSHE. The stunt caused the FCC to come down hard on the station. It cost announcer John Ulett his job as Cardinals public address announcer for a time.

January 30

1821 The City of Alton, Illinois, was incorporated. Alton was named in honor of Alton Easton, the son of city founder, Colonel Rufus Easton. Rufus Easton was the first postmaster general of St. Louis, who saw Alton as an ideal site for a steamboat landing.

1905 Amid debris left over from the World's Fair, classes began at the new Washington University campus "west of Thomas Skinker's Road" and Forest Park. The site was acquired largely through the efforts of Robert Somers Brookings. The building now known as Brookings Hall served as the administration building during the fair.

1982 About 3:30 that Saturday afternoon, forecasters issued a winter storm watch. That meant four or more inches of snow was expected. By suppertime, heavy snow was falling, and a violent thunder snow storm had developed. Officially, 13.9 inches of snow fell by the next day, but unofficial totals were closer to 22 inches.

1982 Jim Hanifan was named as coach of the football Cardinals. He was credited with building the best offensive line in football while serving as Big Red assistant coach from 1973 to 1978.

2000 The Rams brought St. Louis its first Super Bowl title, with a 23-16 win over the Tennessee Titans at the Georgia Dome in Atlanta. Rams linebacker Mike Jones tackled Titans receiver Kevin Dyson at the one-yard line as time ran out to preserve the win.

January 31

1929 The brand new "Fabulous" Fox Theater on Grand was dedicated. The theater cost $6 million to build. It was billed as the second largest in the world at the time. It was refurbished from top to bottom in 1982. The first movie shown at the Fox was "Street Angel," starring Janet Gaynor.

1931 Tom Alston was born in Greensboro, North Carolina. In 1954, he became the first African-American to play for the Cardinals. A battle with depression kept Alston from realizing his potential, and he was out of baseball by 1957.

1982 The entire area was paralyzed by as much as 22 inches of snow. Five people were dead and travel was impossible, except by ski or snowmobile. County Executive Gene McNary and Mayor Vince Schoemehl declared snow emergencies. A Rod Stewart concert that Sunday night at the Checkerdome was cancelled.

1992 TWA filed for reorganization under Chapter Eleven of the Federal Bankruptcy Code. Reorganization was completed in November, 1993. The airline's financial problems began in October 1988, when Carl Icahn used over $1 billion in borrowed money to complete a buyout started three years earlier.

2000 About 100,000 people braved the cold and lined the parade route downtown to honor the Super Bowl Champion Rams. Players rode by in the back of pickup trucks while waving and shaking hands with the crowd. The Anheuser-Busch Clydesdales led Coach Dick Vermeil through the parade.

FEBRUARY

February 1

1819 The first permanent theater in St. Louis opened. William Turner and 15 other citizens had joined to build the 600 seat theater on Main, between Olive and Locust. The first show was Oliver Goldsmith's "She Stoops to Conquer" and the farce, "The Watchman."

1903 Edward G. Lewis, the founder of the University Heights Realty and Development Company, announced his plans for a new headquarters building for his American Women's Magazine. The design called for an octagonal building on Delmar in Lewis' planned community. The building now serves as the city hall of University City.

1959 The *Globe* reported that the area around Boyle and Olive may soon be known as "Gaslight Square." If the city agreed, gas lamps would light the area. The area was beginning to attract a mix of non conformists, night clubs and antique stores.

1970 Jesse "Pop" Haines was named to the Baseball Hall of Fame. He spent 18 of his 19 major league seasons with the Cardinals. His 210-158 record included three 20 win seasons. He threw a no-hitter in 1924.

2000 Less than 48 hours after his team won the Super Bowl, Rams Coach Dick Vermeil announced his retirement. The Rams named offensive coordinator Mike Martz as the new head coach the following day. Vermeil led the Rams to 13-3 record and a world championship in his third season in St. Louis.

February 2

1863 A writer for the Virginia City territorial *Enterprise* signed his pen name to a dispatch for the first time. The tenderfoot writers real name was Samuel Clemens. He chose a steamboating term he picked up during his days as a riverboat pilot here for his nom de plume - Mark Twain.

1865 The Missouri General Assembly chartered the public school library, the foundation of today's St. Louis Public Library. Superintendent of Schools Ira Divoll had been working for years to develop the library. At the time, free public libraries were virtually unheard of.

1876 St. Louis was among the eight teams to sign on as the National Baseball League was founded. The other seven cities were Boston, Chicago, New York, Cincinnati, Philadelphia, Louisville and Hartford.

1923 Albert "Red" Schoendienst was born in Germantown, Illinois. He played second base for the Cardinals from 1945 to 1956 and 1961 to 1963 . Red managed the Redbirds for 12 seasons beginning in 1965. That's the longest tenure of any manager in Cardinal history. As manager, he led the Birds to two National League pennants and a World Championship.

1931 The structure of Bagnell dam was completed, and the Osage River began backing up behind it. The Union Electric dam formed the vast Lake of the Ozarks. The lake is 125 miles long, with 1,300 miles of shoreline and one "Party Cove."

February 3

1902 Seven city firemen where killed in a fire at the American Tent and Awning Company at Third and Chestnut. The assistant chief was among the dead. The wall of the building collapsed on the firefighters just as they were satisfied the blaze was under control.

1928 A crowd of about 1,000 watched as Mayor Victor Miller laid the cornerstone for the new civil courthouse downtown. The cornerstone contains a box of documents detailing the controversy over moving the courts to a new location. The box also contains a medallion featuring a likeness of Charles Lindbergh.

1934 The Cardinals and the Browns announced they were discontinuing radio broadcasts from Sportsman's Park. Games had been broadcast on weekdays only since 1926. The owners of the clubs thought the broadcasts were keeping fans away from the games.

1968 The *Globe* reported that "Gaslight Square ain't what she used to be." The article blamed crime and crowds of teenagers hanging out in front of the "Go-Go" establishments. A dozen clubs had closed since 1967.

2002 The New England Patriots stunned St. Louis with a 20-17 victory in Super Bowl XXXVI. The Rams erased a 14-point deficit but lost on the final play, a 48-yard field goal by Adam Vinatieri. The Rams had been listed as 14-point favorites going into the game.

February 4

1850 The first high school west of the Mississippi opened in a portion of the old Wayman School at Sixth and Locust. Central High at 15th and Olive would be the first building used exclusively for high school purposes. Central opened on March 24, 1856.

1902 Charles Lindbergh was born in Minnesota. He came to St. Louis to take the job as chief pilot for the Robertson Aircraft Company, which flew the mail between St. Louis and Chicago. In 1926, he convinced a group of St. Louis businessmen to back his attempt at the first solo transatlantic flight. Part of the money came from Listerine, the family business of aviation booster Albert Bond Lambert.

1947 The very first public test of a television program in St. Louis. Harold Grams, the program manager of KSD-TV, interviewed two technicians from RCA. The broadcast was seen by RCA executives at the Statler Hotel and a troop of Brownies at the home of the local RCA distributor.

1972 Missouri Governor Warren Hearnes signed legislation creating the Missouri-St. Louis Metropolitan Airport Authority. Hearnes and St. Louis County Supervisor L.K. Roos made the move to thwart Mayor A.J. Cervantes in his plans for a new airport at Columbia-Waterloo. Governor Hearnes said Lambert Field would be adequate for the next 100 years.

1982 Five days after a blizzard dumped up to 22 inches of snow on the area, things were still not back to normal. County Executive Gene McNary asked business owners to keep half of their employees home, and asked public schools to remain closed. The city announced it would pay anyone with a snow plow $45 an hour to help clear the streets.

1830 Fee Fee road was declared an open public road. One of the oldest roads in St. Louis County, Fee Fee is named for Nicholas "Fifi" Beaugenou. (Fifi denoted "son" in French) Beaugenou was one of the 30 men who helped begin construction on the trading post that became the city of St. Louis. He settled in what is now Bridgeton after his wife died.

1845 A group of county residents, led by Wesley Watson, field a petition for a road "from Cooper's Farm on the Old Manchester Roads, thence to the River des Peres near the mouth of the Lick Branch, from thence the most practical route to the ferry landing opposite the town of Fenton." The road would be named after Watson.

1914 Author William Burroughs was born at 4644 Pershing. He was a reporter for the *Post*, and met Jack Kerouac and Allen Ginsburg during the war. Together, they formed the core of the "Beat Generation" writers. Burroughs' most famous work is "Naked Lunch."

1965 The National Park Service announced that the Gateway Arch was now the tallest structure in St. Louis. With the addition of the latest 12-foot section on each leg, the Arch was now 372 feet tall on the North Leg and 384 feet tall on the South. The Southwestern Bell

Building at the time became the second tallest, at 369 feet.

1977 The Blues called up rookies Bernie Federko, Brian Sutter and Rick Bourbonnais. Federko scored three goals in that game, including the winner against Buffalo.

February 6

1837 The Legislature approved a state road from St. Louis to Springfield, following the old Indian "Osage Trail." The road eventually became known as the Springfield to St. Louis Road, the "Wire Road," and eventually, the basis for the route of US Highway 66 and I- 44.

1861 Captain Nathaniel Lyon arrived to take over defense of the United States Arsenal at St. Louis. Lyon moved fast when the state militia began drills at "Camp Jackson" on the outskirts of the city. On May 10th, his troops surrounded the camp. A crowd gathered as the prisoners were marched towards the arsenal. Shots were fired. About three dozen people were killed, many of them civilians.

1927 The *Globe-Democrat* reported that Charles Lindbergh, chief airmail pilot for the St. Louis to Chicago route, "has been discussing with St. Louisans who are interested in aeronautics the possibility of the financing of a New York to Paris flight for the $25,000 Orteig Prize."

1951 The only killing ever reported at Union Station occurred. Several drunken soldiers headed for Korea, got into a brawl with an MP. The MP shot and killed 19-year-old Corporal Robert McKenna of Massachusetts.

1988 The spirit of the Blues, Barclay Plager, died after a long battle with cancer. Plager played in the Blues organization for ten years. He served as coach, assistant coach, scout and even player-coach. His number eight was retired in 1982.

February 7

1897 City Health Commissioner Max Starkloff was promising an investigation into the polluted River des Peres. He pledged to bring a bill before the Legislature to improve the pesky and foul smelling stream. Nothing was done until 1923, when a bond issue paved the way for the river to be channeled and buried in a tunnel.

1898 St. Louis was in a furor over the kidnapping of flamboyant Browns owner Chris Von Der Ahe. Detectives from Pittsburgh, where a pitcher had won a $27,000 settlement against him, forced him into a train in broad daylight. The pitcher came here to recruit a Browns player. When Von Der Ahe got wind of it, he had the pitcher thrown in jail. The pitcher sued.

1870 James B. Eads hosted a "champagne party" for the press in his underwater "air chamber" beneath one of the piers under construction for his bridge. The reporters, except for a few who had a last minute change of heart, descended to the bottom to watch Eads hook up a telegraph for communications with the surface.

1994 A new era began at the Pruitt-Igoe site. Ground was broken for the Gateway Elementary and Gateway Middle School on the former site of the notorious housing project. It marked the first new school in St. Louis in 24 years. The last of the 33 high rises on the site were torn down in 1976. Pruitt-Igoe had been hailed as a model for public housing across the nation when it opened in 1954.

February 8

1820 William Tecumseh Sherman was born in Lancaster, Ohio. In 1850, he reported for duty at Jefferson Barracks. He left the army to try banking and law. When the war broke out, he was managing a St. Louis street railway company. After the war, he returned here to make his home. His funeral in 1891 was one of the biggest in city history.

1851 Katherine Flaherty was born in St. Louis. She married New Orleans native Oscar Chopin, and learned of the Creole culture that would provide the settings for many of her works. Her 1899 novel, "The Awakening," caused a furor with its frank treatment of women's issues.

1853 The Missouri Legislature passed an act incorporating the "Kirkwood Association." Real estate agents Hiram Leffingwell and Richard S. Elliott wanted to promote a suburb along the proposed Pacific Railroad. They hoped to promote their development as an escape from the noise and disease of the city. Kirkwood is the first planned suburban community in the United States.

1947 The first television station in St. Louis signed on the air. At the time, KSD was one of only seven television stations in the country. The first broadcast lasted less than 90 minutes. It featured news with Frank Eschen, ballroom dancers, a wrestler, and an appearance by Joe Garagiola.

1972 Vincent Dobelman received the first heart transplant in St. Louis medical history at Firmin Desloge Hospital. Doctor Vallee Willman, chief of surgery at the St. Louis University School of Medicine, headed the team of surgeons.

February 9

1837 John Ball changed the name of the town he had laid out from "Ballshow" to "Ballwin." Legend says he changed it because of a rivalry with Manchester. Ball was confident his town on the new state road to Jefferson City would "win" over his neighbor to the east. Ballwin was not incorporated until 1950.

1876 The city of St. Louis had two mayors. The city council declared Henry Overstolz the winner of last May's special election. But election officials had declared James Britton the winner, and Britton had been inaugurated. The council said Overstolz won by 77 votes and that there was evidence of "frauds of gross and outrageous character." Overstolz supporters were threatening to march on City Hall.

1903 The *Globe* reported that the Westlake Construction Company had been awarded the contract for a 12-story-tall, 400-room hotel at the Northwest corner of 12th and Locust. World's Fair officials and public-spirited citizens were promoting the $1.2 million Jefferson Hotel.

1966 St. Louis was shocked to learn the National Hockey League was offering the city a franchise. The fifth expansion franchise had been expected to go to Baltimore, but the league said St. Louis already had a suitable building in place and offered a central location. The city had until April 5th to claim the franchise, or Baltimore would get it. Three groups were preparing bids.

1988 The National Hockey League All-Star Game was played at the Arena. Mario Lemieux scored three goals as the Wales Conference defeated the Campbell Conference, 6-5.

February 10

1843 The city council accepted a gift of land from Mrs. Julia Cerre Soulard. As a condition of the gift, the city had to agree that the land would be used as a public market. The city has kept its part of the bargain to this day.

1959 Just after midnight, a tornado ripped through Warson Woods, Glendale, Rock Hill and Maplewood. As it headed towards Forest Park, the twister knocked the Channel Two tower onto an apartment building. It took out one of the twin towers of the Arena, and tore off a chunk of the roof. The worst damage was in the area around Boyle and Olive. Twenty-one people died, over a thousand buildings were damaged, and more than 2,000 people were homeless.

1976 David W. Leeker, the son of the president of the So-Good Potato Chip Company, was shot to death while staying overnight at the Busch Mansion at Grant's Farm. Peter Busch, the 20-year-old son of August Busch Junior would plead guilty to manslaughter. No one doubted that the shooting was accidental, but many questions remained unanswered.

1982 Ozzie Smith became a Redbird. The Cardinals traded the controversial Garry Templeton to the Padres for the acrobatic shortstop. Templeton had made an obscene gesture to fans at Busch Stadium in August, 1981. He was traded on direct orders from Gussie Busch.

1989 Legendary Blues broadcaster Dan Kelly died of cancer at the age of 52. A month before his death, he was awarded the Lester Patrick Award for service to hockey, and was named to the broadcasters wing of the Hockey Hall of Fame.

February 11

1857 The history of Florissant goes back to at least 1786. But this is the date the town charter was granted by the state. The population of Florrissant would remain below 1,000 as late as World War II. It exploded in the '50s and '60s to nearly 70,000.

1856 The United States Supreme Court began hearing the case of Dred Scott. Scott sued for his freedom in St. Louis after his owner took him into Illinois, a free state. The Supreme Court would rule that slaves were not citizens and therefore could not sue. The case further divided the country on the slavery issue.

1901 The *St. Louis Post-Dispatch* "Weatherbird" appeared for the first time. The Weatherbird is the oldest continuous cartoon in American journalism. He appeared without a pithy "bird line" only a few times — following the deaths of Franklin Roosevelt,

John F. Kennedy, Dr. Martin Luther King Jr., August Busch Jr., the Challenger disaster, and after 9/11/2001.

1903 The International Olympic Committee announced that the 1904 games would be held in St. Louis, instead of Chicago as previously planned. The games would be held in conjunction with the World's Fair. The financially strapped city of Chicago raised little objection to the move.

1961 Excavation began on the foundations of the Gateway Arch, nearly 30 years after the monument was first proposed. The first excavation work began on the South Leg of the Arch. Excavation work would be finished late in 1963.

1961 Mr. and Mrs. Ed Ceries signed KSHE-FM on the air from the basement of their home at 1035 Westglen Lane in Crestwood. The call letters stood for "The Lady of FM." The station offered drama and fine arts features, as well as classical and "time tested" lighter music.

February 12

1809 Abraham Lincoln was born in a log cabin in what is now LaRue County, Kentucky. Lincoln came to the St. Louis area several times, most notably for the final Lincoln-Douglas debate in Alton. He spent the night in the National Hotel on his way to

Washington to become a Senator in 1848. As a plaque in the lobby attests, the site is now home to KMOV-TV and KMOX radio.

1926 Joseph Henry Garagiola was born on the Hill. He played for the Cardinals for five seasons. In 1955, he joined Jack Buck and Harry Carey on the Cardinals broadcasts. He took a job with the Yankees, then called baseball for NBC for 27 years.

1955 A new federal grand jury investigation opened in the case of the missing half of the $600,000 Greenlease ransom. The money disappeared the night St. Louis Police arrested Carl Austin Hall and Bonnie Lee Heady for the murder of the six-year old son of a Kansas City auto dealer in October 1953.

1963 The very first stainless steel triangle that forms the first section of the Arch was moved into place. The first section was put in place at the south leg.

1966 "Corky's Colorama" became the first locally produced color television program. Channel Five weatherman Cliff St. James played "Corky". "Corky" had actually made his television debut back in 1956.

February 13

1904 Suffering from depression, brewery magnate William Lemp

shot himself at his South St. Louis mansion. At the time of his death, his estate and brewery were worth $16 million. His daughter Elsa would kill herself in 1920. William Lemp III killed himself in 1922. In 1929, his brother Charles became the fourth Lemp to commit suicide, and the third to die in the Lemp mansion.

1934 August A. Busch Sr., shot himself at his hunting lodge at St. Peters. He had been suffering from heart problems, and was in intense pain. Busch led his brewery through prohibition and turned it into one of the largest in the world,

1937 The National Football League granted a franchise to a group of Cleveland businessmen. The Cleveland Rams had played in the American Football League in 1936, their first season. In their first season in the NFL, they would compile a record of one win and ten losses. Former Pittsburgh Pirate manager Hugh Bezdek was named as the first Rams coach. To this day, he is the only man to coach an NFL team and a major league baseball team.

1959 The National Aeronautics and Space Administration signed a contract with McDonnell Aircraft for the design and construction of the orbital Mercury spacecraft. The "Freedom Seven" Mercury capsule carried Alan Shephard on America's first manned space flight.

1974 James "Cool Papa" Bell was named to the Baseball Hall of Fame by a special committee on the Negro Leagues. James Thomas Bell may have been the fastest runner in baseball history. Teammate Satchel Paige once said that Bell could turn off the light and be in bed before the room went dark.

February 14

1764 Auguste Chouteau and 30 men arrived on the west bank of the Mississippi to begin building a trading post on a site chosen by Pierre Laclede a year earlier. Laclede hoped to establish a post to counter British influence in the area. He also believed the site would one day become a great city. The trading post developed into the city of St. Louis.

1922 KSD radio began broadcasting. "The wireless service of the *Post-Dispatch*" presented an address by Walter P. Upson of the Washington University Electrical Engineering Department. No one had bothered to get a license, so the station had to wait until June 26, 1922 to officially sign on.

1947 KSD-TV aired the first television broadcast of a sporting event in Missouri. The first TV game was a Billikens contest against Oklahoma from Kiel Auditorium.

1964 President Lyndon Johnson came to St. Louis for the activities marking the city's bicentennial. The president heralded St. Louis' accomplishments in overcoming the blight that had defaced so many American cities.

1970 Cardinals slugger Richie Allen was demanding $150,000 to sign for the 1971 season. That would make him the highest paid player in baseball. Bob Gibson was the highest paid Cardinal at $125,000 per year. Carl Yastremski was the highest paid player in baseball, at $130,000.

February 15

1872 Collinsville, Illinois was incorporated as a village. The city is named for the four Collins Brothers who came to the area in 1817, and established many businesses. The area was originally known as Unionville, but another town in Illinois already had that name.

1927 Congress approved a charter for a toll bridge across the Mississippi River at the Chain of Rocks. The bridge cost $1.5 million. The Corps of Engineers ordered the famous bend in the middle, to keep the bridge from hindering navigation.

1930 A bill before the Board of Aldermen would create a board of censors to oversee movies, vaudeville and stage plays. Alderman Samuel Wimer said shows could have "a certain amount of spice." But he added "motion pictures today are getting too raw in their suggestiveness."

1959 Police said drivers on the Express Highway were causing a hazard by stopping to take pictures of the tornado damage at and around the Arena. Officials said sightseers were causing "chaos" in the devastated area around Boyle and Olive.

1978 St. Louisan Leon Spinks defeated Muhammed Ali in a split decision to gain the world heavyweight boxing title. It was one of the most stunning upsets in boxing history. Ali regained the title seven months later. Spinks had won gold medal in light heavyweight division at the 1976 Olympics. His brother Michael won the heavyweight title in 1983, making the Spinks the only brothers to hold world titles.

February 16

1846 This is believed to be the date that William B. Ferguson and his wife arrived in an area north of St. Louis to build homes. He bought 107 acres. In 1855, he offered nine acres to the North Missouri Railroad (later the Wabash), under the condition that the station built on the site be named Ferguson.

1903 Several meetings were held to protest a measure in the legislature designed to clean up the city in time for the fair. The bill called for moving all of the "disreputable houses" to one area. The residents of the near south-side chosen for the new district were not too pleased with the idea.

1946 Construction began on the new $8 million Ford plant on Highway 66 near Lambert Field. Governor Walter N. Davis poured the first concrete. Florissant had moved to annex the area, but backed off when Ford threatened to scrap plans for the plant. In 1949, the local farmers would incorporate the Village of Hazelwood.

1959 Workers began tearing down a home at 3518 Laclede. It was the first of over 2,300 buildings that would be demolished in the renewal of the Mill Creek Valley, 465 acres between 20th and Grand. The plan would displace 20,000 people, 95% of them African-American. The area would be dubbed "Hiroshima Flats" before new buildings began going up.

1960 Robert Hyland unveiled his new programming concept for KMOX radio. "At Your Service" was a radical concept. Top newsmakers would go on-air and field calls from listeners. It marked the birth of what we now know as talk radio.

1999 Police arrested dozens of people as the Fat Tuesday celebration in Soulard got out of hand. Mounted Police maced a crowd that had gathered to watch women bare their breasts in exchange for beads. Mayor Clarence Harmon said such behavior might be accepted in New Orleans, but it would not be tolerated here.

1943 The gangland era came to a bloody end, as William Colbeck was shot to death in his car at Ninth and Destrehan. Colbeck had recently been released from prison. He took over the Egan Gang after powerful politician and gang founder William Egan was killed in 1921. Colbeck led a bloody three-year war against the Hogan Gang on the streets of St. Louis.

1946 Archbishop John Joseph Glennon was elevated to the College of Cardinals. St. Louisans never saw him as a prince of the church. He died while visiting his native Ireland prior to his return trip to St. Louis from Rome.

1957 A fire at the Katie June Nursing home in Warrenton killed seventy-one people. It's the deadliest fire in Missouri history. The home's license renewal had been held up after a state inspector found faulty wiring.

1958 The FCC recommended that KTVI-TV be granted a permanent license to broadcast on Channel Two. WTVI had begun broadcasting on UHF Channel 54 from Belleville in 1953. The call letters were changed when the station moved to studios on Berthold and began operating on Channel 36 in 1955.

1972 A bill before the Board of Aldermen would change the name of Easton Avenue and portions of Franklin Avenue to Martin Luther King Boulevard. Alderman C.B. Broussard was one of the sponsors. He said the measure was part of a concerted drive to name streets after the murdered civil rights leader.

February 18

1859 The city of Pacific was incorporated by the Missouri General Assembly. The town was originally named Franklin. But the name was changed because of the constant mix-ups in the mail between Franklin and New Franklin. The name Pacific was chosen to honor the new Pacific Railroad.

1908 School Superintendent Frank Soldan denied a charge by a Congregational Church Minister that "preliminary steps of dancing" were being taught. Soldan said students were doing calisthenics. But the minister said the calisthenics were similar to dancing, and the same evils could be expected to result from them.

1918 Private David Hickey was killed in France. Hickey was the first St. Louisan to die in World War One. The Soldiers Memorial downtown lists the names of 1,075 St. Louisans who gave their lives in the war.

1972 Minnie Liddell and a group of parents filed suit, alleging that the city school board and the State of Missouri were responsible for the segregation of the city schools. A court of appeals later agreed, and ordered a desegregation plan be put into effect. In 1983, the area became the first in the nation where suburban districts cooperated with a city district in such a program.

1998 Harry Caray died after collapsing at a restaurant in Palm Springs, California. He was 83. Caray was a voice of the Cardinals from 1945 until he was fired in a dispute with Anheuser-Busch in 1969. He was born on "The Hill" in South St. Louis.

February 19

1859 What is today the city of East St. Louis was incorporated. At the time, it was known as "Illinoistown." Captain James Piggott, who set up a ferry across the river from St. Louis in 1797, first settled the town. The name was changed to East St. Louis in 1861.

1904 The first building in St. Louis designed specifically for showing motion pictures opened. The Washington Picture Theater stood on Delmar, between Euclid and Kingshighway.

1948 Eero Saarinen was chosen as the winner of a contest to find a design for the proposed riverfront memorial. His design called for a 630-foot-tall arch of steel. The public got its first look at the design in the Post-Dispatch. Reaction was mixed, to put it mildly.

1966 "The Cheater" by Bob Kuban and the In-Men, already a hit in St. Louis, entered the "Billboard Hot 100" chart. Lead singer Walter Scott would be murdered in December, 1983. James Williams, who had been having an affair with Scott's wife, JoAnn Notheis, was sentenced to life in prison in the case. Williams' wife had died in a mysterious car accident in October, 1983. Jo Ann was implicated in the plot, but cut a plea bargain and served 18 months.

1975 A group of banks and downtown businessmen announced the formation of a corporation to oversee development of a nine-block area north of downtown. A 1966 effort to re-develop the dilapidated old warehouses lining the cobblestone streets on "Laclede's Landing" had gone nowhere.

February 20

1857 As many as 60 people died in a fire at the Pacific Hotel, near what is now the site of Busch Stadium at 7th and Poplar. "Hawkeye Bill," a notorious robber and arsonist, reportedly set the fire. Other sources indicate that it started in some turpentine stored inside a drug store on the first floor of the building.

1865 The state granted the town charter of Kirkwood. An association of businessmen who wanted to escape the crowded city ravaged by fire and cholera founded Kirkwood. In 1853, They bought up land along the proposed Pacific railroad and began promoting their development, the first planned suburb in the United States.

1828 A meeting of 105 citizens in Lebanon, Illinois organized Lebanon Seminary The name was later changed to McKendree College. The institution received its charter from the state in 1834, making it the oldest university in Illinois.

1920 The first Chevrolet rolled off the assembly line at the General Motors assembly plant on Natural Bridge. The plant built 13,873,983 vehicles over the next 67 years. During World War II, the plant made army trucks and amphibious "ducks." The Fisher Body plant made airplane parts. Today, the site is an industrial park.

1942 Lieutenant Edward O'Hare of St. Louis saved his aircraft carrier by fighting off nine Japanese planes singlehandedly. He was awarded the Distinguished Flying Cross and the Navy Cross. O'Hare Airport in Chicago is named after him.

1953 The Board of Directors of Anheuser-Busch approved the purchase of the St. Louis Cardinals. The former owner, Fred Saigh, was forced to sell after he was convicted on income tax charges. The brewery stepped in to keep the team here.

1871 Henry Kiel was born in St. Louis. He was elected mayor in 1913, and was the first to serve three four-year terms. During his term, the "Free" (MacArthur) Bridge was completed, the Zoo and Muny Opera were established, and construction began on the Civil Courts Building and on the Municipal Auditorium. The auditorium would later be named in Kiel's honor.

1947 The Billikens won their first Missouri Valley Conference title with a 47-38 win over Drake. "Easy Ed" McCauley scored 22 points as the Bills won their 11th straight.

1969 West County Center opened at Manchester and I-244, on the site of the old Manchester Drive-In. The design of the center was hailed as a new trend. All of the stores opened into a climate controlled "Mall."

1970 The Army ROTC Building at Washington University was heavily damaged in a fire. Anti-war groups had been protesting the program's presence on campus. A crowd of 200 students cheered as the building burned. More protests would erupt there in the spring.

1980 The "S.S. Admiral" excursion boat appeared to be headed for the scrap heap. The 1980 season had been cancelled. Captain William Carroll said he doubted whether the Admiral would ever return to St. Louis. The boat was in a New Orleans dry dock. The Coast Guard said the entire hull would have to be replaced.

February 22

1854 The Reverend William Greenleaf Elliot organized the board of directors under the charter of Elliot seminary, founded in 1853. At that first meeting, the board chose to name their school "Washington Institute of St. Louis." The name was changed to Washington University three years later.

1918 Robert Pershing Wadlow, "The Alton Giant," was born. The world's tallest man was eight-feet, eleven-inches tall when he died in 1940. The cause of death was an infection caused by a poorly fitted leg brace.

1937 Homer G. Phillips Hospital on Whittier was dedicated. At the time, it was the largest and best health care facility in the nation ded-  icated to the care of African-Americans. It closed amid controversy and violence in 1979. Homer Phillips was an attorney who fought for better health care for African Americans. He was gunned down on a city street in 1931.

1960 Three city firemen were killed, eleven injured, while fighting a general alarm fire in a three story building at Sixth and Chestnut. The building housed the Silver Dollar Bar and Cafe, a popular downtown night spot.

1983 The Environmental Protection Agency announced that the entire town of Times Beach would be bought out and leveled because of dioxin contamination. The dioxin was found in waste oil sprayed on the streets of the town in the 1970's. The site has been cleaned up, and is now Route 66 State Park.

February 23

1819 Edwardsville Illinois, was founded. It is named after Governor Ninian Edwards. Edwardsville was the third town in Illinois to be incorporated. Only Kaskaskia and Cairo preceded it. Those communities were incorporated in 1818.

1834 Johann George Aff was born in Germany. Like many Germans fleeing a failed revolt, he settled in South St. Louis County in 1859. He farmed property on Weber Road and built a store near Gravois and Tesson Ferry. The area around the store became known as "Aff's Town," later shortened to Affton.

1877 Arson was suspected in a fire that broke out at the school house in Florissant. It had caused controversy since a clock was installed that chimed hourly, disturbing the sleepy village of a few hundred. A bucket brigade saved the building and citizens were watching the school to make sure it didn't happen again.

1923 The smoke pall covering St. Louis threatened to drive the Missouri Botanical Garden out of town. The garden was seeking court permission to sell part of Henry Shaw's estate. The money would be used to buy land off Highway 66 in Gray Summit to cultivate plants for display in St. Louis.

1951 The Senate Crime Committee hearings, chaired by Senator Estes Kefauver, got underway in a St. Louis courtroom. KSD-TV televised the hearings live. The coverage prompted some of the subpoenaed underworld figures to claim their privacy was being invaded. The landmark broadcasts helped build an audience for the hearings in New York the following month.

February 24

1829 Auguste Chouteau died at the age of 80. When Chouteau was 13, Pierre Laclede placed him in charge of a group of men building a trading post south of the confluence of the Mississippi and Missouri rivers. Laclede predicted the site would one day become a great city.

1853 Lindenwood College in St. Charles was chartered. It was founded in 1820 by Mary Easton Sibley and named for the grove

of Linden trees in which the campus was set. It was turned over to the Presbyterian Church in 1853.

1902 It was reported that a Pittsburgh syndicate had bought up almost all of Valley Park. They were planning a glass factory and a model town, with homes for about 6,000 workers. The population of Valley Park was expected to explode from about 200 to 10,000 within a few years. It would all wash away during a flood in 1902.

1910 The village of St. Peters was incorporated. The town trustees laid out a set of ordinances, including a five-miles-per-hour speed limit for automobiles. They also made it a misdemeanor to ride a horse or drive a carriage through town "faster than a moderate trot." The population stood at 269. By 1970, only 486 people lived there. The population now stands at about 55,000.

1968 Gary Unger's NHL amazing consecutive games streak began, as he took to the ice as a rookie with the Toronto Maple Leafs. The "Iron Man" would start the next 914 consecutive games, including 662 straight with the Blues. The streak still stands as the second longest in NHL history.

February 25

1922 The *Globe* reported that St. Louis built autos were the hit of the 1922 auto show here. The "Dorris," "Moon," "Gardner," "St. Louis," and "Stanwood" were all built in St. Louis. Trucks manufactured here included the "Eagle," "Luedinghaus," "Power" and the "Traffic."

1966 CBS Television aired the documentary "16 in Webster Groves." The next day, Webster Groves was in an uproar. At first, Webster Groves was thrilled to have been chosen. But the documentary made the teens look shallow and materialistic. Some of the parents looked even worse.

1972 The Cardinals made the worst deal in their history. They sent Steve Carlton to the Phillies for Rick Wise. Carlton would go on to win four Cy Young Awards and 241 games for the Phillies.

1976 Reporters and some of the workers who built it took the first rides on the brand new rollercoaster at Six Flags over Mid America. The "Screaming Eagle" reached speeds of 62 miles per hour on a 3,872-foot course.

1983 Tennesee Williams was found dead in a New York hotel. The author of "The Glass Menagerie," "A Streetcar Named Desire" and "Cat on a Hot Tin Roof" had choked to death on a plastic cap from a prescription bottle. The death was ruled accidental. Williams moved here with his family at age seven. He attended University City High School and Washington University.

February 26

1876 Several people were dead, many missing, after a "cyclone" devastated the business section of St. Charles. Two of the biggest businesses, the saw mill and the woolen factory, were destroyed. The county jail and the gas works was also leveled.

1887 Grover Cleveland Alexander was born in Elba, Nebraska. He is best remembered for coming into the seventh game of the 1926 World Series, with the Cards leading by a run. The bases were loaded with two out. Nursing a hangover, Alexander struck out Tony Lazzeri and held the Yankees scoreless the rest of the game.

1962 East Side organized crime kingpin Frank "Buster" Wortman and two of his henchmen were convicted of evading federal income taxes. One of the associates, Elmer "Dutch" Dowling, was found shot to death near Belleville before a sentence could be handed down. The murder was never solved. Wortman won a re-trial and was acquitted. He retired to his home surrounded by a moat.

1970 The Old Chain of Rocks Bridge was closed for repair work on a hole at the east end. It never re-opened to traffic. Since the new bridge to the north had opened in September, 1966, traffic had fallen to just a few hundred cars per day. The Old Route 66 bridge appeared headed for the scrap heap. But thanks to the efforts of Gateway Trailnet, it is now the world's longest pedestrian bridge.

1994 The Blues beat the Ottawa Senators, 11-1. It was the most lopsided win in Blues history. Just two nights earlier, the Blues had been shut out by Quebec.

February 27

1843 The town of Bridgeton was incorporated. The town had been in existence since 1794. The French called it "Marais des Liards," which means "cottonwood swamp." The Spanish called it "Villa a Robert." The Americans called it Owen's Station, then Bridgeton.

1907 Standard Oil announced plans for a $2 million refinery south of Alton. The planned Wood River Refinery was expected to be one of the largest in the nation. Company agents had already bought up most of the land for the 400-acre plant and the company town of Wood River.

1967 The owners of the new St. Louis National Hockey League franchise unveiled the team logo. The owner's son, Sidney Salomon III designed the Blues logo, which he described as "a flying musical note." It features a quarter-note taken off a cleff, with

some wings added on.

1973 The Spanish Pavilion downtown was sold for $1 to the bank. The association formed by Mayor Cervantes to bring the pavilion here from the New York World's Fair in 1965 owed the bank $3.5 million. The pavilion opened a cultural center in 1969, but closed a year later. The pavilion is now the lobby of the downtown Marriott.

1999 It took less than 15 seconds for explosives to bring nearly 70 years of memories crashing down. Thousands of people gathered hours before the 5:45 pm implosion reduced the Arena to a pile of rubble. The former home of the Blues opened in 1929, and hosted its last event in 1994.

February 28

1788 Ralph Clayton was born in Auguste County, Virginia. He came here in 1820 and bought 700 acres of what is now prime Clayton real estate for $9 an acre. He married Rosanna McCausland, whose family also owned a large tract of land. When the county separated from the city in 1876, he donated 100 acres of his land for the new county seat.

1961 The movie "Hoodlum Priest," had its world premiere at

Leow's State Theatre here. The film was shot in St. Louis. Don Murray starred as Father Dismas Clark, founder of Dismas House. Dismas House is a halfway house for convicts.

1966 U.S. astronauts Elliott See and Charles Bassett were killed when their jet trainer crashed into a McDonnell-Douglas building here. They were flying in for an official visit to Mac, where their Gemini space capsule was under construction. In bad weather, they hit the very building they were to have visited. Eight thousand people got out safely as debris rained down. 15 were hurt.

1996 The "Great One" became a member of the St. Louis Blues. The Blues acquired Wayne Gretzky from the Los Angeles Kings for Roman Vopat, Craig Johnson and Patrice Tardif. Gretzky would just spend the rest of the 1996 season in St. Louis, before signing a free-agent contract with the New York Rangers.

1999 The man police said was the "Southside Rapist" was arrested in New Mexico. Dennis Rabbitt was suspected in dozens of rapes across the St. Louis area over the past decade. Police found him in a hotel with a teenaged runaway.

February 29

1844 The city returned to normal after several days of violence.

It started when boys playing ball stumbled upon dissected bodies at the Medical College of old St. Louis University. A mob destroyed the school, then headed for another medical school. But students there hid the bodies, and the mob went away disappointed.

1904 Cardinal great Pepper Martin was born in Temple, Oklahoma. Known as "The Wild Horse of the Osage," Martin personified the aggressive play of the "Gashouse Gang" team that won the World Series in 1934.

1916 St. Louis voters passed a referendum mandating racial segregation. Under the new law, no one of any race could move to a block where 75 percent of the residents were of another race. The U.S. Supreme Court eventually threw out all such ordinances.

1960 The birthday of "talk radio." KMOX instituted the "At Your Service" program. Jack Buck hosted the show with Mayor Raymond Tucker as the first guest. It was a novel idea to have newsmakers take calls from listeners.

1996 Fifteen-year old Kyunia Taylor was shot to death on her school bus in North St. Louis. Her unborn child was delivered by Cesarean section, but died 23 days later. Her boyfriend, Mark Boyd, would be convicted of hiring a hit man to kill Kyunia because he didn't want the baby.

MARCH

March 1

1903 A St. Louis grand jury announced that disreputable houses, alledgedly operated under police protection, were also being used as centers of bogus voter registration by political bosses. A search of the voter poles found that 259 men who voted in the last election listed their residence at one of 15 such locations.

1912 Aviation history was made in St. Louis. Lieutenant Albert Berry made the very first parachute jump from an airplane. He jumped from a Benoist bi-plane piloted by Anthony Jannus 1,500 feet above the snow covered ground of Jefferson Barracks.

1914 Harry Christopher Carabina was born in St. Louis. He would begin his announcing career as Harry Caray on Cardinal broadcasts in 1945. He was the lead voice of the Cardinals before being fired during a dispute with the brewery in 1969. He went on to broadcast for Oakland, the White Sox, and the Cubs. Carey died in 1998.

1921 The city hosted a public hearing on a proposed bill regulating dance halls. The measure would provide for the creation of a city "Dance Hall Inspector." The bill also called for a ban on "immoral" dances such as the "Shimmy" and the "Bunny Hug."

1932 The infant son of Colonel and Mrs. Charles Lindbergh was kidnapped from the upstairs nursery of the Lindbergh home in Hopewell, New Jersey. The boy was found dead after a ransom had been delivered. Police eventually traced some of the ransom money to Bruno Richard Hauptman. He was found guilty and executed after what was then called "The trial of the century."

1966 KMOX announced a new service, "Operation Stadium Watch." The station's helicopter would broadcast traffic conditions before and after Cardinal Baseball and football games in the new stadium. For MU games, the copter would patrol the roads leading to Memorial Stadium in Columbia.

March 2

1803 Secretary of State James Madison sent credentials to Robert Livingston and James Monroe in Paris. They were now authorized to negotiate with France to buy the port of New Orleans and West Florida. They were stunned when Napoleon offered to sell them all of the Louisiana Territory.

1821 The president approved the Second Missouri

Compromise. The measure cleared the way for Missouri to be admitted to the Union as a slave state and Maine as a Free state. The first Missouri Compromise allowed the territory to draft a constitution. But some northern lawmakers objected to a passage preventing free Negroes from settling in Missouri. The second compromise removed the offending language.

1932 Al Capone offered a $10,000 reward for the capture of the Lindbergh baby kidnapers. Capone was in a Chicago jail cell, awaiting appeal of his eleven-year sentence for tax evasion. Scarface denied that he was involved. He said he could help find the real kidnapers if he wasn't in jail.

1953 Browns officials were issuing heated denials amid rumors that plans were already in motion to move the team to Baltimore. Noting that attendance had nearly doubled in 1952, owner Bill Veeck said "We have no plans to go anywhere."

1966 Two planes left St. Louis. One carried the Gemini Nine Space Capsule, built at McDonnell-Douglas. The other carried the bodies of astronauts Charles Bassett and Elliott See. They were killed on February 28th, when their jet trainer crashed into a building at McDonnell. They crashed into the very building they were to visit to inspect their space capsule. They were to have been aboard Gemini Nine in May.

1805 James Wilkinson was named as the first Territorial Governor here. He was not a popular man. He drank too much and even hatched a treasonous plan to separate the lands west of the Appalachians from the rest of the United States. He was removed from office when the plot came to light in 1807.

1825 President James Madison signed a bill authorizing funds to mark a trail westward to Santa Fe. The first leg of the Santa Fe Trail would follow the "Booneslick Trail" west from St. Charles. (Later the route of U.S. 40 and I-70) A marker in front of the St. Charles Courthouse commemorates the starting point of the trail.

1875 The St. Louis area was hit with a 15-inch snowstorm, the biggest since 1860. Transportation was at a standstill, since the horses couldn't find the streetcar tracks. The *Globe* reported that "thousands of children" were unable to make it to their places of labor.

1961 The Board of Aldermen was considering a bill to change the name of Olive Street between Whittier and Pendelton. The bill would change the name to "Gaslight Square," as the entertainment district there had become known nationwide. Today, nothing remains of the once vibrant area.

1981 Thirty-four-year-old Alderman Vincent Schoemehl won the

Democratic primary, ensuring his election as mayor. Schoemehl had been considered a long shot to defeat incumbent Mayor James Conway.

March 4

1869 The founder of University City was born in Connecticut. Edward Garner Lewis was a flamboyant publisher and something of a con artist. Lewis bought a tract of land along Delmar to build a model city, which he would govern. He built the building that is now city hall to house the headquarters of his women's magazine. He ended up broke and fled to California, where he founded another model city, Atascadero.

1878 The St. Louis County Court ordered a site be cleared for the new county seat. The site would be called "Clayton," after the man who donated much of the land. The streets were to be named after the county townships, Central, Meramec, Carondelet, Bonhomme and St. Ferdinand. St. Ferdinand later became Forsyth, after the family that owned the land along its borders. Bemiston was named for Justin Bemis, who owned the land north of Clayton.

1932 Ground was broken for the "new" terminal building at Lambert Field, on the northwest corner of the airport off Bridgeton Station Road (now Lindbergh). At the time, one city politician was nearly impeached over the plans. Critics thought the huge building, which could handle four planes at once, would never be used to capacity. It was replaced by a modern terminal in 1956 and torn down in 1978.

1974 A survey of police departments by the *Globe-Democrat* found that the streaking fad sweeping college campuses had not taken hold in St. Louis. One cop said "We're hoping to get a female." Up to 40 streakers had been sighted at the University of Missouri at Columbia.

1992 Robert Hyland, Senior Vice-President of CBS Radio and General Manager of KMOX and KLOU, died at the age of 71. Hyland is credited with inventing what we now know as talk radio with the advent of "At Your Service" in 1960. He was one of the most influential and powerful men in St. Louis.

March 5

1790 Daniel Page was born in New York. He became one of the most successful businessmen in St. Louis and a great philanthropist. The second mayor of St. Louis, he served four terms. Page Boulevard is named for him.

1877 The St. Louis Court of Appeals ended the legal battle over the election that separated the city from the county. The initial vote count showed it had failed. But the court instead found that it had passed. The separation is now blamed for many of our area's problems. It would never have happened if the election had not been contested.

1946 Former British Prime Minister Winston Churchill and President Harry Truman traveled by special train from St. Louis to Jefferson City. They then joined a motorcade to Fulton, where Churchill was to deliver a speech at Westminster College. Churchill declared "From Stettin in the Baltic to Trieste in the Adriatic, an Iron Curtain has descended across the continent." Historians see the speech as the beginning of the Cold War.

1974 Six-hundred streakers claimed a world's record at the University of Missouri in Columbia. Streakers struck Washington University, the Penrose Street Police Station, the 8900 block of Riverview and in the Central West End.

1999 The "Spoonball" era at St. Louis University came to an end. Men's basketball coach Charlie Spoonhour announced his retirement. In his seven years at SLU, Spoonhour revived the program and took the Bills to the NCAA Tournament three times. Lorenzo Romar replaced him.

March 6

1815 Residents of the Dardenne area gathered at the home of Etienne Bernard to establish a new Catholic congregation. The first St. Peter's church was built of logs and was later wiped out by the rampaging Dardenne Creek. The settlement that sprang up around the church also took the name St. Peters.

1857 The U.S. Supreme Court ruled in the Dred Scott case. Scott was a slave from Missouri who sued for his freedom after his owner took him into Illinois, a free state. In a trial at the Old Courthouse in St. Louis, Scott lost. He won on appeal, then lost again before the Missouri Supreme Court. The U.S. Supreme Court found that slaves were not citizens and thus could not sue. The case polarized the nation on the slavery issue.

1907 The Western Brewery in Belleville announced the winner of a contest to find a name for its newest brew. Seventeen-year old George Wuller won $25 for suggesting the name "Stag." The named lived on even after the brewery closed for the last time in 1988.

1923 The Cardinals announced that players would wear uniform numbers for the first time, They would be numbered according to the players spot in the batting order.

1973 John Poelker upset incumbent Mayor A.J. Cervantes in the Democratic primary. The defeat ended a 25-year-political career and eight controversial years as mayor for Cervantes. His term was marked by the battle over a second airport, and the ill-fated

Santa Maria and Spanish Pavilion. *Life* Magazine once charged he had ties to the underworld.

March 7

1849 A group of prominent St. Louisans established a cemetery on the site of the Hempstead Farm on Bellefontaine Road. A cholera epidemic soon swept the city, and as many as 20 burials a day took place there. Many of the most famous names in St. Louis history are buried at Bellefontaine Cemetery, including Adolphus Busch, William Clark, Thomas Benton, James Eads and many others.

1861 Adolphus Busch, a former brewery supply salesman, married Lilly Anheuser. She was the daughter of Eberhard Anheuser. He ran the small Bavarian Brewery in St. Louis. In 1865, Busch obtained controlling interest in the brewery. When Anheuser died in 1880, the name was changed to Anheuser-Busch.

1872 After months of debate, the Missouri Legislature approved a bill creating Forest Park. The bill was the result of a campaign by Hiram Leffingwell, a developer who just so happened to own huge tracts of land near the site. Taxpayers and land owners successfully challenged this bill, claiming the park was too far away to be of any use. But in 1874, a new bill made changes required by the court, and Hiram got his park.

1980 Workers wrapped a giant yellow ribbon around the planetarium in Forest Park in honor of the American hostages in Iran. The planetarium is traditionally wrapped in a red ribbon over the holidays.

1988 The Blues made one of the better deals in their history. They swapped Rob Ramage and Rick Wamsley to Calgary for Steve Bozak and some guy named Brett Hull.

March 8

1887 James B. Eads died in the Bahamas at the age of 66. Eads made a fortune when he devised a way to recover valuables from sunken steamships and provided gunboats to the Union that helped win the Civil War. But he is best remembered for the bridge in St. Louis that bears his name. Completed in 1876, the Eads bridge was the first major span made entirely of steel.

1896 St. Louis Browns manager Harry Diddlebock was fired for drunkenness. Owner Chris Von der Ahe managed a couple of games himself before hiring Roger Connor. Von der Ahe went through six managers that season alone.

1901 The cornerstone was laid for the new St. Charles County Courthouse. The building at the top of "Clerk's Hill" was completed in 1903.

1971 Two bombs blasted the ROTC Building on Forest Park Boulevard. Fourteen police officers and firefighters were inside investigating the first explosion when the second bomb went off. Seven policemen and three firefighters were hurt. A few hours earlier, a bomb had shattered the Civilian Personnel Records Center in St. Louis.

2001 The rebirth of the Cupples Station Complex took a giant leap forward. The $75 million Westin St. Louis at 8th and Clark opened its doors. It was part of a redevelopment plan for nine of the ten remaining buildings. The 23 original buildings covered 30 acres. They were constructed between 1891 and 1917, and handled much of the city's wholesale shipping trade.

March 9

1896 Granite City, Illinois, was incorporated. F.G. and William Niedreinghaus named the town for their "Graniteware" kitchen products. By 1899, the Niedringhaus plant was called NESCO, for National Enameling and Stamping Company. It covered 75 acres and employed 4,000. The plant and the immigrants it drew attracted other heavy industrial firms, such as Granite City Steel.

1904 The May Company announced it had installed a new invention in the store at Sixth and Washington. A spokesman for the company said the "Escalader" was a kind of moving staircase that would take shoppers from floor to floor.

1914 The deadliest fire in St. Louis history. Thirty-three people, many of the prominent citizens, lost their lives when the Missouri Athletic Club and Boatmen's Bank Building burned. The fire chief had warned the building was a firetrap. Six days later, one of the walls of the burned out building collapsed and crushed an adjacent building. Six more people were killed. The present Missouri Athletic Club Building was built on the same site.

1946 Archbishop John Cardinal Glennon died in his native Ireland while on his way back to St. Louis from Rome. He was 83. Just 19 days earlier, he had been elevated to the College of Cardinals. Glennon had served as Archbishop of St. Louis for 42 years.

1972 The *Globe* reported on a new gimmick in a price war among gas stations here. A Sinclair station on Olive was offering "mini-service." The attendant just pumped gas. No windshields were washed, no oil checked, but the motorist saved a couple of cents per gallon. The article noted that some stations in Columbia were offering "Self-Serve" gasoline.

1982 The Blues fired coach Red Berenson. President and General Manager Emile Francis replaced him behind the bench. Berenson had led the Blues to their best regular season record in club history just one year earlier.

March 10

1804 The American flag was raised over St. Louis for the first time by Captain Amos Stoddard. The United States had bought the Louisiana Territory from France, but it hadn't been transferred to France from Spain. Captain Stoddard performed that ceremony on March 9th. The French flag flew over St. Louis for one day before he raised the American flag.

1814 St. Clair County officials met to pick a more central site for the county seat. They voted to move it from Cahokia to the farm of George Blair. It was his idea to name the site "Belleville," French for "beautiful village."

1849 St. Charles was incorporated as a city and the first city charter was adopted. Louis Blanchette established a post at the site in April, 1769. The village was originally known as "Les Petite Cotes" or "Little Hills." It eventually took the name of the first church, San Carlos Borromeo. That was eventually anglicized to St. Charles.

1956 The new, ultramodern terminal building at Lambert Field was dedicated by Mayor Tucker. The St. Louis architectural firm of Hellmuth, Yamasaki and Linweber designed the terminal. It replaced a terminal built in 1933, which stood on the north end of the airport at Highway 66 (Lindbergh) and Bridgeton Station Road. The old terminal was torn down in 1978.

1991 St. Louis City Prosecuting Attorney George Peach's troubles began. He was arrested at the Airport Marriott as part of a prostitution sting. He was using the alias "Larry Johnson." By October, Peach had been indicted on eleven counts of misusing public funds.

March 11

1926 St. Louis Comptroller Louis Nolte opposed accepting the generous offer of Albert Bond Lambert. Lambert offered to sell the Bridgeton Flying Field to the city for a fraction of its value. Nolte said the field was too far away to be of use. Nolte said the city had spent thousands on an airfield in Forest Park that was used by airmail pilots for a few months (the Mounted Police Stables are the old hangar building).

1978 A hostile crowd of several thousand prevented a march and rally by the National Socialist Party of America in South St. Louis. About 43 Nazis settled for a ride down Cherokee Street in a truck while the crowd pelted them with snowballs, rocks and bottles.

1980 The landmark riverfront McDonald's opened. The restaurant was built on a 702-ton, 185-foot long riverboat on top of a barge moored on the levee. The restaurant could seat 350 people. The restaurant was closed in 2000.

1984 TWA announced that its landmark hangar at Lambert Field would be demolished to make way for new passenger gates. The massive hangar along I-70 was one of the airport's most visible features when it opened in 1957.

1987 Amid much fanfare, the refurbished "Admiral" riverboat opened as a complex of bars, restaurants and a ballroom. A combination of high costs and low attendance forced it to close in November of 1988, millions of dollars in debt.

March 12

1921 A gunman for William Egan, a saloon-keeper and powerful Democratic city politician, killed a rival over a rum running operation. A political lobbyist was also killed. Egan would be dead by fall, and a bloody war was underway between "Egan's Rats" and the Hogan Gang. The gangs engaged in wild gun battles on the busy streets, while the public fled for their lives. The violence took at least 23 lives over two years.

1963 St. Louisans got their first look at the proposed design for a new downtown stadium. Edward Durell Stone, internationally famous architect and designer, presented the plans along with a scale model. He called the design "suggestive of a 20th century version of the Roman Coliseum. City leaders expected it to be completed by 1965.

1975 The *Globe* reported that the old Chain of Rocks Bridge was doomed. The Madison Village Board had accepted a bid from a Michigan firm to demolish the bridge for $103,000. But a sudden dip in steel prices saved the bridge.

1989 The curtain came down on the Ambassador Theatre. The chandeliers, staircases and even sections of plasterwork were auctioned off. The Ambassador was once the home of the "Skouras Brothers Missouri Rocket Girls," which evolved into the world-famous Radio City Music Hall "Rockettes." It was torn down in 1997 to make room for a plaza in front of the Mercantile Bank headquarters.

1999 Six children were killed in a fire in the 1400 block of Salisbury. Police would later charge Nevelynn Stokes with first degree murder. They said Stokes set the fire after he was beaten up during a quarrel with the woman who lived in the building and her boyfriend.

March 13

1914 Edward "Butch" O'Hare was born in St. Louis. During

World War II, he was awarded the Congressional Medal of Honor for shooting down five Japanese bombers attacking the USS "Lexington." O'Hare was shot down over Tarawa in 1943. Chicago's Airport was named in his honor in 1946.

1947 The St. Louis County Library began operations. The voters had approved a tax creating the library district in April, 1946. On this date, the first book was checked out of a collection of 86,000.

1960 The Chicago Cardinals announced they were moving to St. Louis. Carroll Rosenbloom, owner of the Baltimore Colts, helped persuade the Bidwell family to bring the team here. Joseph Griesedieck, president of the Falstaff Brewery, helped by buying a large minority interest in the club.

1964 The Beatles made their first appearance in St. Louis, sort of. A film of their recent Washington DC concert was shown at the St. Louis Theatre on Grand as part of a "Closed-circuit big-screen TV" hookup in theaters from coast-to-coast. Footage of the Beach Boys and Leslie Gore, neither of whom were at the DC concert, was edited in.

1988 Brett Hull scored his first goal for the St. Louis Blues. It came in a game in Los Angeles against the Kings.

1782 One of the most colorful figures in Missouri history was born. Thomas Hart Benton was a lawyer, politician and statesmen who would become one of the first two Senators from Missouri. He also had a bit of a temper. Benton once took a shot at Andrew Jackson, before Jackson was president. He killed Charles Lucas in a duel on "Bloody Island" in the Mississippi here. (Now part of the East St. Louis riverfront)

1859 It is the birthday of the Missouri Botanical Garden. The Missouri Legislature authorized Henry Shaw to open the garden at his country estate "Tower Grove" to the public. He deeded the land to the city trustees. "Shaw's Garden" quickly became a top St. Louis attraction.

1899 The Browns were sold to Frank de Haas and Mathew Stanley Robison for $33,000 at a sheriff's auction. The Robisons also owned the Cleveland franchise. They swapped players between the two, bringing the much better Cleveland players to St. Louis. The new team was called the "Perfectos," but a sportswriter called them the "Cardinals" after hearing a fan comment on the new uniforms.

1962 MacDonald Construction Company was formally awarded an $11,442,418 contract for the construction of the Arch and the visitor center shell. In ceremonies at the Old Courthouse, the city turned over its $2.5 million share of the construction costs.

2000 A new era began on the former site of the "Old Barn" on Oakland Avenue. Ground was broken for a five-story office building on the site where the Arena once stood. It was to be the first unit of the "Highlands at Forest Park" office complex. The complex was named for the amusement park that once stood next to the Arena.

March 15

1884 The "New" Post Office and Customs House on Olive was dedicated. General William T. Sherman presided over the ceremonies. In 1959, the federal government moved to sell the building to a developer, who planned to tear it down. Public outcry saved the building. The Old Post Office became the first St. Louis building to be placed on the National Register of Historic Places.

1931 More than 8,000 people attended the biggest celebration ever in Rolla. They were celebrating the completion of paving on Route 66 across Missouri. The last mile had been paved back in January in Phelps County near Arlington. At that time, Route 66 traffic used Manchester west from St. Louis to Gray Summit. The new Watson Road and the highway through Valley Park and Pacific opened in 1933.

1961 Chuck Berry was convicted in his second trial for bringing a 14-year old girl across state lines to work as a hat check girl in his St. Louis tavern. The first conviction had been overturned because the judge made racist remarks. Berry was sentenced to three years in prison.

1965 Civil rights activist Ivory Perry snarled traffic as he lay down in front of a car on the Kingshighway exit from Highway 40. Two other protestors blocked traffic at other key intersections to protest the situation in Selma, Alabama.

1983 The Museum of Science and Industry unveiled plans for a $20 million science center in the old Falstaff Building at 5050 Oakland Avenue. Plans called for the museum to move there from Oak Knoll Park if voters okayed a tax increase.

March 16

1881 Saloon owner Chris Von der Ahe announced he had leased the old Grand Avenue Baseball Club. The head of the "St. Louis Sportsman's Club" said the club would include baseball fields, bowling alleys, and running tracks at what would become known as "Sportsman's Park."

1939 Father Joseph Dunne died. At least 20,000 people would file by his bier over the next three days to pay their respects. Dunne founded his home for newsboys in 1906. In 1948, his life story came to the big screen in the film "Fighting Father Dunne." His newsboys home still provides a place for underprivileged boys today.

1958 The call letters of KWK, Channel Four, were changed to KMOX-TV. CBS had taken over in February, 1957 in a $1 million deal. CBS gave up the rights to Channel 11, for which it had been granted a construction permit.

1972 The first building was blown up at the notorious Pruitt-Igoe housing project. The demolition of the 11-story building was a test to see if the entire complex could be demolished using dynamite. Pruitt-Igoe stood as a monument to the well-intentioned but failed social programs of the 1950's and 60's.

1981 The Streckfuss Line said no potential buyers for the "Admiral" had come forward and the boat would probably be cut up and sold for scrap. The St. Louis Board of Aldermen had rejected a plan to allow the Port Authority to issue bonds for the purchase of the boat.

March 17

1820 The first recorded St. Patrick's Day parade in St. Louis. The Irish were the first large group of immigrants to arrive here. By 1820, there were about 100 of them in a population of seven thousand. They included John Mullanphy, the city's first million-aire. The Great Famine of 1845-50 brought more immigrants. By 1851, the Irish made up one-seventh of the population. Many lived in the notorious "Kerry Patch" shantytown, around 14th and O'Fallon.

1886 The first issue of *The Sporting News* hit the stands. Al Spink, a former reporter for the *Post-Dispatch*, established the paper in St. Louis. Spink is credited with naming Sportsman's Park.

1917 The Women's National Bowling Congress held the first women's bowling tournament in the country right here in St. Louis. About 100 women took part. The team title went to the Progress Team of St. Louis. Mrs. A.J. Koester, also of St. Louis, won the all-event title.

1969 The Cardinals traded the hero of the 1967 season, Orlando Cepeda, to the Braves for Joe Torre. Torre would go on to become the National League MVP in 1971. Torre would manage the Cardinals from 1990 to 1995. He was fired in 1995, and went on to manage the New York Yankees.

1998 Workers took down the landmark blue neon McDonnell-Douglas sign at Lambert Field. It was replaced by a three-story-tall neon "Boeing" sign. McDonnell Aircraft was founded in 1939, and merged with Douglas in 1967. The St. Louis institution merged with Boeing in 1997.

March 18

1851 The first big concert event in St. Louis history. Jenny Lind, "The Swedish Nightingale, " came to town. The windows of the packed hall were thrown open, and crowds gathered in the street to hear.

1904 The *Globe* reported that St. Louis showman Zack Mull's "Wild West Exhibition and Congress of American Indians" at the World's Fair would feature 750 Indians representing 51 tribes. 30 "rough riders" would also be featured. Among the Indians participating would be Geronimo, the aged leader of the Apache. Joseph of the Nez Pierce and Lone Wolf of the Kiowas were also expected to appear.

1947 The familiar St. Louis County Library "Bookmobile" made its first run. The first stop was in Florissant Valley. The library founders felt that bookmobiles were the only way to reach the 400 square miles of St. Louis County, which was mostly still rural.

1948 The St. Louis University Billikens beat New York University to win the NIT Championship. At that time, the NIT was the premiere tournament in college basketball.

1999 A St. Louis landmark came back to life. Ninety display apartments were unveiled and the famous Zodiac and Starlight Rooms were re-opened at the renovated Chase-Park Plaza. The

Chase was the center of the city's nightlife from the 1920s until it closed in 1989.

March 19

1920 Elsa Lemp killed herself. Her father, brewery magnate William Lemp, had killed himself in 1904. Her brother, William, killed himself in 1922. Their brother, Charles, committed suicide in 1929. All of the suicides,  except Elsa's, took place in the Lemp mansion. The mansion is now a restaurant and a ghostly Halloween haunt.

1948 Cleanup was underway after tornadoes swept across Missouri and Illinois. Fifty people were dead and 300 injured within a 60-mile radius of St. Louis. Hardest hit was the town of Bunker Hill, Illinois. Nineteen people were dead and 80% of the buildings in town were leveled.

1982 Workers were putting the finishing touches on Richard Serra's $250,000 sculpture on the Gateway Mall downtown. The sculpture consists of eight, ten-by-40-foot structural steel panels. They were designed to rust with age. Serra said he expected initial public reaction to his work to be negative. But he predicted people would soon be entranced.

1994 The screen at the 66-Park-In Theater on Watson Road in

Crestwood was torn down to make room for a supermarket. The landmark opened in 1948 along what was then Route 66.

2001 Johnnie Johnson was inducted into the Rock and Roll Hall of Fame. On New Years Eve 1952, Johnson asked a friend to sit in for an ailing band member. The friend's name was Chuck Berry. They would go on to collaborate on many rock classics. Berry is said to have written "Johnny B. Goode" as a tribute to Johnson.

March 20

1878 Businessmen Alonso and Charles Slayback proposed a yearly pageant to promote the Agricultural and Mechanical Fair. They created the Mystic Order of the Veiled Prophet, modeled after a New Orleans Carnival Society. The annual parade and ball became a show for the rich and powerful, but faded as times changed in the 60's and 70's. In July, 1981, its leaders put on the first "V.P. Fair." The name was changed to "Fair St. Louis" in 1994.

1922 The Aero Club of St. Louis voted to name its new airfield at Bridgeton after Albert Bond Lambert. Lambert was the president of the club and a tireless promoter of St. Louis as an aviation center. He was using his own money to develop the field. Lambert would later sell the field to city for a fraction of its value.

1943 St. Louis Fire Chief Joseph W. Morgan was killed in a fire at the Goodwill Industries Building, 713 Howard. Morgan had climbed a fire escape to order his men out of the building, when the whole thing collapsed.

1965 A crowd of 9,000 Hawks fans turned out for the festivities honoring the great Bob Petit in his final game before retirement. Petit played for the Hawks for 11 seasons. He set numerous records while becoming the first player in NBA history to score 20,000 points.

1975 It appeared a certainty that the controversial Meramec Dam would be built. A federal judge ruled against the Sierra Club in its suit to halt the project near Meramec State Park. Construction was already underway on the site of the proposed 12,000 acre reservoir. But farmers and environmentalists pushed for a referendum on the issue. Over 60% voted against, and the project was halted in 1981.

March 21

1845 Artemus Bullard was sent to organize the First Presbyterian Church of St. Louis. John Marshall donated the land. Bullard named the church Rock Hill, after some nearby rocky outcroppings and the rocky road that ran there from St. Louis. The community that sprang up around the church also took the name.

1904 The new St. Louis water works was completed in a rush, just in time for the fair. The new system brought an end to the days when St. Louis water had "body." Nervous fair officials had installed their own water purification system in case the new water works was not on line in time to keep the fountains from being fouled with the muddy, brown water.

1970 A last minute phone campaign was credited with passage of a bill to keep the musical "Hair" out of St. Louis. The Board of Aldermen voted 16-11 to ban "obscene" plays and movies. Aldermen said they had been deluged with calls in favor of the bill from religious and patriotic groups.

1975 Redbird great Joe Medwick died of a heart attack. Medwick is best remembered as a member of the "Gas House Gang" world champions of 1934. Commissioner Kennesaw Mountain Landis took him out of game seven for his own safety. Irate Detroit fans pelted him with debris after he slid hard into Tiger third baseman Marv Owen.

March 22

1904 The founder of University City, Edward G. Lewis, unveiled the world's largest spotlight. It was brought here from Germany. He planned to put it on top of his Woman's Magazine Building, today's city hall. The light would be visible from 150 miles away.

1922 An article in the *Globe* reported on the growing popularity of radio in St. Louis. The paper said there were now 2,200 receiving sets here, up from just a few hundred the year before. Nationwide, there were about 600,000 sets, up from 50,000 a year earlier.

1934 Legendary athlete Babe Didrickson became the only woman ever to pitch for the Cardinals. She started an exhibition game and gave up four hits and three runs before being relieved by "Wild Bill" Hallahan. Didrickson is one of only two females to pitch in the majors. The other was Lizzie Murphy, who played for an American League All-Star team in 1922.

1952 Bob Costas was born. Costas came to KMOX in 1974, to announce the games of the St. Louis Spirits of the ABA. He joined NBC in 1980. Since then Costas has hosted nearly every type of major sporting event, including the World Series, Super Bowl, and the Summer Olympics in 1992 and 1996. He hosted his own late night talk show from 1988 to 1994.

1976 Elvis Presley made his final concert appearance in St. Louis. He was scheduled to return to Kiel in September of 1977, but died in August.

March 23

1818 William Lindsay Long bought 408 acres along the Meramec River for about $1,200. He laid out the town of Fenton and named it after his Welsh grandmother, Elizabeth Fenton Bennett. Local legend says she was a descendent of the Earl of Fenton.

1806 The Lewis and Clark Expedition began their return trip from the Pacific Coast to St. Louis. They reached St. Louis on September 23, 1806 The round trip took two years and four months, covering over 4,000 miles

1994 Channel Five weatherman Bob Richards took off in his Piper Cherokee 180. He climbed to 440 feet above Spirit of St. Louis Airport, then nosed the plane straight into the runway at over 100 miles-per-hour. His reputation had been tarnished by allegations that he had stalked and harassed a Farmington, Missouri woman.

2000 The Cardinals traded pitcher Kent Bottenfield and infielder Adam Kennedy to Anaheim for outfielder Jim Edmonds. Edmonds would slug 42 home runs in 2000, a Cardinal record for an outfielder.

2000 Workers began taking down the Mercantile signs and replacing them with the Firstar logo. Firstar bought out Mercantile in the summer of 1999. Mercantile had been a St. Louis institution since 1855.

1881 The first concert of the St. Louis Choral Society, a performance of Handel's "Dettigem Te Deum," was presented at the Mercantile Library Hall. The choral society eventually absorbed a local orchestral group. It changed its name to the St. Louis Choral-Symphony Society, the forerunner of today's St. Louis Symphony.

1893 The greatest player in Browns history was born in Manchester, Ohio. George Sisler played for the Browns from 1915 until 1928 and managed them from 1924 until 1936. He hit .407 in 1920 and .420 in 1922, ending his career with a lifetime average of .314. Sisler was one of the original 12 players inducted into the Baseball Hall of Fame in 1939.

1904 The World's Fair Restaurant Concessionaires Association agreed that the price of a beer on the pike would be 10¢. Several members protested it would be holding up the public to charge that much. But a majority wanted the higher price, because "they could get it."

1923 Members of the warring "Egan's Rats" and Hogan Gangs blasted away at each other from speeding cars on Lindell between Grand and Jefferson. A 13-year old boy was run over and seriously injured. Asked to identify the gunmen, Edward "Jelly Roll"

Hogan said, "I'll identify the two men under arrest, with a shotgun." Public outrage against the gangsters was growing.

1970 Washington University was in turmoil. Students were continuing protests against the operation of an ROTC center on campus. Hundreds of students marched on the home of Chancellor Thomas Eliot. Police kept them back, but more rallies were planned.

March 25

1904 A trainload of Filipino "wild people" and "half-savage tribes" arrived to be put on exhibit at the fair. Nearly all of the Igorrotes and savage headhunters were suffering ill effects from the change in climate. The Igorrotes would become a major attraction, since they ate dogs on special occasions. Legend has it that the surrounding neighborhood became known as "Dogtown." It had actually been known as Dogtown since before the Civil War.

1927 The last piece of horse-drawn fire equipment in St. Louis was removed from service. Engine Company Number 25 made the final horse-drawn run, from the firehouse at 16th and Mullanphy.

1957 One of the most notorious corporate move-outs in St. Louis history took place. The Missouri, Kansas and Texas Railroad moved to Texas. Employees arriving to work that day found a terse note informing them they could report the next day for a train to Texas if they wanted to keep their jobs.

1961 The Missouri Highway Department announced plans to extend the Daniel Boone Expressway (U.S. 40) past its dead-end at 20th street. A spokesman said if voters approved a gasoline tax increase, the highway could be ready in time for the opening of the new stadium. It actually took until 1971 before 40 connected with the Poplar Street Bridge.

1965 The Chrysler Corporation announced plans for a multi-million dollar truck assembly plant to be built next to the automobile plant on Highway 66 in Fenton. The company said it would bring up to 2,000 jobs to the area.

March 26

1776 Peter Lindell was born. He became a successful merchant and made a fortune buying up land in what is today the heart of St. Louis. That's where you will find Lindell Boulevard today.

1874 Backers were hailing the signing of a bill establishing Forest Park. The proposal pushed by Hiram Leffingwell had failed before, after critics said the park was too far away to be of any use. Leffingwell said the park was "one of the best things ever done to ensure the city's permanent prosperity." He just happened to own a good chunk of real estate around the park.

1911 Playwright Tennessee Williams was born in St. Louis. At the age of seven, he moved with his family to the tenement at 4633 Westminster Place that served as the setting for "The Glass Menagerie." He won Pulitzer Prizes for "A Streetcar Named Desire" and "Cat on a Hot Tin Roof."

1973 UCLA's Bill Walton hit 21 of 22 shots and scored 44 points as the Bruins beat Memphis State in the NCAA championship game at the Arena. Walton's performance is still considered one of the greatest individual performances ever in an NCAA championship game.

1979 General Motors announced it was moving its Corvette assembly line out of North St. Louis. The St. Louis plant had built Corvettes since the 1954 model year. The move would cost 1,450 jobs and an annual payroll of over $20 million. The Vette plant would be moved to Bowling Green, Kentucky.

March 27

1819 Belleville was incorporated as a town. The town was founded because the county seat needed to be moved. A wave of American settlers had shifted the population of the county. George Blair laid out the county seat on his 200-acre tract,

Compton Hill. He said any town located on the land would become a "beautiful city" or in French, "Belle Ville."

1861 The current St. Louis police system was set up by the state legislature. The ordinance established a board of police commissioners appointed by the state, independent of city government. The system was established to keep the police under control of Missouri's pro-southern governor. St. Louis is the only major city in the country where such a system is still in place.

1968 The pilot of an Ozark D.C. Nine was credited with averting disaster at Lambert Field. He managed to bring his crippled plane in after a collision with a small plane directly over the Ford plant in Hazelwood. The Cessna struck the D.C. Nine's wing. It came down at Lindbergh and I-270. The two people on the small plane were killed.

1981 Southwestern Bell announced plans for a 44-story, $120 million corporate tower downtown. The project would once again give St. Louis the tallest building in Missouri. The 42-story Hyatt Regency in Kansas City had eclipsed the Mercantile Building in July, 1980. The Metropolitan Square Building in St. Louis is now the tallest in the state.

2002 After 96 years, the D'Arcy, Masius Benton and Bowles advertising agency announced it would close its doors by June.

The firm created such advertising icons as the Coca-Cola Santa Claus, The Budweiser Frogs and Lizards and the Ralston-Purina dog food chuck wagon. The firm suffered a major blow, when it lost the Budweiser account in 1994. That was followed by the loss of TWA and Southwestern Bell.

March 28

1899 August Busch Junior was born. As long-time chairman of Anheuser-Busch, he oversaw its growth into the largest brewery in the world. He served as president of the Cardinals from their purchase by the brewery in 1953 until his death in 1990. He was beloved by St. Louisans for his work to keep the Cardinals here and his efforts to revitalize downtown.

1902 Marlin Perkins was born in Carthage. He came to the St. Louis Zoo in 1926 to work with the reptile collection. He left to oversee other zoos, and started the television show "Zoo Parade." He returned to the St. Louis Zoo in 1962 and began a new show, called "Wild Kingdom." He hosted it until 1985.

1923 "Jelly Roll" Hogan gave his pledge to the pastor of St. Patrick's Church that he would try to make peace between his followers and the Egan Gang. Outraged citizens were demanding an end to the bloody gun battles in the streets. The truce lasted a couple of months, until Egan's "Rats" opened fire on a crowd in an effort to kill Hogan. Two bystanders, including State Representative William McGee, were killed.

1958 Composer W.C. Handy died in New York at the age of 84. Handy composed such blues standards as "Memphis Blues," "Beale Street Blues," and of course, "St. Louis Blues." In St. Louis, 16 bands would mass at the Soldier's Memorial to play his signature song at the hour of his funeral.

1963 Mayor Tucker and a group of civic leaders met with Walt Disney in California. Disney was proposing to construct an attraction on the St. Louis riverfront. Plans for "Riverfront Square" fell through due to a lack of financing, and because Walt initially refused to allow beer to be sold. A few months after Disney withdrew from the project in 1965, he announced plans for a development in Central Florida.

March 29

1818 The Reverend William DuBourg, Catholic Bishop of the Louisiana Territory, laid the cornerstone for a cathedral to replace the old log church built in 1777. The growth of the diocese quickly rendered this church obsolete. Work began on a "new" cathedral in 1831. DuBourg's cathedral became a warehouse and burned to the ground in 1835.

1838 The first public transportation system in St. Louis went into operation. The horse-drawn omnibus operated by J.C. Melcher was a failure. The first successful transit line in the city would be opened by Erastus Wells in 1844. Wells lived on a country estate known as "Wellston."

1957 Elvis Presley returned to St. Louis for the first time since he opened for Roy Acuff in 1956. This time, he was the headliner for a show at the sold-out Kiel Auditorium. Tickets were $2 and $2.50. Twenty St. Louis Police officers and 50 auxiliary officers were on hand to keep the crowd in line.

1969 The ill-fated replica of the Santa Maria arrived at the St. Louis riverfront. The ship was part of the Spanish exhibit at the World's Fair in New York. Mayor Cervantes acquired it as a tourist attraction. It sank in a storm in June 1969. Raised and repaired, it was sold and moved to California in 1973.

March 30

1890 The Great Blizzard of 1890 began. Officially, 20.4 inches of snow fell here on the 30th and 31st. That's still the all-time record for the worst snowstorm in St. Louis history.

1903 Mark Twain wrote a letter to the directors of the world's fair, urging that steamboat races be held at the fair. Twain wrote, "As an advertisement for the fair, it would be hard to beat the boat race. As a spectacle, nothing could be added to it, except an old fashioned blow up as the boats entered the home stretch. But this should not be arranged; It is best left to providence and prayer."

1931 The *Globe* reported that Betty Grable of St. Louis had signed a contract that "assured her a pretty salary for five years" and "says she will be developed for talkie stardom." Producers Flo Ziegfield and comedian Eddie Cantor were said to have discovered her in the chorus of the film "Whoopee."

1957 A reviewer in the *Globe* said "Elvis Presley sang, groaned, shimmied and shook his way through 16 offerings" the night before at Kiel. Every seat was filled. It marked the first sell out by a performer "other than Liberace" in recent years.

1977 The long-running controversy over the proposed major airport at Columbia-Waterloo, Illinois was resolved. Brock Adams, the U.S. Secretary of Transportation, reversed a decision by his predecessor. Adams announced there would be no federal funding for such a project. Adams said he was confident Lambert Field was capable of meeting the area's needs until at least 1995.

March 31

1890 Compare this item to the way we cover snowstorms today. As the city dug out from the worst blizzard ever, an item on page six of the *Globe* mentioned that "a spell of weather' had "affected all lines of business and pleasure in a most disagreeable way."

1958 Chuck Berry's autobiographical classic, "Johnny B. Goode," entered the Billboard chart. Berry's family lived on Goode Avenue in St. Louis—hence the title. The song was written in tribute to Berry's piano player and collaborator, Johnnie Johnson. Johnson would sue Berry for royalties on many of their '50s classics.

1964 The seven-month long demonstrations by the Congress of Racial Equality at Jefferson Bank and Trust came to an end. The first large scale civil rights protest here forced the bank to hire five African-American clerical workers. The Congress of Racial Equality (CORE) organized the protests. The bank obtained injunctions against the protestors and many civil rights leaders were arrested and sentenced to jail time or fines.

1977 The new convention center downtown was dedicated. The center was named for former Mayor A.J. Cervantes, who led the push for the $25 million bond issue to get it built.

1984 The HBE Corporation's Adam's Mark Hotel at Fourth and Chestnut downtown opened. A pair of nine-foot-tall bronze horses, created by Venetian Artist Ludovico De Luigi, dominates the lobby of the hotel.

APRIL

April 1

1841 The first luxury hotel in St. Louis opened. The Planter's House was located north of the courthouse on Fourth Street. It hosted the great names of the day, including Henry Clay, Daniel Webster and Charles Dickens. It was the birthplace of the famous "Planter's Punch."

1926 City officials put forward a plan to do something about the smelly River Des Peres in Forest Park. Muny patrons were forced to endure the stench of the polluted river. The plan called for diverting the river into sewage pipes. The Muny Association would pay for the plan, using city labor.

1954 Former patrolman Elmer Dolan was convicted of perjury in connection with the missing Greenlease ransom money. He was convicted of lying to a federal grand jury when he testified that the suitcases containing the ransom were taken to the police station at the same time Carl Austin Hall was booked. Half of the ransom was still missing.

1959 The Missouri State Highway Commission announced tentative plans for a 40-mile "Circumferential Expressway" loop around St. Louis. The highway was to be designated as I-270. Planners called for a new bridge over the Mississippi north of the Chain of Rocks Bridge.

1976 The *Globe* reported on the demise of the Holiday Hill Amusement Park at Brown and Natural Bridge. The property had been condemned a few years earlier. It was purchased by the city for an airport parking lot that was never built. The familiar rides, such as "The Bullet," were gone or had been moved to the Chain of Rocks "Fun Fair" park.

April 2

1838 The first public school in St. Louis opened. The Missouri Legislature had organized a school board and set in motion plans for two school houses in 1837. The first one to open was the Laclede Primary School at Fourth and Spruce. While the first school was public, it was not free.

1896 The city of Webster Groves was incorporated. The town began as five separate communities along the Pacific Railroad. Webster Village grew up around Webster College. The other stops along the line were Tuxedo, Webster Park, Old Orchard and the Frisco Station. The promoters of the subdivision of Webster

67

Park touted their development as "The Queen of Suburbs." The nickname endures to this day.

1923 Gangsters made off with $260,000 in the robbery of an armored mail truck at Fourth and Locust. Several weeks later, they pulled off another mail robbery in Staunton. A member of "Egan's Rats" soon ratted the others out. Twelve members of the Egan and "Cuckoo" Gangs were convicted. The convictions ended the Egan's war with the Hogan Gang that took at least 23 lives over two years.

1953 The first Channel Nine pledge drive began. The St. Louis Educational Television Commission announced a fund-raising plan to put educational television on the air here. The commission said it needed to raise an additional $490,000 to get Channel Nine signed on.

1976 A huge "firestorm" engulfed several buildings just west of downtown. More than 200 firemen fought the blaze in the area bounded by Washington, Olive, 20th and 22nd streets. The flames raged over a six-block area of many multi-story buildings. Eight firemen were injured and a pumper was destroyed.

April 3

1904 A group of St. Louis County farmers and horse owners formed an organization with the purpose of "forcing drivers and automobiles to respect the skittish horse." The horse owners were upset that recent state legislation imposing a nine-mile-per-hour speed limit had not solved the problem.

1936 Bruno Richard Hauptman was executed for the murder of the Lindbergh baby. Hauptman was convicted of the March, 1932 crime mostly on circumstantial evidence. No witnesses were ever found.

1950 The Board of Aldermen moved to stop that great scourge of the 1950s, the comic book. A measure was passed making it a crime to sell lurid comic books or crime comics to kids under 18.

1963 McDonnell Aircraft was celebrating after winning a $436,450,000 contract from NASA. The contract called for Mac to develop and build 13 two-man Gemini spacecraft. 4,481 employees were working full time here on the Gemini program.

1985 The Board of Aldermen of Times Beach voted to disincorporate their dioxin contaminated city. The signs came down along I-44, and nothing remained to remind motorists a town once stood there. Today, the cleaned-up site is Route 66 State Park.

April 4

1918 German immigrant Robert Prager was lynched by a mob in

Collinsville. Prager wanted to join the United Mineworkers, but the union suspected him of trying to bomb the mines. It was later determined that Prager was a loyal American, and had even volunteered to fight the Germans.

1933 Bernard F. Dickmann was elected mayor of St. Louis, the first Democratic mayor here in 24 years. He would call together a group of businessmen to set in motion Luther Ely Smith's plans for a riverfront memorial. The official name for the Poplar Street Bridge is the Bernard F. Dickmann bridge.

1941 A huge crowd turned out for the first Hollywood style premiere in St. Louis. John Wayne, Judy Canova, Jerry Colona, Bob Crosby and Susan Hayward appeared at the premiere of "Sis Hopkins" at the Fox. The crowd was so large along Grand that the stars had to go through an alley to enter the theater.

1968 Martin Luther King Junior was assassinated in Memphis. That night, Mayor Cervantes went from TV station to TV station to appeal for calm. The streets of St. Louis remained quiet. A Senate Committee would later find that James Earl Ray killed King as part of a St. Louis-based conspiracy that posted a reward for his murder. The moneyman was said to be John Sutherland, a St. Louis attorney who lived near Imperial.

1998 A runaway barge slammed into the President Casino on the "Admiral." One of the mooring lines was cut, and the Admiral swung out into the river. At least 50 people were hurt and 2,000 gamblers had to wait for hours to be evacuated by boat.

April 5

1904 The city police chief ordered his officers to strictly enforce the eight-mile-per-hour speed limit on city streets and six-mile-per-hour limit in the parks. He said the spring weather would bring out automobiles of the latest types, and drivers would be using the boulevards and parks as raceways.

1916 The St. Louis Zoo got its first elephant. School children raised $2,300 in pennies to purchase the pachyderm, which was to be named in honor of school board president James Harper. The elephant turned out to be a female, so she was dubbed "Miss Jim."

1939 The last event was held at the old coliseum at Jefferson and Washington. The coliseum had hosted such names as Enrico Caruso, and Billy Sunday. The Democrats nominated Woodrow Wilson for president in the building. The final event was a wrestling match. Jefferson Bank and Trust opened on the site in 1956.

1991 One of the most notorious crimes in recent St. Louis history occurred on the Old Chain of Rocks Bridge. Sisters Robin and Julia Kerry were raped and forced to jump into the Mississippi. Their cousin was also forced to jump, but survived. Antonio Richardson, Marvin Gray and Reginald Clemens were sentenced to death for the brutal crime.

2000 The Blues clinched the President's Cup Trophy for the best regular season record in the NHL. With a 6-5 win over Calgary, the Blues clinched their first title of any kind since winning the Norris Division in 1987. But the Blues would fall to the San Jose Sharks in the first round of the playoffs.

April 6

1917 Congress declared war on Germany. 156,232 Missourians served in World War One. There were 11,172 casualties among them. 1270 were killed in action, 1,075 St. Louisans died in the war.

1926 Ninety voters went to the polls in St. Peters and voted to bring electricity to their town. They approved the awarding of a franchise to the Eastern Missouri Power Company, and okayed a tax increase to pay for it. Many of the 500 or so residents of the town had dreamed of electricity since they saw it at the World's Fair.

1948 St. Ann was incorporated as a city. St. Ann was started as a defense housing project, built by Charles Vatterott. The first 100 homes in Mary Ridge opened in 1940. Vatterolt built 638 more on the site of the Stein farm, and dedicated the development to The Virgin Mary's mother, St. Ann.

1966 The National Hockey League Board of Governors awarded a franchise to St. Louis. The group headed by Sidney Saloman Junior and his son, Sid Saloman III, announced the team would be called "The St. Louis Blues." The Salomans had already reached an agreement to buy the decrepit old Arena on Oakland Avenue.

1993 Freeman Bosley Jr. was elected mayor of St. Louis, replacing incumbent Vincent C. Schoemehl Jr. who, after serving as mayor for 12 years did not run for re-election. Bosley became the first black mayor in St. Louis history, and served until 1997.

April 7

1823 The first city election in St. Louis was held. William Carr Lane was elected the first mayor. The election marked the beginning of city government under a charter granted by the state. Voters also chose the first Board of Aldermen.

1881 The organizers of the new St. Louis Sportsman's Club announced plans to improve the recently purchased Grand Avenue Baseball Grounds. Owner Chris Von der Ahe said he would build a 2,000-seat grandstand. A reporter for the *Globe* said the plan would attract interest in bringing professional baseball back to St. Louis.

1904 The new Hotel Jefferson formally opened. It was the grandest of a dozen hotels rushed to completion for the fair. The 12-story Jefferson boasted 400 rooms. Today, it has been converted into the Jefferson Arms Apartments for seniors.

1933 Prohibition ended at midnight, and the first shipments of legal Budweiser were delivered to an eager city. As horns and factory whistles sounded at 12:01 am, the gates of the brewery swung open. One of the first cases off the line was delivered to President Roosevelt. Because it had diversified during prohibition, AB survived to become the world's largest brewery.

1933 The world famous Anheuser-Busch Clydesdales made their debut. The Clydesdales took one of the first cases of legal Budweiser down Pennsylvania Avenue to present it to President Roosevelt. Today there are six Clydesdale Hitches.

1970 St. Louis County purchased the former Edgar Queeny Estate for a park. Hyacinth Rennard originally owned the 569-acre tract that makes up Queeny Park. He built the house that still stands at 1723 South Mason Road. He named it "Jarrville"

after his ancestral home in France.

April 8

1904 The latest figures from the Census Bureau showed that St. Louis was the fourth largest city in the country. The population of the city was put at 612,279,000. That ranked behind only New York, Philadelphia, and Boston.

1911 Ground was broken for the Jefferson Memorial in Forest Park. The memorial was not built for the fair, as many believe. It was built on the site of the main entrance to the World's Fair. The World's Fair company built it as part of their deal with the city to restore Forest Park following the fair.

1940 The Board of Aldermen passed a strict anti-smoke ordinance. St. Louis had one of the worst smoke palls in the nation because soft coal was burned here. Future mayor Raymond Tucker was charged with ridding the city of the smoke. He had to overcome the coal lobby to get the bill passed. The air improved immediately, but the buildings were still stained black for years afterwards.

1999 "The Big Bumper" signed off his show on KMOX for the final time. Jim White retired after 30 years of entertaining night time listeners.

2000 The Cardinals unveiled plans for a new stadium south of the current ballpark. The $370 million plan called for a retro-style stadium and a "Ballpark Village" development. Team officials said the club would pay a third of the cost. The owners hoped lawmakers would approve the use of money from taxes generated by the development to cover the rest. When lawmakers balked, the Cardinals began considering a move to Illinois

April 9

1899 James Sanford McDonnell was born in Little Rock, Arkansas. In 1939, he opened his own aircraft company with two employees and a rented office at Lambert Field. By the time he died in August, 1980, McDonnell-Douglas employed 83,000 people across the St. Louis area.

1953 Anheuser-Busch announced the purchase of Sportsman's Park from the Browns for $800,000. Gussie Busch wanted to name the field Budweiser Stadium. After hearing that the league might not be thrilled with naming a stadium after a product, Gussie settled for Busch Stadium. AB also said it would spend $400,000 to renovate the ballpark.

1963 Water from the Columbia River in Oregon was mixed with the first concrete poured into the structure of the Arch. The waters were drawn near the site of Fort Clatsop, the westernmost point of the Lewis and Clark Expedition.

2000 It was Willie McGee Day at Busch Stadium. In pre-game ceremonies, Willie received a new pickup. Then rookie Rick Ankiel went to the mound and earned his first victory. The Redbirds pounded out six home runs in the 11-2 win over Milwaukee.

2001 It was a bittersweet day for the "Hometown Airline." The CEO's of American and TWA joined employees to celebrate. They were marking the closing of the $4.2 billion buyout of the bankrupt TWA by American. The deal would create the world's largest airline.

April 10

1847 Joseph Pulitzer was born in Mako, Hungary. He was penniless when he came to St. Louis. He rose to the state legislature and later became a partner in the "Westliche Post," an influential German language newspaper here. In December of 1878, he purchased the bankrupt "St. Louis Dispatch" and merged it with the "Evening Post."

1948 The Board of Aldermen changed the name of the "Express Highway" (now part of Highway 40) to "The Red Feather Express Highway." The move was in honor of a charity drive. Some aldermen were concerned over the use of the word "red." Most St. Louisans were expected to keep calling it the Express Highway anyway.

1978 The Major Indoor Soccer League was formed. The St. Louis franchise would be called "The Steamers." For a time in the late '70s, the Steamers were the hottest sports ticket in town.

1987 The body of Walter Scott, lead singer for Bob Kuban and the In-Men, was found in a cistern in rural St. Charles County. It marked the beginning of one of the most bizarre murder cases in St. Louis area history. James Howard Williams, who was having an affair with Scott's wife, was convicted of killing Scott and his own wife, Sharon. Scott's wife, JoAnn, would plead guilty to hindering the prosecution.

2001 Twisters and hail combined for the most expensive natural disaster in St. Louis since the Flood of 1993. Baseball sized hail ruined nearly every roof in Florissant and Hazelwood. The storm damaged 60,000 cars. TWA cancelled 60 flights to check dented aircraft. Damage was put at over $700 million.

April 11

1842 English author Charles Dickens arrived in Missouri. He was not impressed. He described the Mississippi as "an enormous ditch, sometimes two or three miles wide, running liquid mud." He called St. Louisans "tobacco-spitting, slave-holding, and vulgar."

1877 At least 21 people died in one of the most dramatic fires in city history. The blaze destroyed the huge Southern Hotel. It occupied an entire city block between Fourth and Fifth, (now Broadway) Walnut and Elm, where the Stadium East Garage stands today. A huge crowd watched as guest leaped from windows. Heroic fireman Phelim O'Toole moved from window to window with a ladder, saving many lives.

1898 The new St. Louis city hall opened. Mayor Henry Ziegenheim led a parade of city employees from the old offices at 11th and Chestnut. The new building had been under construction for years. Much work remained to be done, but the mayor declared the city had waited long enough. The building was not completely finished until 1904.

1934 A group of civic leaders formed a non-profit corporation to spearhead development of a riverfront memorial. The Jefferson National Expansion Memorial Association chose Luther Ely Smith as its chairman, and immediately began working on acquiring federal status.

1954 The Cardinals traded longtime star Enos Slaughter to the Yankees for Bill Virdon, Mel Wright and Emil Tellinger. The news here was greeted with a front-page banner headline. Slaughter had been a star here for 16 years. He wept when he was told the news. Bill Virdon would go on to win rookie of the year honors in 1955.

April 12

1892 The current St. Louis National League franchise played its first game. The Browns lost to Chicago 14-10 before 8,160 fans at Old Sportsman's Park. St. Louis had a franchise when the NL was founded in 1876, but the team folded in 1899. In 1882, the Browns joined the American Association. The AA merged with the National League in 1892. In 1897, the owners of the Cleveland Spiders bought the Browns. They swapped the entire team with Cleveland and renamed the club "The Perfectos." When a fan commented that the new team socks were "a lovely shade of Cardinal," a newspaper writer came up with a new nickname.

1952 Jerome Hannah "Dizzy" Dean returned to St. Louis for "Dizzy Dean Week." The highlight of the festivities was the premiere of the movie based on his life, "The Pride of St. Louis." Dean was to broadcast Browns games during the 1952 season.

1958 The Hawks won the NBA championship, defeating the Boston Celtics four games to two. In the final game, Hawks hero Bob Petit scored 50 points. He broke the NBA record for points in a regulation playoff game.

1975 Josephine Baker died in Paris. Born Josephine McDonald in St. Louis, she overcame discrimination and her impoverished roots to become one of the best-loved entertainers in France. She was awarded the Legion of Honor for her work in the resistance during World War II.

1993 The state cleared the way for demolition of the last two blocks of the controversial Gateway Mall downtown. Crews soon began tearing the 9-0-5 liquor store and the Western Union Building. A 1980 plan calling for a block-wide green space from the Old Courthouse to Union Station ignited a battle over two historic buildings. The city ended up with a half-block wide mall. The Buder and Title Guaranty Buildings were demolished.

April 13

1743 Thomas Jefferson was born in Goochland, now Albemarle County, Virginia. No other American president had more impact on the history of St. Louis. It was Jefferson's Louisiana Purchase that paved the way for St. Louis to become the Gateway to the West.

1861 The news from Fort Sumter had St. Louis in a great state of excitement. The "Missouri Democrat" captured the mood.

"The dispatches this morning will thrill the whole country to its hearts core. The war has begun, and it has been inaugurated by the rebel forces. On their heads be the responsibility."

1912 The *Globe* carried advertisements for sailing dates of the new White Star liner "Titanic". The "unsinkable" liner was to sail from New York on April 20th, May 11th and June 1st. The 45,000 ton liner was en route from Southampton on her maiden voyage to New York. 2,200 people were on board.

1934 A huge crowd jammed the streets downtown for the dedication of the new Municipal Auditorium. It would later be named after Mayor Henry Kiel. His contracting firm built the auditorium. The auditorium was torn down for the new Kiel, or Savvis, Center. The adjacent opera house still stands.

1951 The Zoological Board of Control was said to be considering making the chimps at the zoo the first anywhere to get driver's licenses. They were being taught signals and signs. The *Globe* reported that if trial runs in Forest Park worked out, the chimps could drive downtown and apply in person.

April 14

1885 The nude body of Arthur Preller, an English silk salesman, was found in a trunk at the Southern Hotel. Police nationwide were alerted by telegraph to watch for his flamboyant traveling companion, Walter Maxwell. San Francisco authorities reported that Maxwell had sailed for New Zealand. St. Louis Police had to raise the unheard of sum of $500 for a cablegram to Auckland. Maxwell's trial was one of the first to become a national media sensation. He was hanged on August 10, 1886.

1912 The Titanic struck an iceberg and sank, taking over 1,500 lives. Vacationing *Post-Dispatch* reporter Carlos Hurd was on board the "Carpathia," which rushed to pick up survivors. The Carpathia's wireless was too swamped to send the reporter's messages. When the ship docked in New York, Hurd had the story ready. His work was sent around the world as the first complete account of the disaster.

1913 Clayton was incorporated as a city. It was established as the county seat in 1877. The founder of University City, E.G. Lewis, wanted to make Clayton part of his community. But word of his plans leaked out. A group of Clayton residents stayed up all night to prepare the paperwork for incorporation. When Lewis' people arrived at the courthouse, they found the papers had been filed an hour earlier.

1924 Maya Angelou was born as Marguerite Johnson in St. Louis. She first rose to critical acclaim in 1970 with her story of her childhood in segregated rural Arkansas, "I Know Why The Caged Bird

Sings." Angelou today is one of the leading African-American literary figures.

1954 The town of Times Beach was incorporated. Times Beach was founded in the 1920s as a promotion by the old St. Louis "Times" newspaper. Choice clubhouse sites on the Meramec were sold for $67.50, plus a six month subscription. Russell Bliss sprayed the streets with dioxin contaminated waste oil in the 1970s. The federal government bought out the homes in 1983. The cleaned-up site is now Route 66 State Park.

April 15

1899 A completely new St. Louis team opened its season with a 10-1 win before 18,000 fans at League Park. The new owners of the Browns also owned the Cleveland team. During the off season, they had sent the hapless Browns players to Cleveland and sent the Cleveland players here. The new team was called the "Perfectos." By 1900, the "Cardinals" had caught on as the new nickname.

1912 The *Post-Dispatch* listed seven St. Louisans believed to be aboard the Titanic. Among them was 15-year old Georgette Madill, one of the richest heiresses in St. Louis. Former St. Louisan Charles Hayes, now president of the Grand Trunk Railroad, was also on board. The papers here were reporting that most of the passengers had been saved.

1947 Jackie Robinson broke the major league color barrier as he made his debut with the Brooklyn Dodgers. One of the sadder chapters in the story was a potential protest by the Cardinals as their first game against the Dodgers approached on May 8th. According to league president Ford Frick, only a last-minute plea by Card's owner Sam Breadon prevented trouble.

1970 St. Louisans joined the world in prayer for the astronauts aboard the crippled Apollo 13. Special prayers were said at a noon mass at the Old Cathedral. Special masses would be held for the next two days. Pastor John Long said he hoped the final one would be a mass of thanksgiving.

1998 Dozens of people were hurt in the largest traffic accident in Missouri history. At least 98 cars piled into each other on a rain-slickened stretch of eastbound I-70 west of Highway 79. About 40 people were hurt. Amazingly, there were no fatalities.

April 16

1898 With some 6,000 people in the stands to see the Browns and Chicago, fire raced through the stands at Sportsman's Park. The grandstand and the left field bleachers were destroyed. As many as 100 people were injured in the panic. The players spent the night helping clear the debris, so the game could be played the next day. The exhausted Brownies committed eleven errors and lost 14-1.

1904 The buildings at the world's fairgrounds were lit for the first time for the public. The lights had been tested back on the 9th. Meanwhile, the Igorrote tribe at the Filipino Village were preparing for their first dog feast. Five dogs provided by the city pound were being fattened up for the occasion.

1953 The first win for Gussie, as the Cardinals beat the Cubs 3-0 on opening day. It was the first game for the Cardinals under the ownership of Anheuser-Busch. There were some rough spots at the opener. The pre-game fireworks fizzled, the national anthem singer had a sore throat, and the Governor of Missouri couldn't throw out the first pitch because of a sore arm.

1963 The new Planetarium in Forest Park formally opened. The first show was called "New Skies for St. Louis." The decision to build the Planetarium on the site of the old mounted police academy caused a controversy over the use of the park for new buildings.

1978 Bob Forsch pitched the first no-hitter in St. Louis in 54 years, blanking the Phillies 5-0. It was one of the few bright spots of the 1978 season. The official scorer charged Ken Reitz with a controversial error in the 8th inning.

1865 City leaders and members of the Merchant's Exchange met downtown to pay their respects to the murdered president. After the dignitaries addressed the crowd, plans were made for many St. Louisans to attend the funeral of Abraham Lincoln in Springfield two days later.

1918 William Beedle was born in O'Fallon, Illinois. He changed his name to William Holden when he signed a movie contract in 1939. Holden won an Oscar for his role in "Stalag 17" in 1953. He also starred in classics such as "Bridge over the River Kwai" and "Sunset Boulevard."

1945 Red Schoendienst played his first game in a Cardinal uniform. He would play in 2,216 games. Red's first game was also the first for Cards broadcaster, Harry Caray. He broadcast Redbird games until 1969.

1948 The very first baseball game ever on television here. KSD-TV broadcast the "City Series" game between the Browns and the Cardinals at Sportsmen's Park. It was such a success that KSD scheduled another 20 Browns and Cards broadcasts over the next two months.

1961 A show opened at the Crystal Palace in Gaslight Square, featuring the Smothers Brothers. Second on the bill was a "chic singer with vocal prowess unusual for a girl of 18". Her name was Barbara Streisand. Performers such as Woody Allen, Lenny Bruce, and George Carlin played the Palace early in their careers.

April 18

1866 A subcommittee formed by the Merchant's Exchange of St. Louis approved a design by James B. Eads for the proposed Mississippi Bridge. Missouri Senator Benjamin Gratz Brown quickly secured Congressional approval. Construction would begin on August 21, 1867.

1906 City officials demanded that all police officers pay their way into baseball games. Owners were advised to hire private watchmen to provide security. It was reported that as many as 85 policeman at a time had attended some games last year, many of whom were supposed to be on patrol somewhere else.

1945 According to one source, this is the date that the first pizza parlor in St. Louis opened. Italian immigrant Amadeo Fiore is credited with operating the first pizzeria at 204 North Sarah.

1945 The Brown's legendary one-armed outfielder, Pete Gray, made his major league debut. Gray lost his right arm in a child-hood truck accident. Naturally right-handed, he learned to bat and field with his left. Gray played just one season for the Browns, batting .218.

1987 The Cardinals were trailing the Mets 5-0 on "Seat Cover Night" at Busch Stadium. Tommy Herr doubled in the sixth to give the Cardinals the lead, but the hated Mets tied it. Herr came up again in the tenth and hit a grand slam. Thousands of seat cushions rained down on the field.

April 19

1878 The telephone came to St. Louis. George Freeland Durant opened the first exchange at 417 Olive. He had 12 subscribers. They paid $300 for a three-year contract. By the time the first directory was issued later that year, there were 60 subscribers and 72 phones in St. Louis.

1912 The *St. Louis Post-Dispatch* printed the first eyewitness accounts of the Titanic disaster. Carlos Hurd, a vacationing reporter who was on board the Carpathia when it rushed to rescue the survivors, gathered them. Hurd's account was sent around the world. S.W. Silverthorne, a buyer for Nugent's Dry Goods in St. Louis, said he was unaware the ship was in danger at first. He was ordered into one of the lifeboats because there were not enough women nearby to fill the first few.

1925 The first radio commercial ever aired in St. Louis was beamed out over KSD. It was a program called the "Eight in Line Quartet," sponsored by the Gardner Motor Company.

1955 Demolition work began on the city's number one eyesore to make room for a parkway and the Plaza Square Apartments. The $15 million project called for tearing down 87 dilapidated buildings between Chestnut and Olive.

1983 It appeared as if only a miracle would keep the Blues in St. Louis. The Vice-President of Ralston-Purina signed papers selling the team to a group from Saskatoon, Saskatchewan. The deal still required approval from the league.

April 20

1766 The first wedding in St. Louis took place. Toussain Hunaud, a Canadian trapper, married Marie Boujenou, the daughter of one of St. Louis' first settlers. There was no church in St. Louis, so the wedding took place at the bride's house.

1769 The great Ottawa Chief Pontiac was assassinated by Peoria Indians at Cahokia, Illinois. Governor St. Ange sent for his body. Pontiac was buried in St. Louis, near the present site of Broadway and Market.

1875 The Police board approved a proposal by Chief Laurence Harrigan to form a special "Ladies Platoon". The most handsome cops in the city would be assigned to patrol the fashionable Fourth Street shopping district. All of the officers had to be at least six-feet tall. Their duties included helping ladies across the street.

1931 One of the most sensational crimes in St. Louis history occurred. Doctor Isaac Kelley was kidnapped. The crime was master minded by gangsters and socialite Nellie Muench. She was a reverend's daughter and the sister of a state supreme court judge. Her lawyers thought the jury would be more sympathetic if she came to court with a baby. She stole one, and even blackmailed a doctor by telling him he was the father.

1982 Ground was broken for the Bowling Hall of Fame and Museum. St. Louis Hall of Famers Roy Bluth and Myrtle Schulte rolled balls down a simulated alley to trigger explosives at the ceremony.

April 21

1856 The first railroad bridge over the Mississippi was completed. It linked Davenport, Iowa with Rock Island, Illinois. Since St. Louis had no bridge, rail traffic was shifted north. In 1856, St. Louis was much larger than Chicago. But the shift in rail traffic spurred Chicago's growth, and it soon surpassed St. Louis.

1910 Missouri's celebrated humorist, Mark Twain, died at the age of 74 in Redding, Connecticut. His real name was Samuel Clemens. He was known the world over for his works, "Tom Sawyer" and Huck Finn."  Clemens set type for a time at a newspaper in St. Louis, and became a riverboat captain on the Mississippi here. The name "Mark Twain" came from the phrase used to measure river depth.

1952 About 450 people turned out to oppose a plan to extend Highway 40 eastward past its current dead end at Brentwood Boulevard and Eager. At a hearing, they heard details of the newly-planned route through Richmond Heights into downtown. The original plan called for the highway to enter St. Louis north of Washington University. But the Mayor of Brentwood was angry his town would be by passed.

1964 The Board of Aldermen cleared the way for construction of the $45 million Mansion House Apartments on the riverfront. They agreed to insure loans totalling $35,641,000. It marked the largest commitment ever by the St. Louis office of the F.H.A.

1972 Demolition work began on the Pruitt-Igoe Housing Project. When it was built in the 1950s, Pruitt-Igoe was hailed as a milestone. But the vacant and vandalized buildings became a national symbol of the failure of public housing.

1790 The birthday of St. Clair County, Illinois. Governor St. Clair of the Northwest Territory organized the county. At that time, it included 1/2 of what is now Illinois. The creation of Randolph County in 1795, Madison, Gallatin and Johnson Counties in 1812, and Monroe County in 1816 reduced it to its current size.

1857 Washington University was formally inaugurated with ceremonies in the Mercantile Library Hall. The speaker at the ceremony was Edward Everett. In 1863, Everett would speak at a cemetery dedication in Gettysburg, Pennsylvania. But his speech was overshadowed by one Abraham Lincoln made that day.

1877 The man for whom the city of Kirkwood is named died. James Pugh Kirkwood was the chief engineer for the Pacific Railroad. He laid out the path of the railroad in 1853. When a group of St. Louis businessmen formed an association to promote their suburb on the line, they named it Kirkwood.

1955 Many St. Louisans heard "Rock Around the Clock" for the first time. The motion picture "Blackboard Jungle," starring Glenn Ford and Anne Francis opened at the Leow's State Theatre.

1970 Teach-ins and seminars at area colleges marked the first "Earth Day" observances in St. Louis. St. Louis University and Washington University students joined in a "Litter and Survival" march to Forest Park.

April 23

1816 A dozen St. Charles County citizens asked the state to build a public road from St. Charles to the Howard County line (At the time there were no Montgomery, Warren or Callaway Counties). The petition marked the beginning of the pioneer road that followed the Booneslick Trial. The route later became State Highway Number Two, U.S. 40, and eventually I-70.

1912 Titanic survivors Mrs. Edward Robert, Miss Georgette Madill and Elizabeth Allen arrived home in St. Louis. Miss Allen said she couldn't understand the controversy over the actions of White Star Line President Bruce Ismay. Ismay was under fire for boarding a lifeboat when so many went down with the ship. Allen said Ismay was a gallant man who did his part.

1973 Officials predicted record flooding was about to hit the Missouri and Mississippi Rivers here. The rivers had crested just 18 days ago. More heavy spring rains were expected to push the Mississippi back to a record 43.5 feet in just four days.

1998 In a case that attracted national attention, Brian Stewart pleaded not guilty of first-degree assault. Prosecutors said the phlebotomist at a St. Charles County hospital injected his son with HIV tainted blood to avoid paying child support back in 1992. The child was now seven, and had developed full-blown AIDS.

1999 Fernando Tatis of the Cardinals slugged two grand slams in the 3rd inning of a game against the Dodgers in Los Angeles. He became the first player in Major League history to hit two grand slams in one inning. Both blasts came off Chan Ho Park. It marked only the 10th time in Major League history that a player had even managed to hit two grand slams in a single GAME.

April 24

1902 The American League St. Louis Browns played their first game and the first American League game ever played in St. Louis. They beat Cleveland, 5-2. The National League had sued to stop the games, charging that several Cardinal players had violated their contracts to sign with the Browns.

1904 The first attraction on "The Pike" at the World's Fair opened. The Old St. Louis Restaurant and Garden was to be part of the Old St. Louis Village on the Pike, the amusement area at the fair.

1953 St. Louis Police interrupted a daring daylight holdup at the Southwest Bank, at Kingshighway and Southwest. A wild shootout ensued between nearly 100 officers and the bandits. An officer and two of the robbers were wounded. One robber killed himself and the other escaped with no loot. The holdup was re-enacted at the scene five years later for the movie "The Great St. Louis Bank Robbery."

1956 The "Weatherball" atop the General American building downtown flashed its first forecast. The giant neon ball glowed red if the weather was to be warmer, blue for cooler weather. It flashed if precipitation was in the forecast. The giant framework for the weatherball is still there. A developer plans to incorporate it into the design when the building is converted to loft condominiums.

1994 The Blues played their final game at the old Arena. They lost 2-1 to the Dallas Stars in the first round of the playoffs. The Arena had hosted 1,256 Blues games. Over the years 17,702,012 fans attended Blues games there.

April 25

1214 Our city's namesake born near Poissy, France. King Louis IX is best remembered as a great crusader. He took up the sword, vowing to recapture Jerusalem from the Moslems. Domestic troubles forced him to return to France. But he embarked on another crusade in 1270. He got as far as Tunis, where he died of dysentery.

1902 Former Governor David R. Francis, head of the World's Fair company, met with Secretary of State John Jay and fair commissioners in Washington. They discussed postponing the fair for a year to give several foreign governments time to complete their exhibits. Francis reluctantly agreed to postpone the fair until 1904.

1973 Forty percent of St. Charles County was under water, as the flood smashed the Missouri, Kansas and Texas Railroad levee. The Mississippi at St. Louis reached 42.02 feet, topping the estimated record level of 1785.

1978 The Cardinals fired manager Vern Rapp. He was replaced three days later by Ken Boyer. Rapp's tenure is best remembered for his ban on facial hair and sideburns, which infuriated players such as Al Hrabosky and Bake McBride. The end came when he referred to Ted Simmons as, "a loser".

1990 St. Louis became a one-newspaper town again, with the demise of the short-lived tabloid, *The St. Louis Sun*. Ralph Ingersoll II had launched the paper just seven months earlier, with a $100 million bank roll. The *Sun* was known for its splashy graphics, lurid headlines and big color pictures.

April 26

1876 William McKee, the owner of the *Globe-Democrat*, was sentenced to two years in jail and fined $10,000 for his role in the

"Whiskey Ring" scandal. The St. Louis based conspiracy defrauded the government out of thousands in tax revenue. The graft reached into the highest levels of the Grant administration. Ironically, McKee's own paper had exposed the ring.

1921 The first radio station in St. Louis began broadcasting. Station 9YK, now WEW, also aired the first radio weather report. Father George S. Rueppel of Washington University delivered that first report. WEW is acknowledged as the second oldest radio station in the U.S.

1960 "Easy" Ed McCauley was elected to the Basketball Hall of Fame. He led St. Louis University to the NIT title in 1948. He had recently resigned as coach of the Hawks to take over as general manager.

1969 The ill-fated replica of the "Santa Maria" was opened to the public on the St. Louis riverfront. Mayor Cervantes brought the ship here from New York, where it was part of the Spanish exhibit at the World's Fair. The Santa Maria collided with the Becky Thatcher and sank during a thunderstorm later that year.

1974 The St. Louis Regional Commerce and Growth Association kicked off a massive promotion campaign with the theme "St. Louis Has It All From A to Z." Remember the jingles? "Gimme an A....We've got the Gateway Arch, antiques, amusement parks........B..........boat rides and boulevards, baseball and beer."

April 27

1822 Ulysses S. Grant was born in Ohio. After graduating from West Point, he was assigned to Jefferson Barracks. While there he married Julia Dent. The Dent family estate, "Whitehaven," still stands. After he left the Army, Grant built a cabin for his wife on the family land off Rock Hill Road. The cabin was later moved to Grant's Farm, where it stands today.

1896 Rogers Hornsby was born in Winters, Texas. The premiere right-handed hitter in baseball history, his lifetime average of .358 is second only to Ty Cobb. He played for the Cardinals from 1915 to 1926. He won the National League batting title for six years in a row beginning in 1920.

1903 President Theodore Roosevelt arrived in St. Louis for ceremonies marking the dedication of the World's Fair buildings. The fair had been postponed for a year past the planned April, 1903 opening to give several nations more time to complete their exhibits. The dedication ceremonies went on anyway. A future president was also in St. Louis that day. Woodrow Wilson, the president of Princeton University, was here for a speech at the University Club.

1916 Enos Slaughter was born in Roxboro, North Carolina. He is best remembered for his dash from first to third to score the winning run for the Cardinals in game seven of the 1946 World Series.

1943 Ernest Hamwi died at the age of 59. The International Association of Ice Cream Manufacturers credits the Syrian concessionaire with inventing the ice cream cone at the 1904 World's Fair in St. Louis. Other sources credit ice cream salesman Charles Menches. The family of Italo Marchiony claims he invented the treat in New York or New Jersey in 1896 and patented a mold for cones in 1903.

April 28

1836 Francis Macintosh, a free black man, was arrested for interfering with sheriff's deputies. He believed it when one of the deputies joked that he would hang, and stabbed one to death. A mob chained him to a tree and burned him alive. Elijah Lovejoy infuriated the city when he condemned the incident in his presbyterian newspaper, *The Observer*. Amid break-ins and threats, Lovejoy moved his paper to Alton. He would soon become a martyr for freedom of the press.

1907 A group of St. Louisans announced plans to raise $50,000 to preserve the "Grant Cabin" as a Civil War museum. The cabin was located in Forest Park, where it had been moved for the world's fair. Some members of the group were pushing to have the cabin returned to Grant's Farm, now owned by August A. Busch.

1959 St. Louis' first independent television station, KPLR Channel Eleven, signed on the air. KPLR was to air its first program at 7 pm, a telecast of the game between the Cardinals and the Reds. But the game was rained out. The next night, Jack Buck, Harry Carey and Joe Garagiola called the action as the Cards played the Milwaukee Braves.

1973 The Mississippi River at St. Louis reached a record crest at 43.23 feet. The Army Corps of Engineers was estimating damage at $150 million. Three-million acres were underwater. 25,000 people were homeless. The flood of 1993 would shatter that 1973 record.

1980 A crowd of 19,000 ignored a handful of protestors as The Who played at the Checkerdome. A group calling themselves "Parents Against Drugs at Rock Concerts" was calling for a ban on smoking at shows to discourage marijuana use. It was the first appearance by the Who in St. Louis since the death of eleven fans at a concert in Cincinnati.

April 29

1825 St. Louis welcomed the Marquis de Lafayette. A cheering crowd greeted him at the riverfront and lined the streets as he was transported to the Chouteau Mansion. He was then taken to the home of General Clark, were he was to meet with the Indians. There was some concern about using city funds to entertain Lafayette, but the bill came to only $37, so no one complained.

1900 The St. Louis team was referred to as the "Cardinals" for the first time in the *Post-Dispatch*. The team had been known as the "Perfectos." Legend says Willie Hale, a reporter for the "Republic" coined the name after overhearing a female fan comment that the teams new uniforms included a "lovely shade of Cardinal."

1953 Director of Public Safety Miles Dyer requested a ban on bottles at Busch Stadium (until recently known as Sportsman's Park). The request came after a melee during a game between the Browns and the Yankees. Several Browns players had to escort the Yankees to the dugout as bottles rained down from the stands.

1955 Construction began on the new highway bridge over the Missouri River at St. Charles. The four-lane bridge was clogged with traffic soon after it opened. A second bridge was completed next to it in 1979, and both were named for Louis Blanchette, the founder of St. Charles.

1989 Paula Sims told police that her six-week old daughter, Heather, had been kidnapped by a masked gunman from their home near Brighton, Illinois. In 1986, Sims had claimed that 13-day old Loralei was kidnapped in a similar manner. A true crime bestseller called "Precious Victims" was written about the case, and the book became a television movie starring Richard Thomas of "The Waltons" fame.

April 30

1803 The United States and France agreed to the Louisiana Purchase. The territory of the U.S. was doubled for $15 million. That comes to about four cents per acre. At the time, President Thomas Jefferson was roundly criticized for the deal. Many feared the country would be too large to govern effectively and that Jefferson had exceeded his authority. Congress consented to the deal in October, 1803.

1897 City officials were debating a bill to tax baseball parks $3,000 per year. The measure was introduced after Browns owner Chris Von der Ahe failed to send over the customary season passes. The situation was quickly remedied.

1904 It was St. Louis' finest hour, as the great Louisiana Purchase Exposition opened. The fair was held in Forest Park and its environs. At 1:04 pm, President Roosevelt touched a special telegraph key in Washington and the grounds came to life. The fair dazzled the world, and touched off a ten-year building boom in St. Louis. Legend says the hot dog, ice cream cone and iced tea were all introduced at the fair. Doctor Pepper also made its debut at the fair. Over 12 million people would visit the fair, about 1/2 of them from the St. Louis region, before it closed on December 1, 1904.

1926 Highway officials from Missouri and Oklahoma agreed to end their battle with federal officials over the number to be assigned to the highway from Chicago to Los Angeles. They agreed to accept the number "66." The highway was to have been designated as Route 60, but the governor of Kentucky wanted the more important sounding 60 to go through his state. It's a good thing. "Get your kicks on Route 60" doesn't have the same ring to it.

1940 President Franklin Roosevelt authorized the inclusion of the Old Courthouse in the Jefferson National Expansion Memorial. The courthouse was the scene of Thomas Hart Benton's speech that spurred the westward migration. It was also the scene of the Dred Scott trial and the last slave auction ever held in St. Louis.

MAY

May 1

1877 The Brown Stockings played 15 scoreless innings against the Syracuse Stars. A sportswriter called it one of the greatest games ever. By the 15th inning, it became apparent that the game would have to be called because of darkness. The Stars refused to take advantage of the Browns after "such a manly contest," and asked the umpire to declare the game a draw.

1904 The grandest of the two dozen hotels built for the World's Fair opened. The Jefferson Hotel on 12th Street at Locust cost $1 million. The Hilton Corporation bought the hotel in 1950. It was sold to Sheraton in 1955. The last guest checked out in 1975, and the hotel has been converted into apartments for seniors.

1907 Archbishop John Joseph Cardinal Glennon broke ground for the "New" St. Louis Cathedral on Lindell. It was completed in October, 1914. Dedication ceremonies were not held until June 29, 1926.

1946 The USO canteen at Union Station closed. The World War II years saw Union Station handle record numbers of passengers. Up to 80,000 per day passed through the station early in 1945. In 1943, 22 million people came through.

1995 The fate of the Coral Courts Motel was sealed, as Conrad Properties bought the site for construction of the Oak Knoll Manor Subdivision. The Coral Court was constructed in 1941 along Watson Road, US 66. It became notorious for its attached garages as much as its beautiful deco moderne design.

May 2

1861 Missouri's Pro-southern governor, Claiborne Jackson, ordered the state militia to assemble at Lindell's Grove, a site that would soon become famous as "Camp Jackson" (The site is now part of St. Louis University). Jackson asked Jefferson Davis for a large shipment of rebel arms, which were taken to the camp. The Commander of the Union Arsenal, Nathaniel Lyon, marched on the camp on May 10th. The Civil War was about to shatter St. Louis.

1942 Aldermen Gus Hartkopf and Louis Lange announced they were sponsoring a bill to rename the misnamed "Free" or Municipal Bridge in honor of Douglas Macarthur. Tolls had been charged on the bridge since July, 1932. They were originally put in place for unemployment relief.

1953 A fire destroyed most of the Westlake Amusement Park at the Rock Road and Natural Bridge. The popular amusement park stood near where Circuit City is today. It boasted one of the biggest roller coasters in the state, a "Tom Thumb" miniature steam railway and "The Bug," which roared around a circular track.

1954 Stan Musial's greatest day. He slugged five home runs and drove in nine runs in a doubleheader against the New York Giants. Stan set a mark for total bases in a doubleheader with 21. In the crowd that day was eight-year-old Nate Colbert. In 1972, he would become the only major-leaguer ever to equal Stan's feat.

1968 The St. Louis Hawks were sold to Atlanta interests led by the governor of Georgia. Owner Ben Kerner said efforts to find a St. Louis buyer failed because "they just don't want our product here." Fewer than 9,000 fans had turned out for three playoff games here last season when the Hawks were fighting San Francisco for the division title.

May 3

1907 Health officials in Cleveland banned the spitball there after watching Browns pitcher Harry Howell's spitter "working in all its slimy effectiveness." The chief health officer said a player should not have to face "a batted ball covered with microbes coming at him like a shot out of a gun."

1918 An ordinance was introduced in the Board of Alderman to change the name of Berlin Street to Pershing. It was the first of several ordinances purging the city of German street names. Von Versing was changed to Enright to honor one of the area's first war dead. Kaiser was changed to Gresham, Brunswick to January, Wiesenhan to Bonita, Helvetia to Stole and Hasburger to Cecil Place.

1948 The United States Supreme Court upheld the rights of African-Americans to own property in any neighborhood. The case of Shelley versus Kraemer originated in St. Louis. The Shelleys had rented a home at 4600 Labadie. A neighbor sued, seeking to enforce a real estate agreement barring the sale of the property to blacks.

1968 The Blues clinched a berth in the Stanley Cup Finals during their first season. Ron Shock's goal in sudden-death overtime gave the Blues a 2-1 win over the Minnesota North Stars. The mighty Montreal Canadiens swept the Blues in the finals.

2002 St. Louis firefighters Derek Martin and Robert Morrison were killed in a fire at the Gravois Refrigeration Company, 2239 Gravois. They had gone into the burning building to rescue a trapped colleague. It was the first time a firefighter had died in the line of duty in the city since 1977.

May 4

1819 Nineteen-year old Henry Shaw arrived in St. Louis from England. He opened a hardware store and was so successful, he was able to retire at age 40. He dedicated the rest of his life to his botanical garden. When it was opened to the public in 1859, "Shaw's Garden" became a top St. Louis attraction. Shaw donated the land around the garden to the city to establish Tower Grove Park in 1868.

1874 A mass meeting of citizens demanded the resignation of state lawmakers who were instrumental in authorizing the purchase of land for Forest Park. They said the park was too far away to be of any practical use, and would be nothing more than a playground for the rich.

1910 President William Howard Taft visited St. Louis. Mindful of the political fallout if he offended fans of either team, he attended parts of the Cardinal game at Robison Field and the Browns game at Sportsman's Park. A month earlier, the 300-pound President inadvertently started a baseball tradition. In the seventh inning, Taft rose from his seat to stretch. The crowd, thinking he was leaving, rose from their seats to show their respect. It was the first "Seventh Inning Stretch."

1941 A crowd of 15,000 jammed the Arena to hear a speech by Colonel Charles Lindbergh as part of his tour to speak against American involvement in Europe. Lindbergh was roundly criticized for his role in the "America First Committee." He was even called the "Leading Nazi in the United States" by Interior Secretary Harold Ickes after he accepted a medal from the Germans.

1969 The Montreal Canadiens completed a four game sweep of the Blues in the Stanley Cup Finals for the second year in a row. The Blues had won the Western Division Championship the first two years they were in the league, only to run up against the mighty Canadiens.

May 5

1876 Washington Bradley of the Browns shut out the Chicago White Stockings, 1-0, at the Grand Avenue Baseball Grounds. It marked the first shutout in St. Louis. A crowd of about 2,000 braved rough weather to see the game.

1885 A crowd of 300 attended an auction of 40 lots on the eastern boundary of Forest Park, at Laclede and Taylor. The lots were billed as "the future residence of the elite of the city." The lots sold for about $30 a foot.

1893 In one of the most sensational cases in St. Louis County history, a jury acquitted Sheriff Emil Dosenbach of murder. Dosenbach fatally shot County Assessor Winfield Scott Smith at the county courthouse over a political dispute on July 13, 1892. The jury convicted him of fourth degree manslaughter and sentenced him to six months in prison.

1961 Alan Shepard became the first American in space. His Mercury "Freedom Seven" space capsule was built here at McDonnell Aircraft. Hundreds of Mac employees cheered as they watched Shephard splash down on television.

1970 Two-thousand youths protesting the killings at Kent State chanted "let it burn" as they torched the Air Force ROTC building at Washington University. Firefighters and police were greeted with rocks and cherry bombs. Howard Mechanic would be sentenced to five years for his role in the riot. He disappeared, and lived in Arizona under the assumed name of Gary Treadway, until a bid for city council in Scottsdale brought his past to light in February, 2001.

May 6

1917 Belleville native Bob Groom threw a no-hitter for the St. Louis Browns in his very first start. It came in the second game of a doubleheader against the White Sox. Groom had thrown two scoreless innings to wrap up the first game. In 1917, Groom would lose more games than any other pitcher in the American League for the third season in a row.

1953 Bobo Holloman of the Browns became only the third pitcher in major league history to throw a no-hitter in his first start. Holloman would win only three games during his entire career. He was out of baseball within three months.

1967 A struggling radio station next to the 66 Park-In Theater had begun adding "underground" music to its play list. KSHE-FM had started out broadcasting Montovani and 101 Strings from the basement of a house in 1961. Advertising time went for 80 cents per minute. By September, 1967, the transition was complete, and St. Louis had the third progressive station in the country. Progressive stations played long album cuts and tracks from artists not normally heard on the AM Top 40 stations.

1967 Ike & Tina Turner were awarded a gold record for, "Proud Mary." Tina met Ike at the Club Manhattan in East St. Louis. They began performing regularly at spots such as the Club Imperial in Baden. They broke big nationally with "Fool in Love" in 1960.

1986 Julie Bulloch was found dead in the garage of her Ballwin home. She had been bound with duct tape and the house had been set on fire. Her husband, Dennis Bulloch, claimed she died during an act of sexual bondage. He was convicted of involuntary manslaughter. In a second trial, he was convicted of arson and tampering with evidence. The conviction was overturned on appeal. He was sentenced to 12 years after a third trial.

May 7

1849 The first elections were held in the newly-incorporated village of St. Charles. Ludwell E. Powell was elected mayor.

1945 At 8:36 a.m., KSD radio flashed word of the German surrender. The city waited to celebrate until the following morning, when VE Day would be officially declared. The *Post* reported that 1,246 St. Louisans had lost their lives in the European theatre. 621 were listed as missing. The next day, vital war industries continued business as usual. The main gathering was an interfaith service at Memorial Plaza.

1968 The NBA approved the sale of the St. Louis Hawks. Owner Ben Kerner sold the team to Atlanta interests headed by the Governor of Georgia for $3.5 million. The Hawks had moved here in 1955 from Milwaukee.

1968 Politics left plans for the dedication of the Arch up in the air. The National Park Service said it expected President Lyndon Johnson to be the speaker. But Mayor AJ Cervantes had already invited Vice President Hubert Humphrey to town for the dedication dinner. Cervantes was a leading supporter of Humphrey's presidential bid.

1974 Nine-year old Vonda Clark of Shipman, Illinois, became the five-millionth visitor to the Arch. Among her prizes: a case of wine and tickets to the Playboy Club.

2001 The trains were packed on the first workday of service along the new Metro Link extension across St. Clair County. Commuters said high gas prices were driving them to think Metro Link. The project extended the line from the Fifth and Missouri Station in East St. Louis to Southwestern Illinois Community College.

May 8

1884 Harry S Truman was born in Lamar, Missouri. He would fail as a haberdasher in Kansas City before turning to politics. He became a judge in Jackson County and eventually rose to the Senate. He became vice president under Franklin D. Roosevelt and took over when Roosevelt died in April, 1945. As president, Truman made the difficult decision to drop the atomic bomb on Japan.

1898 George P. Dorris founded the St. Louis Motorcar Company, the first automobile manufacturer here. Dorris and his partner, John French, built the first internal combustion automobile seen in St. Louis. The Dorris was one of over 200 makes of automobiles manufactured in St. Louis between 1800 and 1930.

1900 Streetcar workers walked off the job, beginning the most violent strike in St. Louis history. Many people were killed or hurt during the 55-day walkout. The city's elite formed an armed posse of 1,600 citizens to keep order. Crowds pelted replacement operators with stones, cut power lines and obstructed the tracks. Business here ground to a halt. Most of the strikers were replaced, but the strike is seen as the major turning point in local labor history.

1966 The Cardinals played their final game at old Busch Stadium, losing to the Giants, 10-5. Willie Mays hit the final home run in the old ballpark at Grand and Dodier. Alex Johnson hit into a double play to end the game. A parade through the downtown streets followed, and the home plate from the old stadium was flown to the new ballpark in the KMOX helicopter. A crowd of 17,803 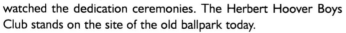 watched the dedication ceremonies. The Herbert Hoover Boys Club stands on the site of the old ballpark today.

1966 The Cardinals made a controversial trade. The Birds swapped pitcher Ray Sadecki to the San Francisco Giants for Orlando Cepeda. Cepeda would go on to win MVP honors in 1967, while leading the Cardinals to a world championship.

May 9

1861 The commanding officer of the federal arsenal at St. Louis, Captain Nathaniel Lyon, decided to move against the pro-southern state militia at Camp Jackson (The site is now part of St. Louis University) Legend says Lyon dressed up in a black dress and rode through the camp in disguise. The next day, his troops marched.

1878 Thousands of people attended the ceremonies marking the laying of the cornerstone for the first county courthouse in Clayton. The county had just been officially separated from the city. A time capsule was placed inside the stone. It was opened when the courthouse was demolished in 1948. But over the years, a seam had ruptured. The contents were a soggy mess.

1895 The city health commissioner said minute organisms in the drinking water were a variety of miniature crab. He said it was harmless, but recommended boiling the water anyway. He said the discovery was actually a compliment to reservoir officials. The water used to be too muddy to see anything in it.

1977 Before a national television audience, Cards pitcher Al Hrabosky went into his psych up routine after coming into a tie game against the Reds with the bases loaded and no one out.

"The Mad Hungarian" proceeded to strike out George Foster, Johnny Bench and Bob Bailey. The Cards won it in the tenth.

1985 The city of Maryland Heights was incorporated. The area was known as Mokeville in the 1850s, after a blacksmith on Fee Fee south of Dorsett. It was also known as Castello for a time. But Dr. Young Hance Bond said the area reminded him of his home in Maryland. In 1914, when Goeke Real Estate subdivided the area around the village, the development was named Maryland Heights.

May 10

1861 The violence of the Civil War came to St. Louis. Captain Nathaniel Lyon, commander of the federal arsenal here, moved against the state militia at Camp Jackson (The site is now part of the Frost Campus of St. Louis University). As Lyon marched his prisoners back to the arsenal, a crowd gathered and rocks flew. No one knows who fired first, but the federal troops turned and opened fire on the crowd. Thirty-three people died. At least 27 of them were civilians.

1904 World's fair officials and the public were disappointed when a group of Apache warriors arrived here for the fair. The Apaches, prisoners from Fort Sill, announced that Chief Geronimo would not make an appearance at the fair unless he was paid $100 per month.

1927 Charles Lindbergh took off from San Diego in his new plane, "The Spirit of St. Louis." He arrived at Lambert Field 14 hours and 25 minutes later, a new record for a flight from the west coast. After a days rest, he took off for New York, breaking the record for a coast-to-coast flight. On May 20th, he took off for Paris.

1957 Annie Turnbo Pope Malone died in Chicago. Her line of Poro Beauty Care products made her one of the richest women in St. Louis, and one of the first female African-American millionaires. She opened Poro College here in 1917. She donated money to open the St. Louis Colored Orphans Home. It was renamed in her honor in 1946.

1970 Bobby Orr's overtime goal gave the Boston Bruins the Stanley Cup and gave Blues fans another heartbreak. A check by Noel Picard sent Orr sailing right after the goal. It was the third year the Blues had reached the finals, only to be swept in four straight.

May 11

1861 The day after the Camp Jackson affair had left over 30 people dead, tensions were running very high in St. Louis. A column of new Union volunteers was marching down Walnut, between 5th and 6th streets, when shots rang out. The recruits fired wildly into the crowd, and nine more people were killed.

1906 A huge crowd watched as the great Ferris wheel from the World's Fair was blown up. It took two explosions of 50 sticks of dynamite each to do the job. The wheel was built for the Columbian Exposition in Chicago in 1893. It was estimated to have carried 6 million passengers at the two expositions.

1940 The Milles Fountain in front of Union Station was dedicated. The "Meeting of the Waters" caused quite a controversy with its nude figures, but it was better than what once stood on the site. Prior to the 1920s, the area on Market in front of the station was lined with saloons and bawdy houses eager to serve the weary rail traveler.

1948 The movie "Fighting Father Dunne" had its world premiere at the Fox Theatre. Pat O'Brien portrayed the founder of the home for newsboys, Father Peter Joseph Dunne. The home was founded in St. Louis in 1906. The home still cares for disadvantaged youth today in Florissant.

1968 The Blues lost game four of the Stanley Cup finals to the Montreal Canadiens, 3-2. The Canadiens swept the Blues in four straight for the second year in a row.

1852 For the first time, a locomotive whistle split the air west of the Mississippi, as the Pacific Railroad received its first locomotive here. The railroad was under construction from St. Louis to what would become the town of Pacific. By May of 1853, the rails reached Kirkwood. In November of 1855, the line was completed to Jefferson City.

1925 Lawrence Peter "Yogi" Berra was born on "The Hill." He played for the Yankees for 17 years, leading his teams to five world series as manager and coach. He was inducted into the Baseball Hall of Fame in 1973.

1966 The new Busch Stadium downtown opened. In the first game, the Cardinals beat the Braves 4-3 in 12 innings. Mike Shannon got the first Cardinal hit at Busch. Felipe Alou hit two home runs for the Braves, as if the new park would be an easy place for sluggers! Gary Buchek scored the first Cardinal run in the new ball park. Don Dennis was the first pitcher to win a game at Busch. Phil Niekro got the first loss. Henry Aaron had the first walk and Ray Washburn got Eddie Mathews for the first strikeout.

1986 The Blues pulled off the "Monday Night Miracle." Trailing the Calgary Flames 5-2 in game six of the Campbell finals, the

Blues came from behind to win in sudden death overtime. Doug Wickenheiser got the game winner. But Calgary won the next game and took the series.

1988 The Metropolitan Square Building was topped out. The tallest building in St. Louis, it stands 539 feet tall. That's just 37 feet shorter than the Arch. The 20-story Third National Bank Building formerly stood on the site.

May 13

1819 The first streamboat to make it up the Missouri River arrived at St. Charles. The "Independence" took 13 days to make the 150-mile trip to Franklin, Missouri. The "Independence" is the boat depicted on the St. Charles city seal.

1946 St. Louis became the first city in the nation to have regular commercial car telephone service. You could get a radiotelephone in your car for $15 a month.

1958 In the sixth inning of a game against the Cubs at Wrigley Field, Stan Musial smacked a double off Moe Drabowsky for the 3,000th hit of his career. Stan was only the eighth player in major league history to reach the 3,000 hit mark.

1965 Harold Gibbons, president of the Teamsters Joint Council 13, announced plans for "the biggest benefit show ever held in St.

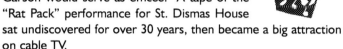

Louis." The June 20th show at the Kiel Opera House would feature Frank Sinatra, Dean Martin, Joey Bishop and Sammy Davis Jr. Johnny Carson would serve as emcee. A tape of the "Rat Pack" performance for St. Dismas House sat undiscovered for over 30 years, then became a big attraction on cable TV.

1966 Seventeen-year old Eric von Schneider was asked what he planned to do with the first home run ball from Busch Stadium. He caught the ball off the bat of Felipe Alou. The lucky fan said he didn't think it was too much to ask $50 for the ball.

May 14

1804 The Lewis and Clark expedition disembarked from the present site of Wood River, Illinois, on their epic voyage of discovery into the Louisiana Territory. The first stop was at the mouth of Coldwater Creek. Two days later, they arrived at Les Petite Cotes (St. Charles). The first three days were sort of a shakedown cruise for the crew. Lewis remained in St. Louis until May 20th.

1901 City planners were noting a decline in construction of skyscrapers over 12 stories tall. It had been found that offices above the 12th floor were difficult to rent. One observer said "Perhaps the rarified atmosphere at that level disagrees with the proper brain vigor necessary for conducting business" (What floor does your boss work on?).

1904 The Olympics came to St. Louis, as the games were held in conjunction with the World's Fair. The first Olympic games held in the United States had little of the pageantry associated with the modern games. The turnout of both athletes and spectators was disappointing. The U.S. captured 24 of the 26 gold medal events. Of the 681 athletes, 525 were from the United States. The games would not be held in the U.S. again until 1932.

1969 The replica of the Santa Maria moored on the St. Louis riverfront was rechristened by Senor Christopher Columbus the 17th of Barcelona, Spain. He was said to be the 17th linear descendant of the man who discovered the new world. The Santa Maria sank during a violent thunderstorm on April 26, 1969.

1988 The Cardinals' Jose Oquendo became the first non-pitcher to get a decision in 20 years. Oquendo was brought in to face the Braves after the Cardinals had used seven pitchers in a 16-inning marathon. Jose held the Braves scoreless for three innings, but was tagged with the loss, as the Cards fell 7-5.

May 15

1793 The founder of St. Charles was buried under the floor of San Carlos Borromeo Church. Louis Blanchette established the trading post that grew into the village, and was also instrumental in establishing the church. His remains were moved to a cemetery on Randolph Street in 1938.

1832 The road from St. Louis to Fenton was declared a public road. A year earlier, William Long had convinced a county court to lay out a road to the town he founded in 1819. Long claimed to be a descendent of the Earl of Fenton. Gravois was made a state road in 1839.

1875 James Britton was declared the winner of the special election to replace Mayor Arthur Barrett, who died of a mysterious ailment after just one week in office. But supporters of Henry Overstolz claimed the election was rigged, and threatened to march on city hall. The ensuing legal battle made St. Louis a national laughingstock. Overstolz was finally declared the winner in February of 1876.

1931 Mayor Victor Miller called for the city to buy the bankrupt Arena. He said the city would be ideally suited to attract conventions and expositions with the new Municipal Auditorium, the Soldier's Memorial and the Arena.

1968 The Cards' Julian Javier borrowed a page from the legend of Babe Ruth. Javier hit a home run just as he had promised a boy he visited in the hospital. The six-year old boy had been injured in an auto accident and was not expected to walk again.

May 16

1804 The Lewis and Clark expedition arrived at Les Petites Cotes, or Village of the Little Hills (Now known as St. Charles). Clark wrote in his journal that the village was "harmonious" and the inhabitants "extreemly kind." Lewis had been detained in St. Louis, and joined the expedition at St. Charles on May 20th. The next day, they headed upriver.

1840 James Milton Turner was born into slavery in St. Louis County. He would one day become the first black diplomat to serve the United States. He founded Lincoln University in Jefferson City, and was appointed the minister to Liberia by President Lincoln.

1970 The gates were closed on the dam as Lake St. Louis was dedicated. Developer R. T. Crowe intended the 600-acre lake to be the centerpiece of a 2,700-acre "New Town," based on developments in Reston, Virginia, and Columbia, Maryland. Crowe ended up bankrupt. The community was incorporated in 1977.

1979 The Streckfuss Lines announced that the Admiral's summer cruise season would be cancelled for the first time since World War II. The Coast Guard had discovered the hull of the ship had been weakened. The Admiral would leave for a New Orleans dry-dock in December, 1979. By 1981, the ship appeared to be destined for the scrap heap.

1998 Mark McGwire launched the longest home run ever hit at Busch Stadium. The 545-foot shot came off Livian Hernandez of the Florida Marlins. The ball nearly landed in the upper deck in center field, shattering the "Post-Dispatch" sign. A three-foot "Band-Aid" would be used to cover the hole in the sign. Just four days earlier, McGwire had broken the old Busch Stadium record, with a 527-foot blast.

May 17

1849 Fire broke out aboard the steamboat "White Cloud," moored at the foot of Franklin Avenue. Within a half-hour, the blaze spread to 23 boats. The worst fire in St. Louis history had begun. The flames lept to the buildings crowd- ed along the levee and the entire business section of the city appeared doomed.

1896 The Reverend Irl Hicks forecast that a tornado would hit St. Louis on this date. He based his prediction on the moon and the planets. Since he had made a similar prediction in 1895, no one paid much attention. This prediction was off by ten days.

1954 Reacting to the Supreme Court ruling barring school segregation, the city Board of Education said it was prepared to integrate the schools next fall. It was also prepared to integrate Harris and Stowe Teacher's Colleges. They were maintained as separate facilities, one for whites and one for blacks.

1960 Steel company executive Harry Kiener died. His will left $200,000 for the erection of a fountain with an athletic motif to be built at a prominent spot in St. Louis. The fountain and the statue of "The Runner" were unveiled in Kiener Plaza in 1966.

1963 Drivers were complaining that the St. Louis area had the only stop sign on Route 66 between Chicago and Los Angeles. It was a four-way stop at Watson Road and Cheshire Lane in Marlborough. The Missouri Highway Department said the sign was put up as an experiment because of a shopping center at the intersection.

May 18

1849 By 8:00 a.m., The Great Fire of 1849 had been contained. Three people were dead, 430 buildings and 23 steamboats were reduced to ashes. Property damage was put at $2,750,000. The fire did clear the crowded riverfront area, spurring much needed improvements. The streets were widened and the wharf was enlarged.

1849 Fire Captain Thomas Targee was credited with saving the business section of the city. He was killed while carrying a large keg of gunpowder to blow up a music store for a firebreak. The action kept the fire from spreading. Targee Street was named in his honor. It once ran south of Market, between 14th and 15th, where Savvis Center stands now.

1876 The owners of the faltering *St. Louis Democrat* announced they were combining their paper with "The Morning Globe." The new paper would be called the *Globe-Democrat*. The first issue hit the streets two days later.

1952 Maybe it was doomed from the start. Bad weather washed out the ground-breaking ceremonies for the Oliver Wendell Pruitt Homes public housing project in the area of Jefferson and Biddle. Plans called for 20 buildings eleven stories tall. By the 1960s, crime and vandalism made the project uninhabitable. The buildings were torn down in the 1970s.

1966 Officials announced a plan to light the Arch at night. Almost immediately, they began reconsidering. After some tests in the fall and winter, the plan was scrapped. The Arch was lit for the visit of Pope John Paul II. Permanent lights were finally installed in November, 2001.

1923 St. Louisans gathered on the streets to witness the first skywriter ever seen here. A British aviator spelled out "Lucky Strikes" in the sky. Skywriting was declared to be the advertising medium of the future.

1927 Charles Lindbergh, frustrated by the weather, planned a night at the theater in New York. But he learned that the weather was clearing over Newfoundland and the Atlantic. He rushed to the field to prepare the "Spirit of St. Louis" for the journey. He turned in at midnight, with instructions to be called at 2 am. But he couldn't sleep.

1961 The Board of Aldermen passed a measure outlawing racial and religious discrimination in places of public accommodation. The board had been regularly turning down such bills since 1954.

1962 Stan Musial pounded out hit number 3,431, breaking Honus Wagner's National League mark. Musial's record breaker came in the ninth inning off Ron Perranoski of the Dodgers. That made 40 league records tied or held by "Stan the Man."

1983 The National Hockey League rejected a bid by Ralston-Purina to sell the Blues to Canadian interests who wanted to move the team to Saskatoon. Within a week, Ralston filed a $60 million anti-trust suit against the league.

1902 It's the birthday of Union Electric. UE was founded on this date with a 6,400-watt power plant that served 2,000 customers. UE soon began work on the huge Ashley Street plant to provide power in time for the World's Fair. UE became part of the Ameren Corporation in December, 1997.

1908 Maplewood was incorporated as a city. James Sutton bought 314 acres of the old Gratiot land grants in 1826. He ran a blacksmith shop at what is now Manchester and Big Bend. One of his daughters sold her share of the land to a real estate company in 1890. The company built a subdivision called Maplewood.

1927 St. Louisans sat by their radios eager for news of Charles Lindbergh's flight. The headline in the *Globe* screamed "Lindbergh off to Paris in Daring non-stop dash." The "Spirit of St. Louis" had taken off from Roosevelt Field, Long Island. The plane staggered under its heavy load of fuel, and barely made it aloft. Thirty-three-and-a-half hours later, he brought the plane down safely at Le Bourget.

1948 Stan Musial's "Stan the Man" nickname was born. A day after going five-for-five, Stan continued a hitting spree against the Dodgers at Ebbets Field. His four hits, including a home run and two doubles, led the Cardinals to a 14-7 win. As he came up to bat, fans were overheard saying "here comes that man again."

1966 Tickets went on sale for the Beatles' August 21st show at Busch Stadium. Sales here were evidently not affected by the controversy over John Lennon's remark that the Beatles were more popular than Christ. All of the 48,000 seats sold out that day, with tickets starting at $4.50.

May 21

1829 A petition was filed to incorporate the village of St. Ferdinand. The Spanish called the town "San Fernando," but the locals used the French name, Florissant. (Settlers declared the area "un vale Fluerissant," meaning "Flourishing Valley" or "Valley of the Flowers") For years, the highway signs read St. Ferdinand. Confused early motorists would ask where Florissant was, only to be told they were already there.

1927 About 3:30 in the afternoon, a wild celebration erupted here as radios flashed the news that Charles Lindbergh and "The Spirit of St. Louis" had landed safely in Paris. Horns honked and whistles sounded in a scene reminiscent of when the Cardinals won the world series in 1926. The bells of Christ Church Cathedral, rung only on great civic occasions, were among the first to sound the news.

1947 Jackie Robinson played his first game at Sportsman's Park. The Dodgers beat the Cards 4-3, with Robinson scoring the winning run in the 10th inning. The Cardinals reportedly had threatened to strike rather than play with Robinson, but National League President Ford Frick credited Cards owner Sam Breadon with avoiding trouble. The Chase Hotel refused to admit Robinson.

1955 Chuck Berry recorded his first hit. "Maybelline" was an adaptation of the country song, "Ida Red." After famed DJ Alan Freed received a co-writers credit, he helped make "Maybelline" a hit. In 1999, "Entertainment Weekly" ranked it as the second most significant moment in rock history.

1966 Car 1628 of the Hodiamont Line made its final run, and the streetcar disappeared from the streets of St. Louis. The last day of the line drew more than 2,500 riders. That compares to the 927,000 that rode the streetcars on the day the World's Fair opened in 1904.

May 22

1926 It was Rogers Hornsby Day at Sportsman's Park. The Cardinals player-manager was presented with the Most Valuable Player award for 1925 and $1,000 in gold. Hornsby had batted .403 and led the league in home runs.

1937 Construction began on the landmark fountain in the Belleville public square. It was dedicated in honor of war veterans on October 10, 1937. The fountain stands on land donated by George Blair for the county seat in 1814. It has hosted a pen for stray cattle, two trees used for whipping posts, and was the site of a lynching in 1903.

1958 What to name the new four-lane highway bridge at St. Charles was a hot topic. There was considerable support for naming it after Harry Truman. The County Court had approved naming it after the first Governor of Missouri, Alexander McNair. The St. Charles Historical Society wanted it named after Benjamin Emmons. Emmons was a St. Charles politician and member of the first state legislature.

1981 Southern Illinois University at Edwardsville announced the cancellation of the SIUE River Festival for the coming summer. Held on a campus hillside since 1969, the festival featured such performers as Bob Dylan, Janis Joplin and the Who. The festival was cancelled because the site was inadequate.

1998 Mark McGwire blasted a home run into "Big Mac Land" at Busch Stadium for the first time. All 47,549 fans were entitled to a free "Big Mac" the next day at Mcdonald's.

1820 James B. Eads was born in Lawrenceburg, Indiana. At the age of 22, he devised the first diving bell to salvage cargo from sunken steamboats. During the Civil War, he built gunboats for the Union at Carondelet. He then designed and supervised construction of the great bridge that bears his name.

1874 The new Eads Bridge was opened to pedestrian traffic. Pedestrians paid a five cent toll. For ten cents, people could buy a promenade ticket and stay on the bridge to enjoy the view and the cool breezes. A great jam was predicted for the coming Sunday, when promenaders would not be disturbed by workmen laying the railroad tracks.

1897 With the Browns mired in last place, owner Chris Von der Ahe opened a "shoot-the-chutes" water slide from a water tower into an artificial lake at Sportsman's Park. Von der Ahe had tried horse racing, a beer garden and even an all-girl band in an effort to draw crowds.

1904 Famed saloon smasher Carrie Nation made another appearance in St. Louis. She spoke at a gospel meeting in a tent at Jefferson and Locust. Nation said she had turned away from busting up saloons. When asked if the she planned to attend the fair, she launched into a tirade, calling it "the devil's carnival."

1932 The city of Ellisville was incorporated. Captain Henry Ferris settled the area before 1837. He built a substantial home that was bought by Vespasian Ellis. William Hereford secured a post office for the Ellis house and named it Ellisville, either after his old hometown in Virginia, or in honor of Ellis.

May 24

1904 The giant Ferris wheel at the World's Fair began operating. The first person in line was a fellow from Milwaukee who claimed to have been first in line when the Eiffel Tower opened in 1889. The Ferris wheel took a full 18 minutes to make a single revolution.

1956 A second federal grand jury recessed without solving the mystery of the missing half of the Greenlease ransom. St. Louis policemen Louis Shoulders and Elmer Dolan were convicted of perjury for testifying that they brought the ransom to the police station the night Carl Austin Hall was arrested. Six-year old Bobby Greenlease was kidnapped by Hall and his mistress, Bonnie Heady on September 28, 1953. Bobby's millionaire father paid the $600,000 ransom, but the child had already been murdered. The rest of the money has never been found.

1969 Amid much fanfare, the Spanish Pavilion opened downtown. Mayor Cervantes led the push to bring the pavilion here from the New York World's Fair. Less than a year after it opened as a cultural center, the foundation formed to bring it here was broke, and the pavilion was closed. Today, it serves as the lobby of the Marriott Pavilion Hotel.

1978 Alan Barklage, chief pilot for Fostaire Helicopters, shot Barbara Oswald to death after she pulled a gun on him in a hijacking attempt 2,000 feet over the U.S. Penitentiary at Marion, Illinois. She planned to force Barklage to land in the yard and rescue her boyfriend.

1983 Ralston-Purina filed a $60 million anti-trust lawsuit against the NHL. The league had refused to approve the sale of the Blues to a group from Saskatoon, Saskatchewan. Ralston argued that the league was forcing the company to operate the team against its will.

May 25

1901 The Glen Echo Country Club opened. It is said to be the first west of the Mississippi. The Olympic golf tournament was held there in 1904. George F. Flynn of Toronto became the first, and only, Olympic golf gold medalist. Golf was dropped after the 1904 Olympics because of the lack of good courses outside of the U.S. and U.K.

1902 The *Post* reported on the new "Loop-the-Loop" ride at the Forest Park Highlands. Some doctors warned that the forerunner of today's roller coasters would stop weak hearts. Riders were pushed to the top of a 50-foot trestle and sped down a 45-degree angle into a 35 feet in diameter loop. The ride was a failure because only four people could ride at one time.

1930 The largest bank robbery is St. Louis history to that date was discovered. The Grand National Bank, at 505 North Grand, had been preparing to move into new headquarters in the brand new Continental Building around the corner. The vault door had alrady been removed, making it easy for the thieves to make off with nearly $1 million in cash, jewelry and securities once they got the keys. The crime was never solved.

1964 Ground was broken for the new Busch Stadium downtown. The cost of the project was estimated at $25 million. Officials said the new ballpark would be ready in time for the start of the 1966 season. Football Cardinals owner Bill Bidwell was threatening to move his team to Atlanta if scheduling conflicts with the baseball birds were not worked out. Eventually, the Big Red signed a lease that was supposed to keep them here until 1996.

1968 Vice President Hubert Humphrey officially dedicated the Gateway Arch. A driving thunderstorm forced the ceremonies indoors. Humphrey and Missouri Governor Warren Hearnes dodged puddles inside as they did the honors. Because of security concerns, the rest of St. Louis was locked out.

May 26

1780 A very famous day in St. Louis history. The British organized an army of of 1,200 Indians and Canadian trappers and marched on the village. Word leaked out, and the village was ready. Fewer than 400 defenders fought back the assault. But some residents were caught by surprise outside of the village. About 60 were massacred or taken prisoner.

1857 Dred Scott and his family won their freedom. Scott was a slave who sued for his freedom in St. Louis in 1846, on the grounds that his owner had taken him into Illinois, a free state. The case went all the way to the U.S. Supreme Court. The court ruled that slaves were not citizens, and thus could not sue. Ownership of Scott passed to Taylor Blow, who granted him his freedom. Scott died a little over a year later.

1926 A fan who had his nose broken by a home run ball off the bat of "Sunny" Jim Bottomley of the Cardinals sued for $7,500. Bottomley was forced to admit in court that he "intentionally hit the ball to create a situation known as a home run." A jury awarded the fan $3,500, but the Cardinals won on appeal in 1928.

1926 Miles Davis was born in Alton. He moved to East St. Louis, and played trumpet in the jazz band at Lincoln High before becoming one of the most innovative jazz artists of all time.

1955 A day that changed the face of the city forever. St. Louis voters approved 23 propositions worth over $110 million in projects. Among the work authorized was the construction of three expressways: The Daniel Boone (U.S. 40), the Mark Twain (I-70) and the Ozark, (U.S. 66, later I-44) Voters also approved money for the Planetarium, the Children's Zoo and the art museum.

May 27

1861 Captain Constantin Blandowski was buried with full military honors. The dashing former European revolutionary was shot in the leg at Camp Jackson, on the western edge of St. Louis, as Union troops marched their prisoners back to the Arsenal on May 10, 1861. Blandowski gave the order to fire on the civilians that day. Over 30 were killed. Blandowski was the first Union officer to be mortally wounded during the Civil War.

1896 The most devastating tornado in city history struck. It first hit the south side, near Lafayette Park destroying City Hospital. The twister then badly damaged the Eads Bridge and sank several vessels on the riverfront before it skipped into East St. Louis, where damage was also extensive. The storm killed 306 people. It destroyed 311 buildings, badly damaged 7,200 and damaged 1,300 more. The total destruction was estimated at $13 million.

1911 Actor Vincent Price was born in St. Louis at 3748 Washington Avenue. He is best remembered for his role in low-budget horror films such as "House of Wax," and his "rap" on Michael Jackson's "Thriller."

1958 The McDonnell F4H "Phantom" made its first flight. The Phantom would go on to establish 15 world's records. It was the most famous plane ever built in St. Louis. Many Phantoms are still in service around the world today.

1973 The Gaslight Square Era officially came to an end, though the area had faded long before. The Board of Aldermen enacted an ordinance changing the name of Gaslight Square back to Olive Street.

May 28

1890 Plans were unveiled for a building at Seventh and Chestnut to house the brewery syndicate of Ellis Wainwright. The first design was rather plain. But Louis Sullivan was eventually hired to design the building. Sullivan's design revolutionized American architecture and ushered in the era of the "skyscraper." The Wainright Building used the steel frame as structural support. In the past, exterior walls had supported tall buildings.

1896 Rescuers were frantically digging through the rubble of the tornado that killed 306 people a day earlier. A long line of people waited anxiously at the old morgue at 12th and Spruce. A crowd at the East St. Louis morgue rioted and stormed the superintendent's office. It was reported that the deadliest spot had been the corner of Seventh and Rutger, where 20 people died in the collapse of two tenements.

1914 A gigantic "Pageant and Masque" celebrating the sesquicentennial of the founding of St. Louis got underway in Forest Park. More than 400,000 people would see the production over the next five nights. The proceeds were used to construct a permanent outdoor theatre in the park, now known as "The Muny."

1950 The New York hypnotherapist hired by the Browns resigned, amid word he was about to be fired. Dr. David Tracy said the players refused to cooperate. Management hired Tracy in the spring to help players deal with a "defeatist complex." The Browns were in last place.

1974 Amtrak announced it was considering moving its operations out of Union Station. Amtrak officials were negotiating to purchase a 15-acre site west of Union Station that could be used as a "temporary" facility. The forlorn "Amshak," cobbled together out of five mobile homes, opened in 1978. It is still in use today.

1896 Two days after the great tornado, rescuers on the east side of the river found the last person to be rescued. A woman named Mary Mock had been buried in the rubble. Demolition and repair work was underway in the devastated area.

1901 The Executive Committee of the Louisiana Purchase Exposition Company began inspecting proposed sites for the proposed 1903 World's Fair. Among the sites under consideration were Carondelet, O'Fallon and Forest Parks.

1925 The St. Louis *Star-Times* was about to launch a new promotion. For $67.50, subscribers could buy a 20-by-100-foot lot in a resort area off Route 66 along the Meramec River. The community soon became known as "Times Beach." A flood and the discovery of dioxin wiped the town off the map in 1982. The buildings were demolished and the soil was cleaned up by the EPA. The site is now Route 66 State Park.

1937 Shaw Park in Clayton was dedicated. The land was formerly part of the huge Davis estate. The park itself is named for Charles Shaw. He was mayor of Clayton from 1933 to 1940. The pool was built with a grant from the WPA.

1977 The Blues great defenseman, Bob Gassoff, was killed in a motorcycle accident on Highway M, south of Highway 100.

Gassoff was a fan favorite for his tough play. In his final season, he finished third in the league in penalty minutes. He was 24 years old.

May 30

1896 Three days after the worst tornado in St. Louis history, 50 police officers were rushed to Union Station to deal with panic in the crowds of out-of-town gawkers who came in for the weekend to see the damage. More than 140,000 people passed through Union Station that day. In East St. Louis, police had arrested 83 people for looting.

1897 The *Post-Dispatch* reported on the first amusement park in St. Louis. Businessman Anton Stuever was bringing "high class vaudeville" to the Forest Park Highlands. The park also boasted a "Scenic Railway," billed as one of the longest tracked rides in the world.

1932 The man who popularized the Missouri state motto died. Congressman William Vandiver of Cape Girardeau listened one night while a colleague poked fun at him before a prestigious audience in Philadelphia. He said he didn't believe his colleague's comments about Philly hospitality. "Frothy eloquence neither convinces nor satisfies me," he said. "I'm from Missouri, you've got to show me."

1972 Six miles of four-lane Highway 40 opened to traffic in the Chesterfield Valley. The highway department had first announced plans to eliminate the treacherous three-lane "suicide lane" stretch in 1962.

2000 Missouri Governor Mel Carnahan signed a bill designating a stretch of I-55 in South St. Louis County as the "Rosa Parks Highway". The bill covered the same stretch of highway between Butler Hill and Lindbergh that had been "adopted" by the Ku Klux Klan.

May 31

1878 The St. Louis Police Board ordered all officers to carry the same type of revolver, a Colt .36 caliber. It was reported that officers currently carried whatever kind of weapon they desired, and some of them resembled small cannons.

1881 St. Louis brewery workers were preparing to walk off the job, demanding a $5 per month raise and a shorter workday. They currently made between $50 and $75 dollars per month for working from 3 a.m. until 6 p.m. But brewery officials pointed out that they got two lunch breaks, at 10 a.m. and 4 p.m., and were entitled to up to 20 glasses of beer per day.

1948 The World War II Court of Honor in Memorial Plaza was dedicated by General Jonathan Wainwright, the hero of

Corregidor. The names of 2,500 St. Louisans who gave their lives in the war are inscribed on 16 granite tablets.

1961 Chuck Berry opened "Berry Park," an outside amusement park in Wentzville. The 30-acre complex included a swimming pool, Ferris wheel, rides and a children's zoo.

1967 Scruggs, Vandervoort and Barney announced it was closing its landmark downtown store and the newer one in Clayton. The block square, seven-story building downtown had been a landmark for shoppers for 117 years.

JUNE

June 1

1890 The first bridge over the Missouri River at St. Charles other than a railroad bridge opened. It was a pontoon bridge, supported by 50 barges. The two center barges, pulled by cables, were opened to allow boats to pass. The bridge was destroyed by ice and rising water after just five months. The permanent highway bridge opened in 1904.

1920 It was announced that National League baseball would return to Sportsman's Park. Cardinals owner Sam Breadon persuaded Phil Bell of the Browns to lease the field so the Cardinals could move from Robison Field. Beaumont High School would be built on the Robison Field site.

1924 City officials took part in the dedication of the new Shriner's Hospital for Crippled Children at Kingshighway and Clayton Avenue. A $2 annual gift from every Shriner in the country would pay for the construction and the operation of the hospital.

1934 Paul and Dizzy Dean claimed they had sore arms that only a pay raise would heal. Rookie Paul was making $3,000, while Ol' Diz got $7,500. The brothers gave in, and went on to win 49 games that season, plus four in the world series.

1988 The city of Chesterfield was incorporated. There actually were three Chesterfields over the years. The first was laid out in 1816 by Justis Post near what is now Wild Horse Creek and Wilson Roads. The second sprang up in the early 1900s next to the railroad tracks that ran beside Olive. The third community developed around the Chesterfield Mercantile on Highway 40 (That building is now the Smokehouse Restaurant).

June 2

1932 The city's reluctance to accept philanthropist C.A. Tilles' offer of his county estate as "a playground for city children" spurred the County Court to action. The Court asked Tilles to donate the land to the county. City officials were afraid that there was not enough money to maintain another park.

1942 The War Department ordered the Village of Madison to repaint the Chain of Rocks Bridge. Parts of the bridge had been painted red. The government said the bridge was too conspicuous from the air, and ordered that it be painted green or another subdued color. The olive green paint is still there.

1958 The city, the Terminal Railroad Association and the Missouri Pacific Railroad signed an agreement removing the final obstacle to construction of the Arch. The deal provided for the removal of the elevated railroad tracks along the riverfront. They were to be placed in a tunnel beneath the memorial.

1958 Chuck Berry was arrested for carrying a concealed weapon in St. Charles. He peeled off $1,250 cash to post bond for himself and an 18-year old woman who was in the Cadillac when he was pulled over. He was later acquitted.

1967 Downtown St. Louis Incorporated awarded first prize in a national contest for a design for the proposed "Gateway Mall." They picked a plan by a Massachusetts firm that called for the demolition of historic buildings along "Real Estate Row" to create an open mall from the Old Courthouse to Union Station. The plan ignited a 17-year battle. When it was over, the city had half a mall, and "Real Estate Row" was gone.

June 3

1812 Persistent earthquakes fanned rumors that the end of the world was near. Following a terrible storm, St. Louis was shrouded in fog. Terrified townspeople heard the church bell ringing at midnight. They fell on their knees when they saw no human hand touched the rope. When the fog cleared, they learned pranksters had tied a rope from the bell across the street.

1875 Business was suspended in St. Louis as residents attended church services and spent the day in fasting and prayer. Governor Charles Hardin had declared a statewide day of prayer for divine intervention to halt a devastating plague of grasshoppers. Within a few days, heavy rains arrived and drove the critters into Iowa.

1906 Josephine Baker was born in St. Louis. She went from a poor child here to become one of the best loved entertainers in France. She was a star of the Follies Bergere and a heroine of the resistance in World War II. Baker only returned to 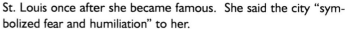 St. Louis once after she became famous. She said the city "symbolized fear and humiliation" to her.

1950 The Cardinals defied a new National League rule and booked a Sunday night game with the Brooklyn Dodgers. It would be the first Sunday night game in major league history. The Cardinals later gave in to pressure from Commissioner Happy Chandler and rescheduled the game as part of a Sunday afternoon doubleheader.

1983 Ralston Purina turned the Blues over to the National Hockey League "to operate, to sell, or otherwise dispose of in whatever manner the league desires." Ralston sued after the NHL Board of Governors refused to approve the sale of the Blues to interests in Saskatoon, Saskatchewan.

June 4

1901 The Executive Committee of the Louisiana Purchase Exposition Company began hearing from advocates of each of the seven proposed sites for the fair. Steel magnate John Scullin argued for a site in Carondelet, where he was a big landowner. But the most powerful men in St. Louis were in favor of a site in Forest Park known as "The Wilderness."

1903 The legislature passed a bill regulating automobiles in St. Louis County. The bill required a $2 yearly license. It also required drivers to announce their presence with a horn or bell, and stop long enough for a rider to dismount and hold his horse. Violations were punishable by a fine of up to a $1,000 or six months in jail.

1916 The *Post-Dispatch* reported on plans for the new Bevo Mill Restaurant on Gravois. August A. Busch said the replica of a Dutch windmill would be a "high class" cafe. The mill was not a success at first. During the war, there were complaints that the place was an attempt to foist Germanic ways on St. Louis.

1940 A crowd of 23,500 saw the first Cardinal night game in St. Louis (The Browns had played one a few nights earlier). The Cardinals got the daylights knocked out of them that night, 10-1.

1964 Big Red Vice-President Bill Bidwell said a research agency was studying whether St. Louis could continue to support a pro football team. He said the study would help him determine whether to accept an offer to move the team to Atlanta.

June 5

1888 The Democratic National Convention in St. Louis nominated President Grover Cleveland for a second term. Cleveland lost to Benjamin Harrison in the general election. But he would be elected president again in 1892.

1916 The first production took place at what is now the "Muny." "As You Like It" was given to mark the tercentary of the death of William Shakespeare. The site chosen sloped down to a natural stage-like area with huge oak trees on either side. The St. Louis Advertising Club offered money to the city to build a concrete auditorium on the site. A presentation of "Aida" for an advertising convention took place there on June 5, 1917. The Municipal Theater Association was organized in 1919.

1937 The Cardinals signed a young pitcher from Donora, Pennsylvania to his first contract. An injury to his arm would necessitate a move to the outfield for Stanley Frank Musial.

1957 The City of Sunset Hills was chartered. The name dates back to 1911, when August Busch Sr. and Eberhard Anheuser built the Sunset Inn. The inn featured a rooftop restaurant, a pool and hunting facilities. The inn eventually grew into the Sunset Hills Country Club.

1971 The "Six Flags Over Mid-America" amusement park opened in Eureka. The 220-acre park was expected to draw nearly 2 million visitors per year and provide a financial windfall for the town.

June 6

1903 The Belleville town square was the scene of a lynching. David Wyatt, a black school teacher from Brooklyn, Illinois, shot and killed the county superintendent of schools, Charles Hertel. Hertel had refused to renew his teaching license. A mob drug Wyatt out of the jail and hanged him from a post.

1903 The *Globe-Democrat* reported that the newest hit song was "The Entertainer," by Scott Joplin. The article noted that the tune was selling thousands upon thousands of copies of sheet music.

1904 The Apache Chief Geronimo arrived at the St. Louis World's Fair. He lived in the Apache Village on the fairgrounds until October 2nd. Visitors paid 10 cents for his autograph and from 50 cents to $2 for a photo.

1944 As the Allied invasion force landed in France, St. Louisans paused for prayer. Archbishop John Glennon presided over an interfaith service at Memorial Plaza. Many schools presented patriotic programs.

1967 The Blues made their picks in the NHL expansion draft. They first chose Glenn Hall from the Blackhawks, making Hall the first St. Louis Blue. Then came Jimmy Roberts and Noel Picard from the Canadiens, Al Arbour from the Leafs and Rod Seiling from the Rangers. The Blues then made their first trade. They sent Seiling back to the Rangers for Gary Sabourin, Bob Plager and Tim Ecclestone.

June 7

1843 Susan Elizabeth Blow was born in St. Louis. Applying the theories of Frederich Froebel, she opened the first public kindergarten in the United States at the Des Peres School at Carondelet in 1873. She was instrumental in establishing kindergartens all over the country.

1896 David Rowland Francis, former mayor of St. Louis and governor of Missouri, suggested an international exposition to mark the 100th anniversary of the Louisiana Purchase. A debate continued for some time before a convention of delegates from the states of the purchase decided on a fair here in 1903 (the date was later pushed back a year).

1963 The replica of the "Spirit of St. Louis" was presented to the Missouri Historical Society. The plane had been built for the motion picture starring Jimmy Stewart. The Historical Society planned to display the plane in the rotunda at city hall or at Lambert Field. After many years at Lambert, the plane now hangs at the Missouri History Museum in Forest Park.

1970 Twenty-thousand hard hats marched down Lindell to show they supported their country. "USA, Love It or Leave It" was a popular slogan of the marchers. They beat up several youthful anti-war protestors. Organizers were disappointed at the turnout. They had hoped for 100,000 marchers.

1983 California business consultant and investor Harry Ornest offered Ralston-Purina $8 million for the Blues. Ralston had turned the team over to the league after the NHL refused to approve the sale of the club to a group from Saskatoon. Ornest said he would keep the Blues here.

June 8

1904 Under heavy police guard, the Liberty Bell arrived in St. Louis for display at the World's Fair. Seventy-five-thousand St. Louis school children had signed petitions requesting the symbol of freedom be sent here.

1911 Tom Benoist made the first flight ever in an airplane built in St. Louis. Benoist had opened the world's first aeronautical supply house at 3932 Olive.

1961 The zoo's worldwide "chimp hunt" was front page news. A Miami court had ruled that the zoo was entitled to the performing chimp "Mr. Moke." His former owner had "chimpnapped" Mister Moke from the St. Louis Zoo. He took the chimp to Miami to perform in the movies. The owner was now believed to have fled the country.

1970 The Linclay Corporation filed plans with the county for a $300 million development on the Missouri River flood plain west of I-270 and I-70. A planning department official said the 1,091 acre "Earth City" development would be "a city within itself."

1980 The Cardinals fired manager Ken Boyer between games of a doubleheader with Montreal. Jack Krol took over as manager for the second game. Whitey Herzog would be named the 31st manager of the Cardinals the following day. Under Boyer, the Cardinals had compiled a record of 166 wins and 187 losses, including an 18 and 33 start in 1980.

June 9

1874 A three-car St. Louis, Vandalia and Terre Haute passenger train became the first to use the new Eads Bridge and the tunnel beneath downtown St. Louis (today, the tunnel carries Metro Link trains). General William T. Sherman drove the last spike for the railroad tracks on the bridge. The bridge was actually dedicated on July 4, 1874.

1927 A special committee announced plans for a three-day celebration to welcome Charles Lindbergh when he arrived back in St. Louis on June 17th. The plans called for a parade from Forest Park to downtown. Lindy was also scheduled to attend the Cardinals game on the 18th and help raise the 1926 championship flag. It would all wrap up with a huge celebration in Forest Park on the 19th.

1927 KSD announced it would be part of a link-up of 57 NBC stations forming a "network" to carry an eleven-hour program covering Lindbergh's arrival in Washington on June 11th. It marked the first time so many stations had been linked to carry such a lengthy program.

1939 The city of Overland was incorporated. Overland is named for the Overland Trail. Originally, the town was to have been named Ritenour City, after a local land owner.

1980 The "Whiteyball" era began. Whitey Herzog was named manager of the Cardinals, replacing Ken Boyer. Herzog would lead the Cardinals to the World Series three times before stepping

down in July, 1990.

June 10

1702 Father James Gravier landed at the mouth of the River des Peres to establish a Jesuit mission. The village there was the earliest European settlement in Missouri. Many French settlers from Cahokia moved to the village when the Kaskaskia Indians built a fort there. By the spring of 1703, the Indians moved away, and so did most of the settlers.

1900 The most violent day yet in the St. Louis streetcar strike. Four strikers were killed and nine were wounded as members of the citizen's police force appointed by the sheriff opened fire on strikers trying to stop a car at Sixth and Washington. The "Washington Avenue Massacre" brought the death toll in the strike to seven.

1922 St. Louis park officials responded to a lawsuit by an African American seeking permission to play golf in Forest Park. They said "when a sufficient number of Negroes expressed the same desire," they would build them a separate golf course.

1950 President Harry Truman dedicated the site of the Jefferson National Expansion Memorial on the riverfront. The site had basically served as a giant parking lot since the buildings were cleared in 1939. The ceremony followed a parade of Truman's old World War I outfit through downtown. The Korean War and a controversy over who would pay to remove the elevated railroad tracks on the riverfront delayed groundbreaking on the Arch for more 12 years.

1999 Missouri Governor Mel Carnahan signed a bill naming part of I-70 in St. Louis in honor of Mark McGwire. A five mile stretch in the city limits was designated as the "Mark McGwire Highway."

June 11

1861 A meeting in St. Louis ended with a declaration of war. Union Captain Nathaniel Lyon and Congressman Francis Blair met with Missouri's pro-southern governor, Claiborne Jackson, and militia commander Sterling Price at the Planter's Hotel. Jackson and Price offered to disband their forces if Lyon would withdraw the home guard. Lyon refused and told Jackson it meant war. Price and Jackson fled to Jefferson City, burning the bridges behind them.

1873 Luther Ely Smith was born in Downer's Grove, Illinois. It was Smith's idea to build a memorial to westward expansion in St. Louis. He took the idea to Mayor Bernard Dickmann in 1933. Their efforts led to the creation of the Jefferson National Expansion Memorial and the Gateway Arch.

1940 The St. Louis Daily "Record" reported that John Carr and architect Adolph Struebig were planning to build ten two-room cabins on Highway 66 at a cost of $7,000. The cabins would form the nucleus of the Coral Court Motel.

1956 The first local color television broadcast in St. Louis was presented by Channel Five. The station showed a film touting the city produced by the Chamber of Commerce.

1974 In a jam against the Dodgers, Cards reliever Al Hrabosky turned his back to the plate and stood behind the mound psyching himself up. He turned around and struck out Tom Paciorek on three pitches, and the "Mad Hungarian" routine was born. Hrabosky became a fan favorite before being traded to Kansas City before the 1978 season.

June 12

1877 St. Louis police had a big round-up on their hands. A court here was debating a law requiring owners of livestock to keep animals on their own properly. A Mrs. Muldoon took matters into her own hands. She led a group of 150 irate citizens to a pen holding 150 stray cows and released them.

1940 The new, streamlined "S.S. Admiral" made its first cruise.

The 375-foot-long five deck Admiral was originally built in 1907 as the steamer "Albatross." Cruising and dancing on the Admiral would be a favorite of St. Louisans for the next 40 years. Once destined for the scrap heap, the Admiral is now a floating casino.

1957 Stan Musial played in his 823rd consecutive game, breaking the National League record held by Gus Suhr. Suhr played in every Pittsburgh Pirates game from September 11, 1931 to June 5, 1937. Stan had played in every Cardinal game since the tail end of the 1951 season, when then-manager Marty Marion rested his star player.

1970 The manager of the Fred Harvey Restaurant at Union Station announced the doors would close forever on June 30th. The restaurant had served travellers since the station opened in 1894. The manager pointed out that there were only 14 trains coming and going from Union Station each day.

1981 Major League Baseball players walked out for the second time in the history of the game. The strike resulted in a split season. The Cardinals were shut out of the playoffs, despite having the best record in the National League East for the entire year.

June 13

1875 Railway service began at the newly opened Union Depot.

It stood on Poplar Street, between 10th and 12th. From the day it opened, it was doomed because of its limited capacity. Almost immediately, plans were in motion for a new depot on the site formerly occupied by Chouteau's Pond.

1921 The famous bear pits at the St. Louis Zoo were opened to the public. The rocks and walls were cast from molds made of actual cliffs near Herculaneum. The waterfalls and fountains were added in 1962.

1956 The State Highway Department awarded contracts for the section of Highway 40 between Brentwood Blvd. and the Red Feather Expressway. Highway 40 was proposed from Wentzville to St. Louis in 1928. It was completed to Lindbergh in 1938. But residents kept it a dead end at Brentwood Boulevard.

1983 The National Hockey League took over the Blues. The league took action after Ralston Purina abandoned the team and sued the league for blocking the sale to interests in Saskatoon. The NHL president said he would move immediately to find a buyer who would keep the team in St. Louis.

1997 The Vatican designated the Cathedral of St. Louis a basilica. The church at Lindell and Newstead was renamed the Cathedral Basilica of St. Louis. St. Louis became one of the few cities in the world with two basilicas recognized by the Vatican. The "old" cathedral downtown is also a basilica.

June 14

1874 A series of tests was being conducted to test the strength of the Eads Bridge. A fellow by the name of John Robinson took a stroll across the upper deck with an elephant. An elephant was selected because it was believed they had tremendous instincts, and would not cross a dangerous structure.

1916 The Democratic National Convention met at the old coliseum on Jefferson. The convention re-nominated President Woodrow Wilson and Vice President Thomas Riley Marshall. It was marked with demonstrations by suffragettes. About 10,000 of them held a "walkless parade" down Locust.

1917 The War Department announced it had selected a site to start construction immediately on a base for aviation cadets. The $1 million facility was to be built on 640 acres in St. Clair County, Illinois. The base would be named in honor of Corporal Frank Scott, the first enlisted man to die in a plane crash.

1927 A special committee preparing to welcome Charles Lindbergh home announced that 15,000 troops would be on hand at Lambert when the "Spirit of St. Louis" touched down. They wanted to prevent mob scenes like those that greeted Lindy across Europe. One hundred thousand people were descending on St. Louis from out of town.

1991 The Riverport Amphitheater opened. The first concert featured Steve Winwood and Robert Cray. One of the premier outdoor concert venues in the country, Riverport entertains more than 500,000 people each year. It can accommodate about 20,000 people per show.

June 15

1927 St. Louis was preparing to welcome Charles Lindbergh that coming weekend. The "Post-Dispatch" reported that Lindbergh pies, luncheons and sundaes adorned menus. There were no fewer than ten popular songs honoring Lindy on display. A Lindbergh display was a feature of nearly every shop window. A huge sign at Grand and Washington declared him "Our Ace of Hearts."

1951 St. Louis became a two newspaper town, as the *Star-Times* ceased publication. The Pulitzer Publishing Company, publishers of the *Post-Dispatch*, bought the Star's circulation lists and printing equipment.

1957 The St. Louis was mopping up after the heaviest rain ever recorded here. 8.7 inches fell downtown in 14 hours. Belleville reported 13.75 inches. The storm was blamed for eleven deaths.

1964 The Cardinals pulled off one of the biggest steals in their history. They traded Ernie Broglio, Bobby Shantz and outfielder Doug Clemens to the Cubs for outfielder Paul Toth—and a fellow by the name of Louis Clark Brock.

1989 The Blues traded away future Hall of Famer Bernie Federko, Bernie went to Detroit for Adam Oates and Paul McLean.

June 16

1896 The Republican National Convention opened at an auditorium erected just for the occasion on Washington near city hall. "The Wigwam" had a seating capacity of 40,000. The convention nominated William McKinley for president and Garrett A. Hobart as his running mate.

1911 The city of Wood River, Illinois, was incorporated. Construction of the Standard Oil refinery in 1906 and 1907 had touched off explosive growth in the area. By 1920, Wood River laid claim to the title of "fastest growing city in the United States."

1919 It was the first successful opening night for the Muny Theatre Association. The first performance of "Robin Hood" the night before was a disaster. A heavy rain sent the River Des Peres rampaging across the stage. The scenery and band instruments were washed away. The following night went off without a hitch, and mayor Henry Kiel appeared in the production as Richard III.

1954 The Missouri Highway Department authorized construction of a new four lane bridge over the Missouri River at St. Charles. The old bridge carrying U.S. 40 had been built in 1904, and was hopelessly overburdened. More than 16,000 cars each day were using the old bridge.

1965 As the Arch continued to rise higher over downtown St. Louis, the Federal Aviation Administration issued a stern warning for would-be daredevil pilots. Any pilot who tried to fly through the legs of the Arch would be dealt with severely. At least ten pilots have done it. Most of them got away with it.

June 17

1845 A committee of citizens from Frankfort, Kentucky came to St. Charles County to exhume the body of Daniel Boone and his wife. They were re-interred in Kentucky. Boone left specific instructions that he was to buried at Defiance.

1861 A little more than a month after the tragedy at Camp Jackson, the violence of the Civil War flared again in St. Louis. Once again, soldiers were fired upon by civilians and returned the fire into the crowd. Six people were killed. The troops had fired into the recorder's courtroom at Seventh and Locust.

1861 The first land battle of the Civil War was fought at Boonville, Missouri (Bull Run did not take place until July 21st). The rebels under Sterling Price and governor Claiborne Jackson were defeated by the federals under Nathaniel Lyon. Price retreated into Arkansas, and northern Missouri was secured for the Union.

1927 Charles Lindbergh returned to St. Louis from his historic flight across the Atlantic. He arrived 20 minutes early, but performed stunts over the city so as not to spoil the welcome planned for him. Light rain kept the crowd at Lambert Field down to just 12,000. A line of 650 soldiers from Scott and 500 National Guardsmen from Jefferson Barracks held the crowd back.

1965 As construction on the Arch reached the 530-foot-level and began creeping over toward the horizontal, the special "creeper cranes" hoisted a 255-foot-wide building strut to the top. The strut was set in place between the legs as a temporary brace.

June 18

1904 Three people were wounded in a real life Wild West shootout on "The Pike" at the World's Fair. Colonel Zach Mulhall, who ran a wild west show, took a shot at a man in charge of his horses. A show cowboy who tried to break it up was wounded, and an innocent bystander nearly died.

1920 The Missouri Aeronautical Society leased a 160-acre corn field on Natural Bridge Road. At his own expense, Albert Bond Lambert drained, graded and developed an airfield on the site. He later offered to turn it over to the city at cost, even though the value of the land had skyrocketed.

1927 It seemed as if the entire city turned out along an eight-mile parade route to welcome Charles Lindbergh back from his epic flight. Troops had to hold the crowd back as the parade headed down Olive amid a shower of ticker-tape. A crowd of 37,000 people at Sportsman's Park cheered as Lindbergh helped raise the 1926 championship banner. A record number of passengers passed through Union Station that day.

1931 St. Louis attorney Homer G. Phillips was shot and killed while he waited for a bus at Aubert and Delmar. Phillips had led the battle for construction of a hospital to serve the black population. Two men were arrested for the crime, but were found innocent. Homer G. Phillips Hospital opened in 1937 and closed in 1979.

2002 Cardinals broadcaster Jack Buck died at the age of 77. Buck had been hospitalized for 5 and 1/2 months, due to complications following surgery for lung cancer. Buck began broadcasting Cardinal games with Harry Caray in 1954. He became the lead broadcaster when Caray left in 1969, teaming with Mike Shannon in 1972. Jack was beloved in St. Louis for his charity work and as the city's favorite Master of Ceremonies.

June 19

1853 The first rail line west of the Mississippi opened, as a Pacific Railroad train made the run from St. Louis to the Franklin County line and the town of Franklin. The town was later re-named Pacific to mark the occasion. It would be 1855 before the line made it to Jefferson City.

1927 Festivities welcoming Charles Lindbergh back to St. Louis continued. Thousands packed Art Hill as Lindy made a fly-by in "The Spirit of St. Louis." The Missouri Historical Society announced it had accepted Lindbergh's offer to give the trophies and awards from his flight for permanent display at the Jefferson Memorial.

1948 The great Babe Ruth made his final appearance in St. Louis. Hundreds of youngsters attended a clinic with the ailing slugger at Sportsmen's Park. The Babe died on August 16th.

1950 The city of Bellefontaine Neighbors was incorporated. In the few years since World War II, a town had sprung up where once there had been only farmland. The village was originally known as "Pull Tight," supposedly because farmers had to pull the reigns while coming down a hill on Parker Road. The French called the area "Bellefontaine," or "beautiful fountain." The name came from a nearby spring.

1996 Ozzie Smith tearfully announced that he would retire at the end of the 1996 season. The 41-year old Smith led the Cardinals to three pennants and a world championship in the 1980s. In 1996, he was battling Royce Clayton for the starting shortstop job under new manager Tony Larussa.

June 20

1808 The Louisiana Territorial Legislature ordered the marking of a pioneer trail running from St. Louis to Ste. Genevieve and New Madrid. The road was to be designated as "The King's Highway." It was the beginning of road planning here in Missouri. Parts of Lemay Ferry, Telegraph and U.S. 61/67 roughly follow the route.

1942 In one of the first civil rights protests ever here, the March on Washington Movement organized a four-mile march to protest discrimination at the small arms plant on Goodfellow. The protests succeeded in forcing the company to hire blacks, but they would work in a segregated facility.

1952 Actor John Goodman was born. The Affton native made his mark in films such as "True Stories" and "Raising Arizona," and starred as Dan on the television show "Roseanne" from 1988 until 1997. He played leading roles in "The Babe" and "The Flintstones."

1981 A headache ball smacked the mural "Lindy Squared" right between the eyes. The popular mural of Charles Lindbergh adorned a parking garage at Tenth and Chestnut that was being torn down to make room for the new Southwestern Bell Building.

1988 Brian Sutter was named coach of the Blues, replacing Jacques Martin. Sutter would coach the Blues for the next four years, setting a Blues record for the most games coached and the most wins in team history.

June 21

1923 President Warren G. Harding, while visiting St. Louis, became the first president to give a speech over the radio. The speech to the Rotarian Convention at the old Coliseum was broadcast over KSD. It was also one of the earliest network programs, picked up by WEAF in New York and WCAP in Washington.

1930 The $4.5 million Civil Courts Building downtown was dedicated. At the time, it was the tallest building in the city. The Greek temple designed building meant the end of use of the Old Courthouse.

1949 The city opened the swimming pool in Fairgrounds Park to African-Americans. A crowd gathered when black youths arrived to swim, and it soon turned into a riot. Twelve people were hospitalized. Police kept the peace later in the summer when the pool reopened.

1957 Just a month out of high school, Von McDaniel of the Cardinals threw a shutout in his first major league start. Von and his brother, Lindy, nearly pitched the Cardinals to a pennant. But Lindy faltered and was shipped out, Von lost his coordination. After the 1957 season, he only pitched two more innings.

1966 An unknown pilot became the first to fly between the legs of the Arch. It is illegal to fly thorough the Arch, so he taped over the registration numbers on the plane. The FAA was conducting an exhaustive search to find the pilot.

June 22

1932 City Health Director Max Starkloff was calling for a ban on dance marathons. He called the craze "the most demoralizing and unhealthful exhibitions" he had ever witnessed. The contests often went on for up to a month. There were three such events going on in St. Louis at the time.

1933 Jimmy Wilson, Bill Hallahan, Frankie Frisch and Pepper Martin of the Cardinals were named to the first National League All-Star Team. The first All-Star game was slated to be held on July 6th in Chicago as a part of the World's Fair.

1971 Lambert-St. Louis Airport was officially designated as St. Louis International Airport. But an outcry arose over the omission of the name of the St. Louis aviation pioneer, and the "Lambert" was eventually restored.

1971 Kurt Warner was born in Burlington, Iowa. The Rams quarterback took the long road to success. He played for the Iowa Barnstormers of the Arena Football League from 1995 to 1997 and for the Amsterdam Admirals of NFL Europe in 1998. He spent 1994 training camp with the Green Bay Packers. Kurt finally signed with the Rams on December 26, 1997.

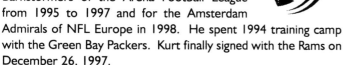

2002 Just 24 hours after funeral services were held for Jack Buck, Cardinals fans suffered another shocking blow. Pitcher Darryl Kile was found dead of heart disease in his Chicago hotel room. Kyle was 33 years old. Teammates received the news moments before they were to take the field at Wrigley. A sell-out crowd had already assembled when Cubs catcher Joe Girardi announced that the game had been called off.

June 23

1814 Ann Lucas married Captain Theodore Hunt. They lived in a home on Gravois later occupied by the Dent family and named "Whitehaven." It was there that Ulysses S. Grant met his future wife, Julia Dent. When Captain Hunt died, Ann married his cousin, Theodore Price Hunt. Ann's father gave them an estate called "Normandy," where you will find Lucas and Hunt Road today.

1933 The St. Louis Central Riverfront Improvement Association unveiled plans for a federal park on the riverfront to "honor the men who helped in the winning of the West." The $90 million plan called for razing all non-historic buildings between the levee, Third, Walnut and Washington. Planners envisioned a huge seawall, parks, boulevards and massive warehouses.

1959 Mayor Raymond Tucker broke ground for work to remove the elevated railroad tracks on the riverfront. It marked the first step in years towards actual construction on the Arch. The battle over who would pay to remove the tracks and budget battles in Washington had delayed the project since the buildings were cleared in the 1940s.

1972 An armed man hijacked an American Airlines 727 on a flight from St. Louis to Tulsa and forced it to return to Lambert. He released 80 of the 103 people on board. After a $500,000 ransom and five parachutes were delivered, the plane rolled towards takeoff. Suddenly, a Cadillac driven by a Florissant businessman crashed through a fence and smashed into the plane's landing gear. The driver was seriously injured, the hijacker got a new plane.

1993 More than 1,000 people boarded the Casino Queen in East St. Louis for the maiden voyage. The casino would allow East St. Louis to refinance millions of dollars in debts, replace worn out police cars and fire trucks, and give city workers a raise—while cutting property taxes.

June 24

1770 The first church in St. Louis was dedicated by Father Pierre Gibault. That first small log church stood on the same block at Second and Market where the Old Cathedral stands today.

1844 The Mississippi River hit the all-time high water mark here. During the 1844 flood, the water stood ten to 20 feet deep over what is now East St. Louis. The river was ten miles wide at Cahokia. It was 38 feet above the low water mark, which is how they measured it back then.

1876 Forest Park was officially opened to the public. The *Globe-Democrat* reported that more than 50,000 people attended the dedication ceremonies. That's about one out of every seven St. Louisans. The ceremony was highlighted by the unveiling of a statue of Edward Bates, U.S. Attorney General under Abraham Lincoln. Critics were blasting the location as too far away to be of any use. At the time, nearly all of the park's 1,326 original acres was virgin forest.

1932 The last streetcar left Belleville. Gerald Phillips took that last ride. The local grocer had ridden on Belleville's first streetcar on June 4, 1899.

1993 A day after the Missouri rose over flood stage at St. Charles, the County Emergency Management Agency warned 800 families from the Lincoln County line to West Alton to move to higher ground. Ten inches of rain fell in Southern Iowa, prompting officials to warn the rivers could top the record crest of 1973.

June 25

1849 St. Louisians packed a public meeting to deal with the Cholera epidemic. In June alone, 1,200 people had died. Those at the meeting voted sweeping powers to a new committee of Public Health. But the disease raged unchecked. Eventually, the disease would kill about 1/10 of the population.

1965 The National Park Service announced that the Gateway Arch was now the tallest man-made national monument. The addition of another 12-foot section on the North Leg brought the Arch up to 562 feet and two inches. That was six feet taller than the Washington Monument.

1989 The St. Louis Walk of Fame on Delmar was dedicated. The first inductees were Chuck Berry, Katherine Dunham, James B. Eads, T.S. Eliot, Scott Joplin, Charles Lindbergh, Stan Musial, Vincent Price, Joseph Pulitzer and Tennessee Williams.

1993 The Corps of Engineers reported that heavy rains in the Missouri and Mississippi River Basin could cause some flooding at St. Louis. Parts of North Dakota, Kansas, and Iowa had received 150% of their normal rainfall.

1999 Jose Jimenez became the eighth Cardinal to throw a no-hitter. His masterpiece came against the Arizona Diamondbacks in Phoenix. The Cardinals won the game, 1-0. Jimenez allowed two walks and hit a batter.

June 26

1922 Radio Station KSD was formally dedicated. The station had signed on back in February, but someone forgot to get a license. KSD would become the first station to broadcast from the Muny, the Veiled Prophet Ball, and the St. Louis Symphony.

1937 The Daniel Boone Bridge carrying U.S. 40 over the Missouri River was dedicated. Back then, Highway 40 through the Chesterfield Valley was two lanes, with a third "suicide lane" in the middle. The highway ran between Wentzville and Bellefontaine, on Clayton Road.

1950 The last streetcar run was made over the "05" Creve Coeur Line to Creve Coeur Lake. When the streetcars were retired, a good portion of the old line was paved over and re-named Midland Boulevard.

1972 McDonnell-Douglas unveiled its newest fighter, the F-15 "Eagle." The F-15 was scheduled to begin flight tests in July. If the tests were successful, the Air Force planned to order 729 planes. Nine thousand workers were involved in the F-15 program.

1981 The John Carpenter film, "Escape From New York" opened. The movie was largely filmed in St. Louis. The Chain of Rocks Bridge, Union Station and other sites filled in for 1997 New York City, which had been turned into an armed maximum-security prison camp. On opening day, co-star Isaac Hayes appeared at several St. Louis area theatres.

June 27

1926 About 40,000 Cardinal fans packed Sportsman's Park to see the debut of pitcher Grover Cleveland Alexander in a Cardinal uniform. Alexander had been acquired from the Cubs a few days earlier. He threw a four hitter as the Cards moved into first place.

1962 Shortly after 5:00 a.m., a worker gave the signal, and trucks began pouring the first concrete for the foundations of the Arch. The first pour was made into a 44-foot excavation for the south leg.

1983 Omni International Hotels announced plans for a 550-room world class luxury hotel at Union Station. The hotel would complement the $125 million station redevelopment project. City officials were predicting that Union Station would become one of the city's top attractions.

1985 Route 66 passed into history as officials decertified the route and voted to remove the few remaining signs. They had come down in Missouri in 1977. When it was first commissioned in 1926, 66 followed Manchester Road west. The route was shifted to Gravois, Chippewa and Watson in 1932. In 1935, that route was renamed "City 66" and the main route shifted to cross the Chain of Rocks Bridge, following what is now Dunn Road and Lindbergh to hook up with City 66.

2000 Nelly's "County Grammar" CD was released. Born Cornell Haynes Jr. in Texas, Nelly spent his early years in Spain, before his family moved to St. Louis, then University City. In 1993,

he formed the "St. Lunatics" with his high school friends. "County Grammar" would go on to sell nine million copies and score three Grammy Nominations.

June 28

1844 The rampaging Mississippi began to recede following the worst flood in St. Louis history. 1993 was a trickle compared to this one. At the height of the 1844 flood, the Mississippi was ten miles wide at Cahokia, all of what is now East St. Louis was under water, and the business section of St. Louis was flooded as far west as Broadway.

1926 Over 100,000 people lined the route of a grand procession to mark the dedication of the magnificent "new' cathedral on Lindell and the 100th anniversary of the St. Louis Diocese. The New Cathedral was declared a basilica in 1997, making St. Louis one of the few cities in the world with two basilicas.

1960 Jerry Lewis and his film company agreed to delete a scene for the movie "The Bellboy" featuring the St. Louis Zoo's famous performing chimp, "Mr. Moke." At the time the scene was filmed, Mr. Moke had been "chimp-napped" from the zoo by his former owner.

1969 During a violent thunderstorm, the riverboat restaurant

"Becky Thatcher" was torn from her moorings and drifted down the river with 100 terrified people on board. The replica of the "Santa Maria," brought here by Mayor Cervantes from the 1964 World's Fair, also broke free. The Becky Thatcher ended up snagged on a Monsanto dock and the passengers were rescued. The badly damaged Santa Maria ran aground in Illinois.

1972 The FBI was combing the fields near Peru, Indiana. Farmers had found a submachine gun and a bag containing the $500,000 ransom paid to a man who hijacked a plane at Lambert Field on June 23rd. Authorities speculated that the shock of bailing out at over 300 miles per hour caused the hijacker to drop the gun and the money.

June 29

1906 The city was embroiled in a legal battle with the sculptor of the plaster statue of St. Louis. The sculpture had become a popular attraction during the fair. The city wanted to cast the sculpture in bronze and place it in Forest Park. But Charles Niehaus demanded more money.

1966 The first day game at the new Busch Stadium downtown created one of the worst traffic jams in city history. Downtown was not ready to handle the crowds during the day, when the

parking was already taken by the workforce. The Stadium West Garage had not opened yet. At that time, Highway 40 dead ended at 18th street.

1972 Martin McNally was arrested near his home in suburban Detroit and charged with the hijacking at Lambert Field six days earlier. The shock of bailing out at 30-thousand-feet over Indiana caused him to drop the $500,000 ransom.

1976 A crowd of 38,000 rock fans came to Busch Stadium for "Superjam 76." It was the largest rock concert here since 1966, when the Beatles came to Busch. Superjam featured Jefferson Starship, Fleetwood Mac, Ted Nugent and Jeff Beck.

1980 Ground was broken for the new $500 million General Motors plant in Wentzville. It was scheduled to begin operations in 1982. The plant replaced the 60-year old facility at Natural Bridge and Union.

June 30

1870 The famous steamboat race between the "Robert E. Lee" and the "Natchez" began in New Orleans. On July 4th, the victorious Robert E. Lee arrived in St. Louis. The trip from New Orleans took three days, 18 hours and 14 minutes.

1916 A landmark in St. Louis closed its doors. Since 1871,

Faust's Restaurant was where the elite met. In 1878, "Tony's" became the first building in St. Louis to have electric lights.

1946 Jefferson Barracks was officially removed from the War Department roles as a military post. In 1950, it became Jefferson Barracks County Park. Jefferson Barracks was established on October 23, 1826, as a training post. Five American presidents served there, as did Robert E. Lee, William T. Sherman and John J. Pershing.

1979 Mayor Conway ordered Homer G. Phillips Hospital closed and consolidated with City Hospital Number One. The move ignited a firestorm of protest in the black community. The last patients were moved in August, 1979. Vince Scheomehl was elected mayor after promising to open the hospital. But he changed his mind once he took office.

2000 Mark McGwire passed Ray Lankford to take over number one on the all-time Busch Stadium home run list with 104. Big Mac's season would end on July 13th, due to tendonitis in the right knee. The 2001 season would be his last.

July 1

1826 The east-west streets in St. Louis were given new names. Mayor Lane persuaded the Board of Trustees to adopt the Philadelphia system of naming streets for trees. Market Street was the only one to keep its original  name. The new names were, Olive, Locust, Vine, Laurel, Prune, Oak, Hickory, Pear, Willow and Walnut. The north-south streets had already been assigned numbers.

1917 Whites in a speeding car fired into homes in a black neighborhood of East St. Louis. When two detectives arrived, the crowd mistook them for the gunmen and opened fire, killing them. White residents went on a rampage when they heard the news of the shootings. At least 39 blacks and eight whites died in the riots. Thousands of blacks fled East St. Louis.

1920 The Cardinals moved back to Sportsman's Park from deteriorating Cardinals Park at Natural Bridge and Vandeventer. They had played there since 1892. At that time, the Browns were the better team and owned Sportsman's Park. The Redbirds paid rent. Sportsman's Park became Busch Stadium in 1953, after the brewery bought the Cardinals and the Browns moved to Baltimore.

1959 The new $50 million Chrysler Assembly Plant on Highway 66 in Fenton began operation. The first models produced there were Plymouths, Dodge Darts and Chrysler's compact Valiant model. At the time, St. Louis was the second largest producer of automobiles in the nation.

1998 An era ended for St. Louis Blues fans, as Brett Hull became a free agent at the stroke of midnight. Two days later, Brett would sign with the Dallas Stars. Hull holds the team record for career goals with 527. He shattered team records with 86 goals and 131 points during the 1990-91 season.

July 2

1900 A settlement was finally reached in the 55-day old streetcar strike. At least 15 people had died, business ground to a halt and 1,600 St. Louisans were pressed into service as citizen's police officers to keep order. A week later, the workers walked out again. The union eventually gave up, but the strike is seen as an important turning point in St. Louis labor history.

1901 Because of a drought, every wagon in the village of St. Peters was pressed into service to haul water from the "Cave Springs." They were named after a man-made cave on the Stille farm, from which a spring flowed. The springs were later covered by the I-70 interchange that now bears the name.

1917 Much of East St. Louis was in flames. Rioting touched off by the killing of two white detectives was sweeping the city. Mobs of whites pulled blacks off the streetcars, clubbing and stoning them to death, while police and government officials stood idly by. The exact death toll will never be known, but at least 39 blacks and eight whites were killed.

1973 Betty Grable died of lung cancer at the age of 56. She was born on December 18, 1916 in St. Louis. Grable was the daughter of a wealthy stockbrocker and a mother who had given up show business. Betty lied about her age at 13 to win a spot in the chorus line at the Fox Theatre.

1991 Concertgoers at a Guns n' Roses show at the Riverport Amphitheater went wild after Axl Rose stormed offstage. Rose yelled at a security guard to confiscate a fan's camera, then plunged into the crowd before walking off. Fans tore up seats, destroyed two video screens, and much of the band's equipment.

1861 John C. Fremont was named commander of the Western Department of the Army, headquartered in St. Louis. Fremont put St. Louis under martial law, and ordered the slaves of Confederate sympathizers freed. Fearful of upsetting the border states, President Abraham Lincoln rescinded the order and had the controversial Fremont removed.

1934 The bankrupt Arena and the Forest Park Highlands were sold for $848,000 to a reorganization firm at a foreclosure auction. The Arena opened in 1929, just months before the stock market crash wiped out the promoters. For a time, the building was in danger of being torn down.

1959 McDonnell Aircraft unveiled its newest fighter, the F-4 "Phantom." The sensitive radar gear in the plane's nose was protected by aluminum. The dignitaries failed to break a bottle of champagne over the nose three times. They gave up and poured the champagne over the plane.

1981 The first V.P. Fair opened on the Arch grounds. Fair officials said more than 1.5 million people attended "America's Biggest Birthday Party." In a sign of things to come, a torrential downpour would turn the grounds into a sea of mud.

1993 The Missouri River at St. Charles rose over flood stage for the second time in 1993. Residents of Northern St. Charles County and in Grafton, Illinois, began moving out. The V.P. Fair opened on the St. Louis riverfront with some of the attractions moved to make room for the rising Mississippi.

July 4

1851 Ground was broken for the first railroad west of the Mississippi. After a grand procession, St. Louis Mayor Arthur Kennett turned the first shovelful of dirt for the Pacific Railroad. When the tracks reached the town of Franklin, 35 miles to the west, the town was renamed Pacific to honor the occasion.

1862 Ceremonies were held marking the completion of the building we now know as the "old" courthouse. The first courthouse on the site was built in 1828. Expansion was begun in 1839, and the east and west wings were completed. But the dome was not finished until 1862.

1870 At 11:24 a.m., cannons boomed on the riverfront as the steamboat "Robert E. Lee" arrived in St. Louis, ahead of the "Natchez." The Lee made the trip in three days, 18 hours and 14 minutes. The Natchez arrived six and a half hours later.

1874 The Eads Bridge was dedicated. More than 300,000 people gathered for the ceremonies honoring the engineering marvel of the age. That was nearly the entire population of the city at the time. William T. Sherman drove the golden spike, symbolizing the linking of East and West.

1904 July 4th at the World's Fair was marked with an elaborate military parade and a speech by William Jennings Bryan. A dramatic recitation of the Declaration of Independence was made next to the Liberty Bell, on display in the Pennsylvania Building.

July 5

1808 The leading citizens of St. Louis asked to be incorporated as a town. A petition was filed with the Court of Common Pleas of the Indiana Territory, of which St. Louis was still a part. The petition included 80 signatures out of a possible 101 "taxable inhabitants."

1879 Dwight F. Davis was born in St. Louis. An excellent tennis player, he served as the city parks commissioner and installed tennis courts in Forest Park. They were the first public courts in the nation. In 1900, he donated the "Davis Cup" for the international lawn tennis competitions.

1925 The St. Louis Police Department fired its female telephone operators. A spokesman said the move was part of a "return to normalcy," meaning pre-war conditions when there were no female employees. The women protested, but the police board said the station house was "not a desirable environment" for women.

1974 Both Chuck Berry and St. Charles County officials said no more rock concerts would be held at Berry Park in Wentzville. A July 4th festival was a disaster because of stolen tickets, low attendance and no-shows by some of the acts. Enraged fans pelted Berry's home with rocks when Leon Russell failed to appear.

1981 Robert Herman, Chairman of the Vieled Prophet Fair, said he would push for a similar celebration on the riverfront in 1982. He said the first fair was a success, despite a downpour that wiped out most of the fireworks and a concert by Loretta Lynn. Fair organizers said about 1.5 people had attended over three days.

July 6

1763 Maxent, Laclede and Company of New Orleans was granted exclusive rights to the Indian trade in the Mississippi Valley. In August, Pierre Laclede and his grandson, Auguste Chouteau, would journey up the river to choose a site for their trading post. The site would become the city of St. Louis.

1880 One of the most colorful characters in St. Louis history was killed. A fire extinguisher exploded in the hands of firefighter Phelim O'Toole as he fought a small fire in a vacant building. O'Toole became a legend during the terrible Southern Hotel fire

on April 11, 1877. He climbed a horse-drawn hook and ladder and rushed from window to window, saving dozens of lives.

1939 The birthday of McDonnell Aircraft. James S. McDonnell founded the aircraft company in a small rented building at Lambert Field. The firm began with one employee and no contracts. In August 1940, McDonnell received its first manufacturing order, for $7,600 worth of parts. McDonnell merged with Douglas Aircraft in 1967, and became the world's largest producer of military aircraft. The firm merged with Boeing in 1997.

1990 Whitey Herzog announced he was stepping down as manager of the Cardinals. He had piloted the Redbirds since 1980, leading them to the World Series three times. Joe Torre was named as his replacement on August 2nd.

2000 Cardinals rookie catcher Keith McDonald became only the second player in major league history to hit two home runs in his first two big league at bats. But the Reds won the game at Busch, 12-6. Bob Nieman of the Browns hit two home runs in his first two at bats back in 1951.

July 7

1851 Christian Von der Ahe was born in Hille, Prussia. The flamboyant saloon keeper owned the Browns during the 1880s and 1890s. He was ahead of his time, devising wild promotions, including a "shoot-the-chutes" ride at the ballpark, a beer garden, an all-girl band and horse racing.

1906 According to some sources, Satchel Paige was born. (no one knows for sure) He is reported to have won 104 of 105 games pitched in the Negro Leagues in 1934. Paige pitched at least 55 no hitters. In 1952, he became the oldest pitcher in major league history to throw a complete game. He was 46 at the time, and pitching for the Browns.

1915 A tornado left seven people dead, and virtually destroyed the small towns of O'Fallon and St. Peters. St. Charles was hit hard as well. Officials were thankful that the twister had hit such a sparsely populated area.

1929 Transcontinental Air Transport inaugurated coast-to-coast air and railroad service along a route from Los Angeles through St. Louis laid out by Colonel Charles Lindbergh. In 1930, TAT merged with Western Air Express to form TWA.

1993 The Army Corps of Engineers warned the flood would surpass the record crest of 1973 within three or four days. Their latest predictions didn't include the downpours that swept across the area that day. The levee protecting West Alton gave way.

1931 One of the oldest firms in St. Louis became a victim of the automobile age. The Weber and Damme Wagon Company declared bankruptcy after 70 years in business. There were now only five wagon making firms left in St. Louis, once a center of the industry.

1944 One of the first organized "sit-ins" for civil rights took place in St. Louis. Forty-five women, including 15 whites, staged a sit-in at the lunch counters at Stix, Baer and Fuller, Famous-Barr and Scruggs, Vandervoort and Barney. The stores closed the counters rather than serve the demonstrators.

1954 The second television station in St. Louis signed on the air. KWK TV broadcast on Channel Four from the *Globe-Democrat* Building.

1982 Representatives of the Gateway Redevelopment Corporation, Landmark Redevelopment, labor and Mayor Scheomehl created the Pride of St. Louis Redevelopment Corporation to try to reconcile the competing plans for the Gateway Mall. Pride would eventually decide to go ahead with the demolition of the historic Buder and Title Guaranty Buildings.

2000 The *Sporting News* named St. Louis as the Best Sports Town in America. The magazine cited "The success of the Rams, Blues and Cardinals, not to mention the extraordinary fans."

July 9

1841 A crowd of 20,000, 3/4 of the city's population, witnessed the hanging of four black men on Duncan's Island. The men were convicted of killing two clerks and torching a bank during a robbery. The city was in an uproar, amid rumors that the men had ties to abolitionists, and the "black underground." City leaders said they were pleased that the men were not lynched.

1860 The first recorded organized game of baseball in St. Louis was played under rules set out by the National Convention of Baseball Players. The "Morning Stars" beat "The Cyclones", 50-24, on a field just west of present-day O'Fallon Park.

1940 The National League won the All-Star Game at Sportsman's Park. The final score was 4-0. It was the first shut out in All-Star history. Max West of the Boston Bees hit a three run home run in the first inning.

1957 The All-Star Game was played here at old Busch Stadium. The American League won, 6-5, in dramatic fashion. Both teams scored three runs in the ninth. But Minnie Minoso's catch in the bottom of the ninth with the bases loaded snuffed the NL rally.

1993 The flooding Missouri River inundated a power station in St. Charles, cutting power to thousands. In Lemay, water topped a levee along Kayser Creek, inundating more homes. Over the next few days, hundreds more families would be forced from their homes.

1997 Ground was broken on the long-awaited Page extension into St. Charles County. The project lost federal funding twice due the controversy over running the freeway through the edge of Creve Coeur Lake Park. Opponents lost their fight when St. Louis County voters approved the plan in November, 1998.

July 10

1839 Adolphus Busch was born in Mayence-on-the-Rhine, Germany. He came to America and was selling brewing supplies in St. Louis when he married Lilly Anheuser, daughter of Eberhard Anheuser, who ran the small Bavarian Brewery. Adolphus obtained a controlling interest in the brewery in 1865.

1871 The City Council passed the "Social Evil" ordinace. The measure authorized the Board of Health to license and regulate prostitutes. Doctors were told to attempt to lead the wayward to a life of virtue. The ordinance sat up the "Social Evil Hospital and House of Industry" at Arsenal and Sublette. The measure was repealed in March, 1874.

1923 Cardinal rookie pitcher Johnny Stuart went the distance and won BOTH games of a doubleheader. Stuart tossed a three-hitter to win the first game, 11-1. He won the second game by a score of 6-3.

1970 KTVI-TV fired Charlotte Peters, known as "The First Lady of St. Louis Television." Her show had been on Channel Two since October, 1964. She appeared on KSD from 1956 until 1964. On her final show, she urged viewers to write the mayor and the Board of Aldermen to prevent the "Yippies" from holding their "Festival of Life" in Forest Park.

1994 The final hockey game was played at the Arena. It was a match between the North and the South teams in the gold medal game at the U.S. Olympic Festival. South defenseman Ashlin Halfnight scored the last goal in the Arena, an overtime goal at 5:52 p.m.

July 11

1739 Louis Pierre Blanchette was born in Canada. A trapper and trader known as "Le Chassuer," he was chosen by the Spanish to open a trading post on the Missouri River. He chose a site that would become the city of St. Charles.

1873 The City Council passed a law regulating the driving of cattle through the city streets. Drives were banned except during the hours of 10 pm through 6 am., and were limited to 25 head or less. Critics complained that the measure would drive the cattle business to East St. Louis.

1911 Cardinal manager Roger Bresnahan averted a tragedy when he complained that his players couldn't sleep because of noise on a train from Washington to Boston. The Cardinals car was moved to the back of the train, just before it plowed into a viaduct and went down an embankment. Fourteen people died. The car that took the Cardinals place at the front of the train was mangled beyond recognition.

1966 With St. Louis in the grip of a terrible heat wave, Union Electric began to shut power off to areas for up to two hours at a time, in order to save the overloaded power grid. The shutdowns continued for two days, and resulted in something of a scandal. By the time the heat wave ended, 146 people had died.

1984 The new $42.7 million Jefferson Barracks Bridge opened. At the time, St. Louis area drivers were also waiting for work to be finished on the new 70/270 interchange and the eastbound lanes of the Vandeventer overpass on U.S. 40.

July 12

1808 The first newspaper west of the Mississippi was published in St. Louis. The weekly *Missouri Gazette* was a one-sheet paper, about eight inches wide and a foot long. Joseph Charless started his paper with 174 subscribers, some of whom paid in "flour or corn." By 1819, he had 1,000 subscribers, about a fourth of the population of St. Louis. The paper evolved into the *Republic*, which was absorbed by the *Globe-Democrat* in 1919.

1901 The "Richmond Heights" subdivision was sold for $200,000 to a St. Louis real estate syndicate. They planned to sell of the site in individual lots. At the time of the sale, there were about 20 homes on the site, the former Ranken farm.

1966 The All-Star Game was played in the brand new Busch Stadium. The National League won 2-1 in ten innings as Tim McCarver scored the winning run. The temperature that day hit 105°. When someone asked honorary coach Casey Stengel what he thought of the new ball park, he said "it holds the heat well." 125 people at the game were treated for heat-related problems.

1973 A general alarm fire swept the Military Records Center on Page in Overland. Irreplaceable records covering servicemen discharged between 1912 and the early 1960s were lost. The fire haunts the military establishment to this day.

1993 As the flooding here worsened, Vice President Al Gore toured flood-damaged areas in Grafton and Lemay. All three network news shows originated from St. Louis. Tom Brokaw anchored from East St. Louis on NBC. Dan Rather anchored on CBS from Grafton, and Peter Jennings on reported from a boat on ABC. In the Midwest to this point, 24 people had died, and damage was estimated at over $4 billion.

1999 About 250 protestors sat down in front of rush hour traffic and closed down I-70 in North St. Louis. Led by the Rev. Al Sharpton, they called for more minority hiring on the I-70 construction project. About 150 were arrested during the protest.

July 13

1925 The birthday of TWA. The airline was founded in Los Angeles as Western Air Express. It merged with Transcontinental Air Transport in 1930 to become Transcontinental and Western Air. The name was changed to Trans World Airlines in 1950. TWA merged with American in 2001.

1932 The first terminal building at Lambert Field was dedicated by Myrtle Lambert, the daughter of aviation pioneer Albert Bond Lambert, and by the conqueror of the Antarctic, Rear Admiral Richard Byrd. The old terminal stood on the north side of the airport on Lindbergh. It was replaced by the present terminal in 1956, and was torn down in the late '70s.

1948 The American League beat the National League 5-2 in the All-Star Game at Sportsman's Park in St. Louis. Stan Musial of the Cardinals hit a home run. St. Louis native Hoot Evers of the Detroit Tigers also added a homer.

1963 The University of Missouri Board of Curators approved the purchase of the grounds of the old Bellerive Country Club grounds in Normandy for the establishment of a St. Louis campus. Some classes were already being held at the old country club.

1992 Ground was broken for the $260 million expansion of the Cervantes Convention Center (America's Center and the TWA dome, now the Edward Jones Dome). Politicians sweated as they gripped shovels in the summertime heat at the ceremony.

July 14

1732 Daniel Boone was born in Pennsylvania. He came to what is now St. Charles County in 1799, three years after his son. The Boones were the first "American" settlers there. The Spanish Lieutenant Governor gave him 1,000 arpents of land for bringing 50 families to settle in Missouri, and appointed him syndic or magistrate, in 1800.

1936 July 14 is traditionally the hottest day of the year in St. Louis. In 1936, the high was 108°. It was the sixth day in a row with a high over 100°, and the tenth day out of eleven. The heat had already taken 139 lives. The total from 37 days that summer with highs over 100° would reach 471.

1954 The mercury here hit 115° —The hottest reading ever recorded in St. Louis. The 115° reading was recorded at Lambert Field. It was 112° downtown. Many businesses closed before noon. Twenty-eight People died from the heat that day alone.

1964 Two civil rights activists climbed the north leg at the construction site of the Gateway Arch. Percy Green and Richard Daly climbed 100 feet to dramatize their complaint of job discrimination at the construction site. They came down after four hours and were arrested.

1980 The death toll from the 12-day heat wave was nearing 100. The temperature hit 103°, the hottest day of the heatwave so far. City Hospital and the Morgue were running out of room for the bodies. The next day, the high hit 107°.

July 15

1925 The city shut down the free auto camp in Forest Park.

Such camps had served intrepid auto travellers in the early days of motoring, but they had begun to attract the homeless and a bad reputation. Commercial auto camps were beginning to spring up along the highways into St. Louis.

1959 The link between the Daniel Boone Expressway and the Red Feather Express Highway was opened (now Highway 40, between Brentwood Boulevard and Clayton Skinker). It was now possible to drive from Vandeventer to Boonville, Missouri, on four-lane highway (40 still ended east of Vandeventer).

1980 The temperature in St. Louis hit 107°, the hottest day of the heat wave. It was also the hottest day in St. Louis since July 1954. The 13-day heatwave had killed one-hunred-thirty people so far. Police were called in to help the City Morgue handle the bodies.

1984 Workers began removing salvageable items from the Buder and International Buildings. Preservationists were preparing to return to court to block the demolition of the buildings for the Gateway Mall.

1993 The flood of 1993 surpassed the record crest of 1973, as more rain fell on the area. Union Electric had to shut off utilities to threatened homes in South St. Louis along the River des Peres.

1875 The news reached St. Louis that Mark Twain had been arrested. The humorist saw a boy steal his umbrella and jokingly offered a reward of $205, $5 for the umbrella and $200 for the lad's "remains." He was arrested when a corpse turned up at his home, along with a note claiming the reward. It turned out that some pranksters at a medical school had sent the corpse.

1925 Truly a landmark day. The first White Castle restaurant in St. Louis opened, at 18th and Olive. The first White Castle in the nation opened in Wichita, Kansas, in 1921.

1963 St. Louis County Supervisor L.K. Roos called on the State Highway Commission to launch a crash building program to end the terrible toll on the "Dead Man's Stretch" of Lindbergh. Twenty-two people had been killed and nearly 800 injured over the past 18 months between Midland and Olive.

1970 Plans were announced for a $30 million, 42-acre "Business City' at what was then I-244 and Page. The development would be called "Westport Plaza."

1993 The record floods worsened as a levee broke near St. Charles. The Missouri now joined the Mississippi 20 miles upstream from their normal confluence. Seven-thousand people were homeless in St. Charles County. Officials were urging some 1,000 residents along the River des Peres to evacuate.

July 17

1908 Auto enthusiasts D.R. Calhoun and Roy Button suggested that the AAA move its 300-mile Vanderbilt Cup Race from the crowded roads of New Jersey to St. Louis County. They said their proposed course over North and South, Clayton Road, Baxter and Olive was "ideal for high-speed racing."

1924 Jesse "Pop" Haines of the Cardinals threw the first no-hitter by a St. Louis pitcher since 1876. The 5-0 masterpiece over the Braves on "Tuberculosis Day" at Sportsman's Park was the first National League no-hitter ever here.

1993 President Clinton came to St. Louis for a flood summit of Midwestern governors. Before the meeting at Fox High School in Arnold, the president flew over the devastation in St. Charles County. By this time, the Mississippi was 15 miles wide there, and cresting at 36.7 feet. Downtown, the river was 2/3 of the way up the Arch steps. A levee gave way in St. Louis County, rejoining Creve Coeur Lake with the river.

1994 The Blues stunned the hockey world as they announced the hiring of Mike Keenan to become the new Blues coach and general manager. St. Louis fans were elated, as Keenan had just led the New York Rangers to the Stanley Cup.

2001 Alderwoman Irene Smith embarrassed the city when she apparently relieved herself in a trash can on the floor of the Board of Aldermen. Smith was taking part in a filibuster to kill a proposed redistricting plan. Smith was told she would lose the floor if she left to use the restroom.

July 18

1826 The Catholic diocese of St. Louis was erected, separated from the diocese of New Orleans. Joseph Rosati would be named as the first Bishop. Forty-five dioceses would eventually be formed from the vast area originally covered by the St. Louis diocese, leading St. Louis to be labeled "Rome of the West."

1964 The Bidwell brothers were threatening to move the Big Red to Atlanta. Sources in New York and Atlanta reported that the team was "as good as gone." But the Bidwells reconsidered when several minority shareholders threatened a lawsuit. Politicians also helped the team win more favorable scheduling in their lease at Busch Stadium.

1969 It was announced that work had begun on a $22 million amusement park near Eureka. The 200 acre park had another 302 acres set aside for future expansion. It was expected that the new

"Six Flags Over Mid-America" would prove to be an economic boon to Eureka.

1980 Two-hundred National Guardsmen were ordered to St. Louis to search door-to-door for heat victims. One-hundred-eight people had died from the heat in the city alone since the heat wave began on July 2nd. Governor Joe Teasdale asked President Jimmy Carter to declare St. Louis a disaster area.

1993 At 9 p.m., the Mississippi river crested here at 46.9 feet, 3.7 feet higher than the record crest of 1973. Water was flowing past the Arch at the rate of 7.5 million gallons per second. Also that day, a levee along the River des Peres was breached, sending water surging into the South St. Louis neighborhood. It looked like the worst was over, but there was more to come.

July 19

1820 Missouri's first constitution was signed at the Mansion House Hotel at Third and Vine. Missourians were confident of being admitted to the union quickly. But some eastern Congressman were offended by language in the document relating to slavery. After a bitter fight, the Second Missouri Compromise changed the offending language. Missouri became a state on August 10, 1821.

1940 All businesses in Alton were shut down, in memory of the "Gentle Giant." Robert Wadlow's 1,000 pound casket required 18 pall bearers, with eight other men assisting. Over 40,000 people attended the funeral. The "Guinness Book of World Records" acknowledged Robert as the tallest person in history, at eight-feet-eleven inches.

1946 The English Teachers Association of Missouri had ignited a firestorm after complaining to the FCC about Dizzy Dean's assault on the language during his baseball broadcasts on WIL. The teachers said he was a bad influence on students. Hundreds of telegrams poured into WIL in support of Ol' Diz.

1963 The city's most popular amusement park went up in flames. Generations of St. Louisans had enjoyed the Forest Park Highlands, on Oakland Avenue immediately west of the Arena. The spectacular fire destroyed nearly everything in the park, except for the roller coaster. That too would be leveled to make room for Forest Park Community College.

1993 The Mississippi River was still at a record crest of 46.9 feet. Hundreds were fleeing the flood waters after a levee gave way along the River des Peres. At least 26 people were dead in the Midwest, and 10 million acres were underwater. Even more rain was predicted here for the next day.

July 20

1929 The new $2.5 million Chain of Rocks Bridge opened. The bridge carried Route 66 traffic around St. Louis from 1936 to 1965. The unique bend in the middle was ordered by the government to prevent the span from hindering navigation. The bridge was closed to traffic in 1968 and appeared headed for demolition. But Gateway Trailnet saved the bridge, now the world's longest pedestrian span.

1969 St. Louisans were glued to their TV sets as Neil Armstrong became the first man to walk on the moon. St. Louis Police reported an increase in burglaries that night. The moon walk kept the crowd at the Mississippi River Festival in Edwardsville down to just 700, the smallest crowd of the season.

1980 The temperatures continued to soar. But for the first time since July 2nd, no heat-related deaths were reported in St. Louis. Karl J. Reid, Deputy Director of the Disaster Operations Center, was blunt in his assessment. He said "the old and weak" had died off.

1985 The St. Louis Science Center on Oakland Avenue opened. The Center was originally housed in Oak Knoll Park. Today, kids enjoy 650 hands-on exhibits at the free facility. The center is connected to the James S. McDonnell Planetarium in Forest Park by a walkway over Highway 40.

1993 A thunderstorm dumped two inches of rain on flood-ravaged St. Louis. The River des Peres swept away a mile-long section of levee along Gravois and Morganford, adding to the devastation. The Mississippi reached a new record high of 47.05 feet. The worst was yet to come.

July 21

1836 A mob attacked the offices of the St. Louis *Observer*, a weekly Presbyterian paper. Elijah P. Lovejoy, an outspoken critic of slavery, edited the paper. After the attack, Lovejoy moved to Alton and continued publishing, even after three presses were thrown in the river. Lovejoy was killed while defending another press on November 7, 1837. Today, he is remembered as a martyr for freedom of the press

1901 A sportswriter for the *Globe* commented on what he called "an unpleasant innovation permitted at league park." During a Cards game, they were selling beer to fans!  The writer said "it was doubtless the bilious practice was indulged in without the consent of Messrs. Robison (the owners of the club), but it was indulged in, and caused considerable adverse comment."

1969 At 12:54 p.m., as the "Eagle" lifted off from the moon, a tense crowd that included Mayor A.J. Cervantes watched a TV set up in the window of One Memorial Drive by KMOX-TV. They were on their way back from a special moon mass, celebrated at the Old Cathedral by Auxiliary Bishop Joseph McNicholas. Robert Hyland, general manager of KMOX radio, read Psalm Eight.

1981 Six Flags Over Mid-America announced it was shutting down the Skyway ride forever. The park blamed lack of ridership and the fact that the ride needed $10,000 in maintenance. Three people died on the ride in 1978, when a cable snapped.

1983 The National Hockey League approved the sale of the Blues to California businessman Harry Ornest and a group of local investors for $12 million. Ornest pledged to keep the team in St. Louis.

July 22

1928 The Lewis Bridge over the Missouri and the Clark Bridge over the Mississippi at Alton were opened to traffic. The bridge owners touted their spans as the safest way to travel to St. Louis, since it eliminated several railroad and grade crossings. But by the 1950s both were hopelessly outmoded. The new Clark Bridge was dedicated in January, 1994.

1959 It was reported that east side rackets kingpin Frank "Buster" Wortman had moved from his digs at an East St. Louis hotel. Wortman moved into a home southwest of Collinsville that was surrounded by a moat.

1968 Cardinals great Joe "Ducky" Medwick was inducted into the Baseball Hall of Fame. Medwick had a lifetime average of .324 and won the triple crown in 1937. But he is best remembered for being taken out of game seven of the 1934 world series for his own protection. Tiger fans pelted him with debris when he returned to his position after sliding hard into Tiger third baseman, Marv Owen.

1989 The "Red Head," Red Scheondienst, was among several players inducted into the Baseball Hall of Fame. Red played for the Cardinals from 1945-56 and from 1961-63. He managed the Birds from 1965 until 1976, leading them to the World Series twice.

July 23

1904 This is one of the dates sources report the ice cream cone was invented at the World's Fair. This particular legend has Charles Menches putting scoops of ice cream into folded waffle cones on a hot day at the fair. Other sources say a Syrian concessionaire, Ernest Hammi, invented the treat on July 29th. Members of the Marchiony family claim Italo Marchiony invented it.

1955 The first tenants moved into the gleaming new William L. Igoe public housing complex. Combined with the Pruitt Apartments, the project had a capacity of nearly 3,000 families. Pruitt-Igoe was a catastrophe. Plagued by crime and vandalism, it was razed in 1975.

1959 The seven Mercury astronauts were in St. Louis to visit McDonnell Aircraft. McDonnell was building the capsule to carry them into space. Lieutenant John Glenn of the Marine Corps, Air Force Lieutenant Commander Alan Shepard, Air Force Captains Virgil Grissom and Gordon Cooper, Navy Lieutenant Scott Carpenter and Lieutenant Commander Wally Schirra were joined by Air Force Captain Donald Slayton.

1973 In the worst air disaster in St. Louis history, an Ozark Airlines Fairchild-Hiller turboprop slammed into a hillside in Normandy during a thunderstorm. Thirty-eight people died as the plane went down near Florissant Road and Highway 70 on the campus of Mount Providence School. Investigators later blamed a severe downdraft, what we know today as "wind shear."

1993 Officials here indicated the worst could still be ahead in the great flood. They were predicting that the Mississippi could reach 48 feet. That same day, four boys and two adult counselors from a St. Louis boy's home drowned in a flash flood at Cliff Cave Park in South County. The park had been closed because of the flooding.

1800 Henry Shaw was born in Sheffield, England. He came to St. Louis in 1819. Shaw was such a successful businessman, he was able to retire at age 40 and build a country home he called "Tower Grove." Shaw established his botanical gardens in 1857, and gave the city the land adjoining it for a park in 1870. When he died in 1899, he left his estate to support Shaw's Garden.

1933 Cards pitcher Dizzy Dean received a half-dozen neckties as a gift from bandits who had held up a St. Louis drugstore the previous week. Ol' Diz had walked in on the holdup and was lined up with the rest of the victims. According to Dean, the robber called him, and said he would send the neckties to show it was nothing personal.

1967 The unique trams that take visitors to the top of the Gateway Arch were dedicated, nearly two years after the Arch was finished. The National Park Service was about to give up on allowing trips to the top, due to lack of funds, when Bi-State stepped forward. Financial difficulty, and administrative bickering within the agency delayed the completion.

1969 Hundreds of people stood shoulder to shoulder in the television department at the Famous-Barr downtown and cheered as the Apollo 11 astronauts returned safely to earth. McDonnell-Douglas built the Apollo 11 SVB One booster, the third stage of the Saturn Five rocket. The astronauts left behind a moonquake detector, built by Monsanto.

1985 The last Route 66 signs came down in Missouri. Without ceremony, Highway Department workers removed the shields from a 14-mile stretch from the I-44 turn-off at Scotland, west of Joplin, to the Kansas line.

July 25

1873 Steamboat operators in St. Louis were suing to halt constrcution of the Eads Bridge. They claimed it would be a hazard to navigation. James B. Eads said his bridge posed no threat, even to the largest boats.

1900 A group of citizens expressed their outrage over the "automobile menace." They were upset over an incident on Locust when something broke on a car, sending it careening down the crowded street while pedestrians ran for their lives. The driver managed to slow the car by sticking his cane into its gears. The car was tipped over onto its side, where the *Globe* reported, "it was soon subdued."

1934 Seventy-three more heat-related fatalities brought the number of dead here to 217. For eight days straight, the temperature had risen above 100°. Thousands of people were sleeping in Forest Park, or along the highways in St. Louis County to escape the heat.

1968 Bob Gibson set a Cardinals team record with his 11th straight win. The 5-0 win over the Phillies was Gibson's 12th straight complete game. He had allowed just two runs over the last 92 innings pitched.

1972 Democratic vice presidential nominee Thomas Eagleton revealed that he had received psychiatric help and shock treatments while a Missouri state official. He said the treatments were for nervous exhaustion and fatigue. Presidential nominee George McGovern expressed full confidence in Eagleton. But less than a week later, Eagleton was out.

July 26

1892 A huge explosion ripped a 20-foot deep, 1,000 foot long trench along Chouteau avenue, killing six people and tossing freight cars around like toys. The opening of the Mill Creek sewer was covered with floodwater, trapping fumes from a refinery fire that had been washed into the sewer. When a saloonkeeper at Fourth and Chouteau entered his cellar over the sewer with a candle—Ka boom!

1978 Three people, including two girls aged ten and fifeteen, were killed when a gondola on the sky ride at Six Flags plummeted to the ground. Firefighters had to rescue more than 100 people stranded in midair, many of them for several hours. A support beam from one of the towers carrying the cables snapped.

1988 A ceremony on I-255 north of Granite City marked the completion of the Interstate loop around St. Louis. Construction on the Missouri side began in 1962, and was finished by 1969. The 38-mile Missouri loop was divided into I-270, 244 and 255. In 1974, officials considered naming the whole thing after John F. Kennedy, then decided to designate it as 270 on the Missouri side, 255 in Illinois.

1998 With a 452-foot shot against the Rockies in Colorado, Mark McGwire became the all-time single season Cardinal home run king. Johnny Mize set the old Redbird mark, hitting 43 in 1930.

2002 The abduction and murder of a six-year old Valley Park girl made national headlines. Cassandra Williamson disappeared from her father's home. Her body was found in the abandoned glass factory. Police charged Johnny Johnson with the crime. He was a transient, who had stayed at her father's home.

1817 The first steamboat arrived in St. Louis. The "Zebulon M. Pike" took six weeks to make the trip from Louisville, because it could only run during the day. A big crowd greeted the boat on the riverfront. The Indians fled at the site of the fire-breathing monster. The arrival of the steamboat would transform St. Louis into one of the great cities of the U.S.

1953 Dizzy Dean was inducted into the Baseball Hall of Fame. Ol' Diz was a legend as much for his broadcasting as for his pitching. He mortified local English teachers with such descriptions as "he slud into third." The teachers tried to have him taken off the air. Diz pitched for the Cardinals from 1930 to 1937. He won two games of the 1934 World Series and his brother Paul won the other two.

1953 As the Korean Armistice took effect, the *Post-Dispatch* reported that 317 St. Louisans were killed in the conflict. Ninety-nine were reported missing in action and 1,078 were wounded.

1977 Ralston-Purina announced they were buying the Blues. Emile Francis was named to head the hockey operation. The Arena would be re-named "The Checkerdome" under Ralston. Six years to the day after it had bought the club, Ralston-Purina announced it had sold the Blues to Harry Ornest. Say what you will about the Ornest era, but he did save the club from moving to Saskatoon and he hired Ron Caron.

1996 Dan Dierdorf was inducted into the NFL Hall of Fame. Dierdorf anchored the Big Red offensive line from 1971 until 1983. He was a five-time all-pro player.

July 28

1849 The Committee of Health declared the cholera epidemic at an end. At the time, 8,423 people were reported to have died from cholera, about one tenth of the city's population. About 4,000 of those deaths were actually attributable to other causes. The epidemic spurred the city to begin building sewers and draining the sinkholes that dotted the area.

1901 A popular gathering place since 1852 would soon be history. "Uhrig's Cave" was to be demolished to make room for a monumental hotel at Jefferson and Washington, to be built for the fair. Uhrig's Cave was named for the caves beneath the beer garden, used to keep the beer cool in those days before refrigeration.

1909 The contract was let for the Municipal Free Bridge over the Mississippi. The bridge was formally opened in January, 1917. For the first time in the history of the city, people could cross the Mississippi for free. The bridge was renamed for General MacArthur in 1942.

1961 The Mark Twain Expressway between St. Charles and downtown was completed with the opening of a four-mile section between Palm and Division. Traffic engineers hailed the new "reversible" lanes that would carry eastbound traffic into the city during the morning rush and westbound traffic in the afternoon.

1969 The greatest Cardinal of them all was inducted into the Baseball Hall of Fame. Stanley Frank Musial came into the Cardinal organization as a pitcher. An injury made him move to the outfield. He played for the Redbirds from 1941 to 1963, winning the National League MVP in 1943, '46 and '48. "The Man" won a total of seven batting titles and has a lifetime average of .331.

July 29

1902 Thomas Skinker wrote his wife that he had leased his land and the road that ran through it to the World's Fair company. Skinker said the road was destined to become "one of the main thoroughfares of the fair and would thereafter rival Westmoreland and Vandeventer Places."

1904 This is the date the International Association of Ice Cream Manufacturers says the ice cream cone was invented at the World's Fair. This source credits a Syrian concessionaire, Ernest Hammi, with inventing the tasty treat. But another source says

Charles Menches invented it six days earlier. Yet another legend credits one Italo Marchiony. But it is Hammi who is credited with giving the ice cream cone widespread acceptance.

1941 McDonnell Aircraft was awarded the first contract for a plane completely designed and built by the five-year old firm. The "XP-67" was a failure. But by 1943, the company was working on its first jet, the FH-1 "Phantom."

1965 Workers took down the landmark 148-foot-tall steel tower at the Forest Park Highlands Amusement Park. The tower with its eight-foot-tall electrical American flags was visible for miles at night. The site was being cleared for Forest Park Community College.

1985 Cardinal greats Lou Brock and Enos Slaughter were inducted into the Baseball Hall of Fame. Brock was baseball's all-time leading base burglar before Rickey Henderson came along. Slaughter is best remembered for his mad dash from first to home on a single by Harry Walker in the eighth inning of the seventh game of the 1946 World Series.

July 30

1920 Babe Ruth smacked a home run called the greatest ever seen in St. Louis. It was higher than the grandstand at Sportsman's Park as it cleared Grand Avenue. The Yankees beat the Browns that day, 19-3. Just a couple of weeks earlier, Ruth broke his own single-season home run record with his 29th.

1929 Dale Jackson and Forest O'Brine landed their "St. Louis Robin" at Lambert Field, after establishing a new aerial endurance record. They stayed aloft for 420 hours, 21 minutes. Their exploits were front page news across the nation. In July, 1930, two Chicago aviators beat the record. So the "Robin" took off again, regaining the record in August, 1930.

1933 Dizzy Dean struck out 17 Cub batters, setting a record that would stand for another 26 years (of course they were Cub batters, so it's not as impressive as it seems). The last Cub batter that day took a pitch with two strikes on him. The umpire called it a ball, but the batter shook his head and walked back to the dugout.

1974 The Centers for Disease Control identified a toxic agent that had killed horses and birds at several sites in Eastern Missouri sprayed with waste oil by Russell Bliss. It was identified as dioxin, a little known and unwanted impurity formed in the manufacture of other chemicals.

1993 The great flood entered another devastating phase, as the Monarch Levee gave way, inundating the Chesterfield Valley. Spirit Airport and 500 businesses were swamped. Highway 40 was underwater, cutting off the Boone Bridge as a route into St. Charles County. Thousands were being evacuated in South St. Louis as 51 propane tanks were floating in the floodwaters. Officials feared an explosion.

July 31

1981 The last Corvette rolled off the assembly plant at the General Motors Plant in North St. Louis. The plant had built about 700,000 Vettes since 1954. GM moved the Corvette assembly line to Bowling Green, Kentucky.

1993 It was a surreal day in St. Louis. Dramatic live television footage showed helicopter rescues from the flooded Chesterfield Valley. City workers were pumping concrete into the floodwall protecting North St. Louis. A tornado swept across the flooded areas near St. Peters, Portage des Sioux and West Alton, adding to the destruction.

1993 A planned benefit concert by John Cougar Mellencamp and Blind Melon at Riverport was cancelled because of the flood. Bob Dylan had also been slated for an appearance at "The Concert for the Heartland." But the break in the Monarch Levee had closed Highway 40. Officials were fearful of tying up traffic on the Blanchette Bridge, the only available river crossing for miles.

1993 Lost amid all the bad news from the river was some good news for commuters. The Metro Link light rail system was opened from East St. Louis to the Hanley Road station. It was extended to Lambert Field in 1994. Within a year, the number of riders had exceeded the wildest projections.

1997 A big day for Redbird fans. The Cardinals acquired Mark McGwire from Oakland for pitcher T.J. Mathews and two minor leaguers. Cardinals GM Walt Jocketty expressed confidence that the Cardinals would be able to sign the slugger to a long-term contract.

August 1

1831 The cornerstone was laid for a "new" cathedral at Third and Walnut in St. Louis. The building we now know as the Old Cathedral was completed in the fall of 1834. A church has occupied the site of the old cathedral since the very beginning of the city.

1904 The St. Louis Police Department became the first in the nation to use the fingerprint method of identification. It had been demonstrated at the World's Fair by Scotland Yard detectives, who said it was foolproof.

1943 St. Louis Mayor William Dee Becker and nine other dignitaries lost their lives in the crash of new a glider during a test flight at what was to be a festive unveiling at Lambert Field. A crowd of over 5,000 watched in horror as the wing fell off the glider, built by Robertson Aircraft Corporation.

1993 The flood of 1993 hit its peak here, as the Mississippi crested at 49.58 feet, 6.58 feet above 1973 record. Over 400 million gallons of water were flowing past the Arch every 60 seconds. The raging waters knocked the Burger King riverboat and the minesweeper Inaugural from their moorings. The Inaugural wedged under the Poplar Street Bridge, and eventually sank. There was panic along the River des Peres, where water was lapping at the top of sandbags protecting thousands of homes.

1993 A levee broke in Monroe County, near Columbia, Illinois. News helicopters sent dramatic pictures back as a house was swept away, one of the most enduring images of the flood. Just before midnight, the water crashed through a levee and inundated the town of Valmeyer and a 20-mile area.

1997 The $16.3 million merger between McDonnell-Douglas and Boeing officially took effect. The McDonnell-Douglas sign at the world headquarters in Hazelwood was dismantled. Twenty-three-thousand St. Louis employees were now working for Boeing.

August 2

1902 Construction had just begun on a permanent highway bridge across the Missouri at St. Charles. A pontoon bridge was built in 1896, but it was destroyed by ice. Four men died building the highway bridge, which was finished just in time for the 1904 World's Fair. The bridge survived a devastating fire in 1916, a train that hit its approach on Main in 1936, and a ramming by an excursion boat in 1990. The bridge was closed in 1993, and dynamited in 1997.

1943 The *Globe-Democrat* reported on an unusual use for the Arena. The Laister Kauffman Aircraft Corporation had moved its base to the Old Barn on Oakland Avenue and was producing gliders there. The CG-4A Glider could hold 15 soldiers. It became the most widely used glider during the war.

1956 The state of Missouri awarded bids for the very first interstate construction in the nation. The first contracts covered I-70 in St. Charles and a section of I-44 in Laclede County. The first actual construction on a U.S. Interstate would take place on I-70 east of Highway 94.

1990 Joe Torre was named manager of the Cardinals. He replaced Whitey Herzog, who resigned on July 5th. Red Scheondienst had served as interim skipper.

1993 Army Corps of Engineers intentionally breached a levee upstream from Prairie du Rocher, Illinois. The strategy flooded thousands of acres of farmland, but relieved pressure on the levee protecting the town. Massive traffic jams were predicted in St. Louis. The Poplar Street Bridge was closed because the minesweeper "Inaugural" was lodged beneath the bridge. Six miles of Highway 40 were closed in the Chesterfield Valley because of flooding. The Missouri set a new mark at St. Charles, cresting at 39.6 feet. Eleven-thousand people were out of their homes near the River des Peres, because officials feared an explosion. The floodwaters had lifted several propane tanks from their mounts.

August 3

1763 Pierre Laclede left New Orleans on a trip to establish a trading post on the Mississippi. After three months, his party reached Ste. Genevieve. They spent most of the winter at Fort des Chatres. In December, Laclede took his stepson, Auguste Chouteau, up the river to find a spot suitable for the post. The site would become the city of St. Louis.

1901 A delegation of automobile owners called on Mayor Rolla Wells to protest two proposed ordinances. One would set an automobile speed limit of eight miles per hour on city streets, six in the parks. They told the mayor autos could travel safely at speeds of up to 15 miles per hour. The other proposed ordinance would have set an auto tax of $10.

1932 Work began on the Municipal Auditorium. The cornerstone was laid on November 11, 1932. The auditorium was dedicated on April 14th, 1934. It was later named for Mayor Henry Kiel, whose firm built it. In 1992, the convention hall was torn down to make room for Kiel Center. The auditorium remains.

1938 The Art Museum announced the purchase of a $14,000 Egyptian bronze sculpture of a cat. The cat purchase ignited a controversy that captured national attention, at a time when the city was still suffering the effects of the depression. The papers were bombarded with letters to the editor, and the city threatened to cut the museum tax rate in half.

1943 All business in St. Louis was halted for one minute at 2 p.m., the hour of the funeral for Mayor William Dee Becker. Becker and nine other people died on August 1st in the crash of an Army glider at Lambert Field. A wing came off while the dignitaries were on a demonstration flight.

August 4

1955 The owners of the Washington University Cyclotron were seeking a new dumping ground for the radioactive waste. For the past ten years, the waste has been dumped "at a safe 20 feet underground" in the backyard of Chancellor Ethan Shepley.

1961 The *Globe* reported that Gaslight Square was becoming a well-known tourist destination. The article cited restaurants such as Le Quartier Francaise, Marty's and the Golden Eagle Saloon, where hot tuba player Singleton Palmer was appearing.

1965 A spectacular fire burned two city blocks, and for a time threatened the Busch Stadium construction project. The blaze began in the Shapleigh Hardware buildings, part of the Cupples Complex. Eight buildings were destroyed. The stadium site was saved, but construction was delayed for a week.

1968 The bronze statue of Stan Musial in front of Busch Stadium was dedicated. In pre-game ceremonies honoring Stan, he donned his old number six and joined his 1941 teammates on the field as a capacity crowd cheered.

1997 Ceremonies in Berkeley marked the launch of the new Boeing, following the buyout of McDonnell-Douglas. Boeing CEO Phil Condit said the military aircraft operations and the missile systems would be headquartered in St. Louis.

August 5

1936 The first major air disaster in St. Louis. The Chicago and Southwestern airliner "City of Memphis" crashed in heavy fog north of Lambert Field. Eight people were killed. The plane crashed in farmer George Behlmann's field, 300 yards east of Howdershell and a half-mile north of Utz.

1938 The controversy over the art museum's $14,000 Egyptian cat sculpture heated up. The *Star-Times* printed a picture of the statue under the photo of a homeless family living in Forest Park. The purchase was criticized because the city faced a $3 million deficit.

1966 The *Globe* reported on security plans for the Beatles August 21st concert at Busch Stadium. Extra officers, a small army of private guards and five-foot-tall barricades were all part of the plans. Management at KXOK and WGNU were quoted as saying their stations would continue playing Beatles records, despite the controversy over John Lennon's remarks that the Beatles were more popular than Christ.

1983 The northwest wall of the five-story Welsh Baby Carriage Factory collapsed onto Interstate 55 during a violent thunderstorm. A woman was killed and two others hurt as the rubble smashed a car that had pulled to the shoulder because of the poor visibility.

1999 Mark McGwire became the 16th player in Major League history to hit 500 career home runs. Number 500 came in the third inning of a game at Busch Stadium. Number 500 was a 451-foot shot off Andy Ashby of the Padres

August 6

1856 Nicholas Krekel arrived to open a store on land he had bought from his brother in St. Charles County, along right-of-way he had donated for the new railroad. Colonel John O'Fallon, head of the Northern Missouri Railroad, gave Krekel the honor of naming a depot to be located there. Krekel named it after O'Fallon.

1924 "Sunny Jim" Bottomley of the Cardinals set a major league record with 12 RBI's in a single game. Bottomley went six for six in a 17-3 win over Brooklyn. Mark Whiten of the Cardinals would tie the record in 1993.

1931 The *Globe* reported on an examination of Robert Wadlow of Alton by physicians at Barnes Hospital. The doctors said the 13-year old stood seven-feet, four-and-a-half inches tall. He had grown by five-and-a-half inches in just one year.

1966 The Big Red played their first game at the new Busch Stadium. Quarterback Charlie Johnson led the Cardinals to a 20-10 win over the Atlanta Falcons. A crowd of 34,303 saw the game.

1970 The St. Louis County Council allowed the city of Black Jack to incorporate. A ten-year battle over incorporation began when the city voted to allow only single-family housing units, in an effort to head-off a proposed federally assisted apartment complex. The fight went all the way to the U.S. Supreme Court. The name "Black Jack" comes from two massive black "Jack Oak" trees that stood at Parker and Old Halls Ferry in the 1800s.

August 7

1846 The birthdate of the St. Louis Police Department. The Board of Aldermen passed an ordinance organizing the old City Guard, the City Marshall, Day Police and the "Keeper of the Calaboose" together into a City Police Department.

1861 The Union awarded a contract to St. Louis engineer James B. Eads to build seven new iron clad gunboats. The contract required the boats to be finished by October 5th, with Eads forfeiting $200 per boat for each day past the deadline! It was a nearly impossible task under wartime conditions. But the first one, the "St. Louis," was launched on October 12th.

1905 The new city hospital at 14th and Lafayette opened its doors. Three-hundred-sixty patients were moved from the dilapidated building at 17th and Pine that had served as the city hospital since the 1896 tornado. The 1905 building still stands, although it has been abandoned and stripped by vandals.

1961 Stix, Baer and Fuller opened its lavish new store in the River Roads Shopping Center at Jennings Station and Halls Ferry. It was the first unit of the ultra modern shopping center that even boasted a monorail indoors. River Roads now sits largely vacant, the victim of changing times and traffic patterns.

1987 A blue Silverado pickup truck rolled off the assembly line, the last vehicle built at the General Motors plant on Union in North St. Louis. The GM plant had built 13,873,983 vehicles since 1920. GM moved to a new plant in Wentzville. The old plant is now an industrial park.

August 8

1877 Browns catcher John Clapp was hit in the face with a foul tip. His replacement, Mike Morgan, donned a mask as he came into the game. This may have been the first use of a catcher's mask in the National League (they had been used before in the International Association).

1977 The bitter fight over the proposed Meramec Dam came to an end. Voters rejected the proposal in an unprecedented referendum on the issue. The dam at Sullivan would have created a 12,600 acre lake. The government had already bought or acquired 280,000 acres for the project.

1985 The $176 million St. Louis Centre Mall opened its doors amid high hopes for the future. Mayor Vincent Schoemehl spoke at the opening ceremonies and Bob Hope even made an appearance. The opening ceremonies for the largest enclosed downtown mall in the nation at the time featured brass bands, homing pigeons and thousands of balloons. Today, the mall is mostly empty.

1993 Hundreds of Lemay and South St. Louis residents were allowed to return to their homes. They were cleared out when the flood ripped several propane tanks from their retaining straps. Among the evacuees were elderly and sick residents of the Community Care Center of Lemay.

1997 Mark McGwire made his Busch Stadium debut in a game against Philadelphia. He smashed a 441-foot home run off the left field foul pole at the Stadium Club level.

August 9

1834 "The Road to St. Charles" was declared a public road. Perhaps the oldest road in the county, it was laid out as early as 1772. It was made a toll road in 1837, and improved with rock in 1865. Since then, it has been known as the St. Charles Rock Road.

1869 Annie Turnbo Pope Malone was born in Metropolis, Illinois. Her line of Poro beauty care products made her one of the first female African-American millionaires. In 1918, she opened Poro College in St. Louis. She used part of her fortune to help establish the St. Louis Colored Orphans

Home. The home was renamed in her honor in 1946.

1905 The St. Louis Police Department unveiled its second automobile. "Skidoodle Wagon Number Two" was expected to help nab "scorchers" who had the laugh on Number One. The new car could hit 50 miles per hour while enforcing the eight-mile-an-hour speed limit. The old auto was one of the first police cars in the country, but had a top speed of 15 miles per hour.

1907 A committee planning President Theodore Roosevelt's visit to St. Louis in October rejected a proposal to use automobiles to transport the presidential party. No committee member had ever heard of the president riding in an automobile.

1951 President Truman approved a $21 million dollar slum clearance and public housing project for St. Louis. A 12-block area regarded as one of the worst slums in the country would be cleared. Over 1,600 families in the area between 18th and 20th, Cass and Cole, would be relocated, and the new Vaughn Apartments would be built on the site.

August 10

1821 President Monroe signed the bill admitting Missouri as the 24th state, after years of struggle over the balance of free and slave states in the union. When Missouri first petitioned Congress for admission in 1818, there were eleven free and eleven slave states. It took two Missouri Compromises before Maine was admitted as a free state, and Missouri was admitted with no restriction on slavery.

1902 The citizens of St. Louis were enthusiastically supporting Mayor Rolla Wells in his call to clean up the city for the World's Fair. The *Globe* reported that smoke from bonfires could be seen in every direction and vehicles of every type were being pressed into service to haul away dirt and trash. St. Louis at that time had a reputation as one of the dirtiest cities in the nation.

1904 The first vehicles from a 69-car caravan that had left New York City on July 25th began arriving in St. Louis, prior to "Automobile Day" at the fair. Many of the cars in the procession were still hopelessly mired in muddy roads in Illinois. The route was changed to run through Collinsville and Edwardsville because the roads were marginally better.

1933 About 2,000 garment workers in St. Louis walked off the job. The strike spread to nearly all of the shops in the garment district along Washington Avenue. The violent strike was settled in September. The workers won recognition of their union, a key turning point in St. Louis labor history.

1953 The second television station in St. Louis signed on the air with a broadcast of the annual "Community Chest" game between the Browns and the Redbirds. WTVI in Belleville broadcast on UHF Channel 54. It moved to St. Louis, switched to Channel 36 and changed call letters to KTVI in 1955. Broadcasts began on Channel Two in 1958.

August 11

1872 An astronomer's prediction that a comet headed towards earth was about to hit St. Louis was causing panic here. Many residents were packing up and leaving. Young boys added to the disorder in the streets by standing on street corners and occasionally yelling "here she comes!"

1899 John Forsyth removed a barrier that had stood across the road between Skinker Boulevard and Clayton for ten years. He donated the right of way through his farm on the condition that a fine road be built. Forsyth barricaded his road when he wasn't happy with the work.

1949 Luke Easter joined the Cleveland Indians, becoming the first black player from St. Louis to play in the Major leagues. Easter led his fans to believe he was born in St. Louis, but his birthplace was acutally in Mississippi.

1966 Famous-Barr reported no noticeable drop-off in ticket sales for the August 21st Beatles concert at Busch Stadium in the wake of John Lennon's remark that the Beatles were more popular than Christ. Beatles records were being burned, Capitol records stock had dropped sharply, and officials in Memphis had requested the cancellation of the concert there.

1981 Reputed mob enforcer Paul Leisure was maimed when a car bomb exploded as he drove away from his South St. Louis home. The attack was in retaliation for a bomb that  killed underworld figure James Michaels Senior. Two more rivals would die, and two more would be hurt in two years of warfare between the Leisure and Michaels families.

August 12

1904 "Anthropology Days" got underway at the World's Fair. The games featured "costumed members of the uncivilized tribes" competing against each other. Competitions included spear throwing, mud fighting, rock throwing and pole climbing. It was also "Automobile Day" at the fair. A parade of 250 machines, 150 of them from St. Louis, paraded from the Jefferson Hotel to the fairgrounds. Police Chief Mathew Kiely led the parade, in the department's new "auto catcher."

1905 Parks commissioner Robert Aull called for a zoo "second to none in the country" to be located in Forest Park. Aull wanted the giant bird cage from the U.S. government exhibit at the world's fair to serve as the centerpiece. He had already acquired a herd of elk and deer, plus some bears and monkeys.

1963 The greatest Cardinal of them all announced he was retiring at the end of the 1963 season. The Cardinals announced that Stan Musial would take a job in the front office starting in 1964.

1967 The football Cardinals announced that quarterback Charley Johnson had been drafted. He had played under the threat for a year, but injuries kept him out of the service. The Big Red announced that a former SIU-Carbondale player with just 17 plays experience in the NFL would take over. His name was Jim Hart.

1974 Negro League great James "Cool Papa" Bell was inducted into the Baseball Hall of Fame. Bell played for the St. Louis Stars, among other teams. He was the fastest man ever to play the game, once clocked rounding the bases in just 12 seconds. Bell once stole 175 bases in under 200 games.

August 13

1904 Secretary of War William Howard Taft was a guest at the World's Fair on "Philippine Day." Taft once served as governor of the Philippine Islands. The highlight of the visit was a tour of the native villages, including the home of the Igorrote tribe. The tribe had made headlines here with their diet of dog meat.

1934 The Cardinals played an exhibition game in Detroit, a preview of the world series. Paul and Dizzy Dean refused to make the trip, having pitched the day before. Dizzy was fined $100 and Paul was fined $50. The next day, they were suspended. Dizzy tore up a uniform, then ripped up another for the benefit of a photographer who missed it the first time.

1947 Willard Brown hit an inside the park home run for the St. Louis Browns, the first American League home run by a black player. Brown and his teammate, Henry Thompson, were cut after just five weeks. The Browns hoped the black players would boost attendance, and released them when it didn't work.

1956 Construction began on a short stretch of I-70 in St. Charles, near the present-day Fifth Street exit. Those few miles of I-70 were the very first over 40,000 miles of interstate built in the United States. At the time, the population of all of St. Charles County was about 40,000. The construction of the interstate launched a population boom that continues to this day.

1979 Lou Brock of the Cardinals got his 3,000th hit. The record-breaking blow came off Dennis Lamp of the Cubs in the fourth inning of a game at Busch. Lamp had knocked Brock down on the previous pitch. Brock became the 14th player in major league history to reach 3,000 hits.

1904 There was a near-riot at the wild west show on "The Pike" at the World's Fair. Officials with the Humane Society tried to arrest the cowboys for inhumane treatment of the steers. The cowboys and Indians attacked the officers, and the crowd piled onto the field to protest the cancellation of the show.

1908 The St. Louis County Sheriff was searching for a mob who attacked a physician. The doc had collided with a farmer's wagon while speeding on Olive to aid a patient. The angry farmers in the area had been at war with automobile "scorchers" in the area for some time. They overturned the doctor's car.

1930 A huge crowd at Lambert Field cheered St. Louis aviators Forest O'Brine and Dale Jackson. They set a new endurance record, remaining aloft for 554 hours so far. The aviators planned to stay in the air as long as the engine on the "St. Louis Robin" held up.

1945 As KSD flashed the news that Radio Tokyo was reporting Japanese acceptance of the surrender terms, a premature celebration broke out downtown and on the Hill. The streets were covered with paper and traffic came to a halt. At 6 p.m., President Truman made it official, and the celebrations continued into the night. A large crowd gathered in front of the Soldier's Memorial downtown, and danced to a live orchestra.

1971 Bob Gibson threw the only no-hitter of his illustrious career, an 11-0 masterpiece over the Pirates in Pittsburgh. Jose Cruz made a great catch off Milt May in the late innings to preserve the no-hitter. Gibson walked three, struck out ten and even contributed three RBI's of his own.

August 15

1797 Captain James Piggott petitioned the Spanish Commandant for permission to establish the first ferry between Cahokia and St. Louis. In the winter of 1792-93, Piggott erected the first buildings on the site of what is now East St. Louis, but was originally known as "Illinoistown."

1963 A week of racial tension and protest in East St. Louis peaked with the arrest of 110 negroes during a demonstration at the First National Bank. Demonstrators were demanding the immediate hiring of 50 blacks by leading East St. Louis banks and savings and loan institutions. The banks eventually agreed to hire 20.

1964 Crews were demolishing the Winter Garden on DeBaliviere. Built in 1903 as a jai alai fronton for the world's fair, it was converted to an ice rink in 1916. Two generations learned to skate at the Winter Garden. The building was torn down to make room for a shopping center.

1980 St. Louis was sweltering under a killer heatwave that had begun back on June 23rd. The heat had claimed 147 lives. The death toll across 20 states was at 1,272. Damage to crops was set at about $12 billion.

1993 The westbound lanes of Highway 40 reopened across the flooded Chesterfield Valley. The eastbound lanes re opened the next day. The highway had been closed since a levee break on July 30th. Hundreds of businesses and Spirit of St. Louis Airport were swamped. The closure of Highway 40 forced the cancellation of a John Cougar Mellencamp Flood Benefit concert at Riverport.

August 16

1921 Regular air-mail service began between St. Louis and Chicago. The first pilots flew the route from Aviation Field in Forest Park to Chicago. Their hangar today serves as the mounted police stables. Charles Lindbergh would later fly the mail between here and Chicago, but he never flew out of Forest Park.

1958 The new 3,900 foot-long highway bridge over the Missouri River at St. Charles was dedicated. Within two years, it was already jammed with traffic, and plans were in motion to build a new one. The second span was completed in 1979, and both bridges were named for Louis Blanchette, the first settler of St. Charles (the westbound bridge is the old one).

1961 Work on the Arch began in earnest with the first blasting for the foundations. Two-hundred-twenty pounds of dynamite were set off 16-feet underground near Memorial and Chestnut.

1965 A big day for St. Louis shoppers. Sears opened its brand new store at the 73-acre Northwest Plaza, at By-Pass U.S. 66 and St. Charles Rock Road. Sears was the first unit to open at one of the largest shopping centers in the country.

1994 The St. Louis Vipers Roller Hockey team lost to the Tampa Bay Tritons, 7-6. The game was the final sporting event held in the Arena. A crowd of 12,249 saw the game.

August 17

1936 A big day for beer drinkers. Anheuser-Busch introduced Budweiser in cans. It was such a novel idea that the first Bud cans included opening instructions on the side.

1938 The Board of Estimate and Apportionment proposed slashing the Art Museum tax rate by 50 percent. The board was also calling for budgetary control over the purchase of art objects. The museum was under fire for spending $14,000 for an ancient Egyptian cat at a time when the city faced a $3 million deficit.

1953 Hundreds of school children came out to watch as the last horse-drawn milk wagon on the streets of St. Louis was retired.

Quality Diary retired its 38 horses and replaced them with a fleet of modern trucks.

1977 Record dealers here reported a sudden shortage of Elvis records, the day after "The King" died in Memphis. The manager of Bootheel records in Lemay said it was a shame, but the death of Elvis was good for business. The manager of Peaches in Dellwood said the latest Elvis album, "Moody Blue" had not been selling well until now.

1979 The last patients were removed from Homer G. Phillips hospital in North St. Louis. Alderman Freeman Bosley Senior was among 18 protestors arrested. Mayor Conway had ordered the hospital closed and consolidated with City Hospital Number One; amid protests from the black community.

August 18

1774 Meriwether Lewis was born in Virginia. After the famous expedition, President Jefferson named Lewis Governor of the Louisiana Territory. His term here was named by battles with local leaders. Depressed and in financial trouble, he died under mysterious circumstances on the Natcher Trail while on the way to Washington. His death was ruled suicide.

1892 Browns outfielder Cliff Carroll misjudged a ground ball. Somehow, it ended up in his pocket. While he fished it out, the runner ended up at third. Brown's owner Chris Von der Ahe fined Carroll $50 and suspended him for the rest of the season—without pay.

1935 Nellie Muench announced the birth of a son. The Central West End socialite was under indictment for masterminding the kidnapping of a Portland Place doctor by gangsters. Reporters discovered that Muench had stolen the child, in an effort to appear more sympathetic to the jury. She even extorted money from another doctor, convincing him that he was the father. The papers had a field day. A judge from Cape Girardeau named Rush Limbaugh heard the custody case.

1936 The temperature here hit 108°, matching the highest reading during the killer heatwave of 1936. The heatwave is the deadliest ever in St. Louis. At least 471 people died as the temperature topped 100° 37 times that summer. That week, the average high in St. Louis was 103°. People were sleeping outside, even driving out to the county and camping out along the highways to escape the heat.

1960 Placement of plants began in the ultra-modern "Climatron" at the Missouri Botanical Garden. The geodesic dome was designed to be the new home for the garden's tropical plants. The first arrivals were palm trees from Florida.

1900 Oliver "Patsy" Tebeau resigned as manager of the Cardinals. They were mired in last place, despite owner Frank Robinson's "lavish" spending of $20,000 on five players, including the great John McGraw. McGraw was offered the manager's job, and turned it down.

1926 Doctor Benjamin Duggar of the Missouri Botanical Garden startled the scientific community with the announcement that he had discovered a lower form of life than any known at the time. He blamed the "virus" for several diseases in the plant world and said further research might link them to diseases in the animal kingdom.

1951 St. Louis Browns owner Bill Veeck pulled his most famous promotional stunt. On "Falstaff Day," he sent three-foot-tall midget Eddie Gaedel up to pinch hit for Frank Saucier in the second game of a doubleheader at Sportsman's Park against Detroit. Pitcher Bob Cain walked him on four straight. The story ends on a couple of sad notes. Gaedel died in 1961, after he was mugged in Chicago. A shady baseball memorabilia collector swindled Gaedel's mother out of the bat and uniform her son wore

1955 The shopping center billed as "the first auto age shopping center in the St. Louis area" opened for business. The Northland Center, at Lucas and Hunt and West Florissant, was located on what were then the fringes of suburbia.

1998 Less than one hour after Sammy Sosa of the Cubs took the home run lead in the fifth inning, Mark McGwire tied it at Wrigley Field with his 48th home run of the season in the eighth inning. McGwire then belted a game-winning home run in the ninth.

August 20

1902 The first baby was born on the grounds of the World's Fair. O'Leary Wampler was born in a construction worker's tent. At age 95, she appeared at ceremonies marking the release of a postage stamp commemorating the fair in January, 1998. She turned 100 in 2002.

1915 The River des Peres swamped a large part of South St. Louis in another flash flood. Twelve people drowned. Forty people had to be rescued by boat near Manchester and Hampton. This latest flood prompted more cries for something to be done about the temperamental stream. A huge sewer would be built to put the river underground as it flowed through Forest Park.

1956 Stix, Baer and Fuller announced plans to build a huge store at Clayton Road and Brentwood Boulevard. The store would be the first unit of the planned 34-acre "Westroads" shopping cen-

ter. Today, the center is known as The Galleria.

1962 A near-disaster downtown, as a huge fire engulfed the eight-story Carson-May-Stern building at 12th and Olive. Flaming debris fell on rooftops all over downtown, starting fires at eight other locations. More than 300 firemen were called in, 13 were injured or overcome by the heat.

1986 Mark McGwire made his major league debut for the Oakland A's. He would finish his rookie season with a batting mark of .189. He made six errors playing third base.

1993 The Coral Court Motel closed its doors for the last time. The owner said it just wasn't worth it to spend the $1 million in needed repairs. The Coral Court was one of the most famous hotels on Route 66, known for its art moderne design — and the attached garages.

August 21

1867 Construction began in earnest on the Eads Bridge, with the first work to build a cofferdam for the west abutment. A convention of engineers was meeting in St. Louis at the time. They condemned the design by James B. Eads as "perilous."

1877 The first recorded use of the telephone here. G.W. Stockley, the manager of a telegraph supply firm, tested the new invention. It was reported that conversations were clearly heard between phones installed in the offices of the *Globe-Democrat* and "The St. Louis Republican."

1891 Today could be considered the birthday of the St. Louis Zoo. New Forest Park Commissioner Jonathan Fechter bought a herd of elk, "Clint the dromedary," and several other animals. They were placed with a buffalo and other animals on display in a yard and blockhouse built by the Forest Park Zoological Association.

1924 John Francis Buck was born. He began broadcasting Cardinals games in 1954. For his first 16 years in St. Louis, Buck served as a backup for Harry Carey. Jack was named to the broadcasters wing of the Baseball Hall of Fame in 1987.

1966 A crowd of 23,143 Beatlemaniacs braved a drenching storm and the controversy over John Lennon's remarks that the Beatles were more popular than Christ to attend the Beatles show at Busch Stadium. The Del-Rays, Bobby Hebb, the Ronettes and the Cyrkle were also on the bill. The promoters rushed the Beatles on third to beat another storm, leaving the Ronettes and the Cyrkle to play afterwards!

August 22

1831 Spencer Pettis challenged Thomas Biddle to their famous

duel. Pettis was running for Congress and criticized Biddle's brother, the manager of the St. Louis branch of the Bank of the United States. Biddle attacked Pettis in his hotel room. Pettis issued a challenge after the election. Four days later, Biddle accepted, and both men died on "Bloody Island."

1848 Ulysses S. Grant married Julia Dent. Grant was serving in the Fourth U.S. Infantry at Jefferson Barracks. He built a cabin at the Dent family estate, "Whitehaven," in what is now Rock Hill. His cabin was moved to its present site after the 1904 World's Fair.

1915 The rampaging Meramec River devastated the booming community of Valley Park. The 20-acre St. Louis Plate Glass Plant, which had caused the boom in the area, was wiped out. More than 2,000 people were homeless. Before the flood, the population of Valley Park was 3,500. Only about 500 moved back.

1982 Glenn Brummer made his memorable steal of home with two out in the 12th inning of a pivotal game against the Giants, giving the Cardinals a 5-4 win. Brummer only had four steals in his entire career.

1994 Ground was broken for the Thomas Eagleton U.S. Courthouse in downtown St. Louis. The fourth tallest structure in the city, and the largest courthouse in the nation was completed in September, 2000.

August 23

1876 William Dierberg was born in Creve Coeur. He worked as a blacksmith before buying Creve Coeur House, a general store and livery stable on Olive near Craig in 1911. That roadhouse would become the first Dierberg's Market.

1958 St. Louisan Teddy Nadler became the all-time quiz show champion. He won a total of $252,000 on the CBS show, "The $64,000 Question". Nadler quit his job as an $80-a-week public servant. His record would stand for 22 years.

1969 A St. Louisan hit the big time, with an appearance on "American Bandstand." Gayle McCormick of the group "Smith" was from St. Louis. Smith had a top five hit that summer with their remake of the Shirelles' "Baby it's You."

1971 On the first Monday rush following the opening of the new elevated section of Highway 40, police said about 70% of the traffic was still exiting at 20th Street. Highway 40 was a dead end at 20th before the double-deck highway was completed. Some drivers were complaining about the sharp turn on the 11th Street exit, and the fact that it was on the left-hand side of the highway.

1990 Preliminary census figures showed that the population of St. Louis had fallen below 400,000 for the first time since the 1880s. The current population stood at 393,109, a loss of 60,000 since 1980. The population of St. Louis peaked at 856,756 in 1950.

August 24

1936 A thunderstorm brought a temporary end to 13 straight days of 100° plus highs for St. Louis. Four-hundred-seventy-one people died during the heat wave. The Mississippi fell a foot below zero level. The storms did not end the heat wave, as the highs still hit 98° and 99°, then topped 100° again three days later.

1951 Brown's owner Bill Veeck pulled another of his famous stunts. On "Fan Manager's Night," Browns coaches held up placards to the fans, who voted on the play! It actually worked. The Brownies beat the Kansas City A's, 5-3, before about a 1,000 managers.

1951 Mayor Darst cut the ribbon as the landmark South Town Famous-Barr opened at the corner of City Route 66 (Chippewa) and Kingshighway. The distinctive building was torn down in 1995 to make room for a Builder's Square that was never built. The land still stands vacant today.

1965 The huge "PDM" letters on the stabilizing strut between the legs of the Arch were removed, ending a dispute between the National Park Service and Pittsburgh-Des Moines Steel. The Park Service claimed the letters were an advertisement for the prime contractor on the job.

1966 The *Globe* reported that business at the clubs in Gaslight Square was down by 25% compared to 1965. Businessmen blamed publicity over crime, loss of tourists due to the airline strike, and teenagers drawn by the "Go-Go" clubs.

August 25

August 25 is the feast day of St. Louis, observed by the Catholic Church. King Louis IX of France became king at age 12. He was beloved for his work with the poor, and made two crusades to the middle east. On the second crusade in 1270, he was captured, fell ill and died. He was canonized in 1297.

1793 Five people, including the wife and sons of Antoine Riviere Junior, were massacred by Indians outside Florissant. Indians were a constant danger to the settlers of the Florissant Valley. One legend tells of the townspeople holding off an attack behind the walls of a stockade along Coldwater Creek until reinforcements arrived from St. Louis.

1900 The 12th U.S. census showed that St. Louis was the fourth largest city in the nation. The population of the city had increased more than 123,000 since 1890, placing it behind only New York, Chicago and Philadelphia.

1984 Thousands watched as the Buder and International buildings downtown were imploded to make room for the Gateway Mall project. Preservationists had lost a court fight to save the historic buildings that once made up "Realty Row." The city would settle for a half mall, instead of the uninterrupted open space originally proposed between the Old Courthouse and the Civil Courts Building.

1986 A's rookie Mark McGwire hit his first major league home run. It was a 450-foot blast off Walt Terrell of the Detroit Tigers.

August 26

1831 Major Thomas Biddle and Congressman Spencer Pettis mortally wounded each other in a duel on Bloody Island (now part of the East St. Louis riverfront). While campaigning, Pettis criticized Biddle's brother, who ran the Bank of the United States here. Biddle barged into the Congressman's room and horse-whipped him.

1904 It was "St. Charles Day" at the World's Fair. Two-thirds of the population of 10,000 packed up and left St. Charles for the day. Business came to a halt. At the fair, there was a huge parade, and a special program was held in the Missouri Building.

1950 Ground was broken for the new veteran's hospital on the site of Vandeventer Place. Guarded by huge gates on Grand Avenue, Vandeventer Place was once the site of the most luxurious mansions in the city. Residents included David R. Francis, former mayor, governor and president of the world's fair. The hospital occupies the eastern half of the place. The western part was later torn down for a children's detention home.

1974 Charles Lindbergh died of cancer in Hawaii at the age of 72. On May 21, 1927, he brought world wide acclaim to St. Louis with his flight across the Atlantic. The kidnapping and murder of his infant son drove Lindbergh out of the country in 1932. While in Europe, he became convinced that the Nazi air forces were invincible and spoke out against U.S. involvement in the war. But once the U.S. was in, Lindbergh flew 50 combat missions in the Pacific at the age of 40.

1981 Garry Templeton was fined and suspended indefinitely by Whitey Herzog after he flipped fans the bird when they booed his lack of hustle. After two more gestures later in the game at Busch, he was kicked out.  Whitey pulled him into the dugout and the two scuffled. Templeton was soon on his way to San Diego for a fellow named Ozzie Smith.

1832 Carondelet was incorporated as a town. The village was founded in 1767. It was nicknamed "Vide Poche" or "Empty Pocket" by the French. The name was either a comment on the poor residents, or on their gambling abilities, depending on which source you believe. Carondelet was annexed by the city of St. Louis in 1870.

1920 Alfonso J. Cervantes, "The Salesman Mayor," was born in St. Louis. He served as mayor from 1965 until 1973. He led the fight for a convention center, but lost a bid to locate a second airport in Illinois. Cervantes also brought the ill-fated Spanish Pavilion and the replica of the Santa Maria to St. Louis from the New York World's Fair.

1933 Lieutenant Tito Falconi, an Italian aviator, flew from St. Louis to Joliet—upside down! He set a record for inverted flight at three-hours, 16 minutes. He admitted being a little scared when one of the three straps holding him in his seat broke.

1956 Dorothy Richer, author of the teen column in the *Globe*, was harsh in her assessment of newcomer Elvis Presley. She wrote, "he cannot sing and his whole performance is crude and disgusting....his face is devoid of expression except when he snarls. My guess is that in a comparatively short time he will be forgotten."

1991 Clarence Harmon became the first black Police Chief in the 130-year history of the St. Louis Police Department. Harmon started out as a patrolman in 1969 and spent a total of 26 years on the force. He was elected mayor of St. Louis in 1997, serving one term.

August 28

1818 Jean Baptiste Pont du Sable died virtually penniless in St. Charles. The African-American from Haiti built the first permanent settlement at a place the Indians called Eschikagou, meaning "place of bad smells." The settlement grew into the city of Chicago. In 1800, he sold the property on what is now Michigan Avenue for $1,200.

1904 World famous race car driver Barney Oldfield crashed while competing for the Louisiana Purchase trophy at the World's Fair. Blinded by dust, he drove into the fence at 60 miles an hour, killing two spectators. Oldfield vowed never to race again, but later changed his mind.

1970 A zookeeper cleaning a cage in the reptile house at the St. Louis Zoo left a drain open, and a deadly king cobra slithered away. Amazingly, they re-opened the reptile house to the braver members of the public. They figured the snake was trapped inside, and cobras are nocturnal, so there was no danger. The snake was found unharmed 40 days later.

1999 The Rams season appeared doomed, as starting quarterback Trent Green suffered a season-ending injury in an exhibition game. His replacement was a little known former quarterback for the Iowa Barnstormers of the Arena Football League and the NFL Europe franchise in Amsterdam. Kurt Warner would go on to win the league MVP honors and lead the Rams to a world championship.

2000 A St. Louis-based Internet company announced a $70 million deal for the naming rights to the Kiel Center. The home of the Blues would be known as Savvis Center.

August 29

1946 Adolphus Busch III died after a brief illness. August A. Busch Junior, "Gussie," took over the brewery. Gussie Busch would become beloved in St. Louis. He oversaw the brewery's rise to number one in the world. He kept the baseball Cardinals here and was a tireless worker for St. Louis University and the redevelopment of downtown.

1971 Nine people, including three policemen, were injured in a melee at a Kiel Auditorium concert featuring the group "Ten Years After." Local promoters were predicting the death of concerts in St. Louis because "the crazies" were getting out of hand.

1977 Lou Brock broke Ty Cobb's career stolen base mark, swiping his 893rd in a game at San Diego. The Redbirds lost the game, 4-3. Rickey Henderson now holds the major league record. But Lou still holds the National League mark.

1977 St. Louis became the first major city without an amusement park as the "Chain of Rocks Fun Fair" park closed. The park on the bluff overlooking the Route 66 Chain of Rocks Bridge opened in 1924. A favorite site for school picnics in the '60s and '70s, the park faded after Six Flags Over Mid-America opened in 1971.

1985 Marching bands, speeches and fanfare marked the re-opening of a St. Louis landmark. After a $150 million renovation, Union Station was re-born as a retail center. After the last train departed in 1978, the station fell into disrepair, its gloomy interior a haven for the homeless.

August 30

1904 Thomas J. Hicks of Cambridgeport, Massachusetts, was declared the winner of the marathon at the World's Fair (after it was disclosed the fellow who came in first had hitched a ride in a car). The route began at Francis Field, took Forsyth to North and South, then Manchester, Ballas, Olive and Clayton Road back to Forsyth and the field. Hicks won with a time of three hours, 28 minutes and 53 seconds. His trainers had given him brandy, and several doses of strychnine mixed with a raw egg along the route.

1908 St. Louis was in the grips of pennant fever. The Browns were two games out with only 40 to play. Mayor Rolla Wells issued an order forbidding city employees from talking about baseball during working hours. He said "constant conversation and argumentation about baseball" had brought work to a halt at city hall.

1958 The very first McDonald's restaurant in Missouri opened at 9915 Highway 66 (Watson Road). Bill Wyatt and partner Don Kuehl brought the golden arches to St. Louis. The first store was a walk-up location only.

1963 Pickets went up at the Jefferson Bank and Trust Company downtown. The seven-month-long demonstration by members of the Congress of Racial Equality was aimed at forcing the bank to hire black workers. Several of the protesters were arrested, including William Clay. The protests were the first large-scale civil rights demonstrations here. Afterwards, 1,000 companies agreed to an equal opportunity employment program.

1998 The statue of Jack Buck outside Busch Stadium was dedicated. Cards fans were enraged after a rookie umpire threw Mark McGwire out of the game the day before. Buck urged fans to show class when the umps took the field that day. Cards fans responded with a standing ovation.

1793 Louis Blanchette died. In 1769, he established a fur trading post on the Missouri River. With his Indian wife, he built three cabins at what he called "Les Petite Cotes," or Village of the Little Hills." He helped establish the first Catholic church there, which was called San Carlos Borromeo. The name was anglicized to St. Charles a few years later.

1872 A group of property owners sued real estate promoter Hiram Leffingwell and the others instrumental in proposing the 3,000-acre "Forest Park." Land owners such as Thomas Skinker, Robert Forsythe and Charles Cabanne said the park would destroy the value of the little land they would have left.

1956 Over 125,000 people jammed downtown for a parade and fireworks marking the dedication of the "Mid-America Jubilee." The month-long, 37-acre exhibition on the riverfront was billed as the biggest show in St. Louis since the 1904 World's Fair.

1972 Mayor Cervantes unveiled a proposal to develop a 3.1. mile stretch of the River des Peres into a concrete lined boating and recreation area. The $14 million plan called for a green belt between Lansdowne and Morganford. Cervantes said it was "one of the most unusual and unique plans ever imagined for the city."

The public ridiculed the plan as the "River des Peres Yacht Club."

1995 The new football stadium downtown was officially named the Trans World Dome. The name would stick until the American buyout of TWA. St. Louis based brokerage firm Edward Jones purchased the naming rights in 2002.

SEPTEMBER

September 1

1880 The predecessor of the St. Louis Symphony was founded. The St. Louis Choral Society would absorb the St. Louis Musical Union in 1890, and change its name to the Choral Symphony Society. In 1907, choral music was dropped, and the name was changed to the St. Louis Symphony Society.

1881 The *Globe-Democrat* reported that Henry Shaw was planning a special horticultural exhibit at his garden, "far away in the southwest outskirts of St. Louis." Shaw offered prizes for outstanding plants. He also promised to purchase any suitable specimens for exhibition in his garden.

1894 The magnificent Union Station opened. Architect Theodore C. Link's building cost $6.5 million to build, and was twice as big as any railroad depot in the world at the time. The station closed in 1979. In 1985, it was renovated and turned into a unique shopping area. Today, the station is one of the top attractions in St. Louis.

1966 At 2 p.m., the new I-270 Chain of Rocks Bridge opened to traffic. Almost immediately, toll takers on the old bridge to the south said traffic was off by 80%. The new bridge was to have opened in November, 1965. But construction was beset by labor troubles and other delays.

1975 A sellout crowd honored Bob Gibson on a special day at Busch Stadium. Gibson heard salutes by Commissioner Bowie Kuhn, August Busch Jr., and a congratulatory telegram from President Gerald Ford. Gibson had announced he would retire at the end of the season.

September 2

1821 St. Ferdinand's Catholic church in Florissant was consecrated by Joseph Rosati, the first Bishop of St. Louis. St. Ferdinand is the oldest Catholic church between the Mississippi and the Rockies. The Old Cathedral was built 13 years later.

1850 Eugene Field was born in the house that still stands at 634 South Broadway. He is best remembered for his children's verses, including "Little Boy Blue" and "Wynken, Blynken and Nod." The home was saved from demolition in the 1930s and is now a children's museum.

1894 At 1:02 a.m., the very first train arrived at the newly-dedicated St. Louis Union Station. It was the St. Louis, Vandalia and Terre Haute "Fast Mail." The last train to use Union Station left on October 31, 1978.

1948 Los Angeles Rams running back Fred Gehrke hand painted Rams horns on the side of his leather helmet. It was the first time a team emblem appeared on a helmet in the NFL.

1993 The "John Larroquette Show" premiered on NBC-TV. The former "Night Court" star played a recovering alcoholic who took a job at a seedy St. Louis bus station. The dark comedy and urban issues made the show a hit at first. But NBC gradually removed or cleaned up many of the interesting characters. The show was cancelled in October, 1996.

1994 The Old Barn on Oakland Avenue closed its doors for good. The final event at the Arena was a concert by Christian recording star, Carman Licciardello. The Arena was built in 1929, as the home of the National Dairy Show. The old barn hosted the Rolling Stones, Ronald Reagan, Blues Hockey, Spirits Basketball and Gypsy Caravans.

September 3

1848 The St. Louis *Republican* became the first paper here to print a Sunday edition. After the great fire of 1849 and the cholera epidemic, some ministers said God had visited St. Louis with fire and pestilence because the newspaper was violating the Sabbath.

1856 Architect Louis Sullivan was born in Boston. Considered the dean of American architects, Sullivan believed that form should always follow function. The "Father of the Skyscraper" designed the Wainwright Building, constructed here in 1890-91 and now used for state offices.

1900 Sally Benson was born in St. Louis. Her novel based on her own childhood memories was called "Meet Me in St. Louis." Benson was also known for her contributions to the "New Yorker," short stories, book reviews, and screenplays such as "Anna and the King," "Bus Stop" and "National Velvet."

1904 The Olympic games in St. Louis came to a close. The games were not really international. Out of the 681 athletes, 525 were from the U.S.A. Athletes had to pay their own way. Marathon runner Felix Carvajal begged for donations in Havana. He lost it all in a New Orleans crap game and hitchhiked to St. Louis. Carvajal ran the race in street shoes and came in fourth. He might have won if not for a detour into an orchard, where the green apples gave him cramps.

1904 The contract to construct the bird cage at the St. Louis

World's Fair was awarded to the St. Paul Foundry Company for $14,634. Frank Baker of the Smithsonian's National Zoo designed the cage. The cage is 228 feet long, 84 feet wide and 50 feet high. After the fair, the Smithsonian made an effort to send the cage to Washington, D.C. But the city purchased it for $3,500. The purchase led to the establishment of the St. Louis Zoo in 1916.

September 4

1809 The governor of the Louisiana Territory, Meriweather Lewis, left St. Louis for Washington. Ailing and facing money problems, he was making the trip to convince the federal government to repay his expenses from the Lewis and Clark Expedition. Lewis would die under mysterious circumstances on the Natchez Trace. His death was ruled a suicide—even though he took a bullet in the back.

1906 University City was incorporated. Edward Garner Lewis, the flamboyant publisher of "Women's Magazine," bought 85 acres for his model city in 1902. The building that now serves as city hall was the magazine's headquarters. Lewis spent his fortune defending himself on fraud charges. He left his planned city to start another one in California.

1966 Willie McCovey of the Giants blasted a mammoth home run off the Redbirds' Al Jackson. It sailed into the upper deck at Busch Stadium, and was estimated to have travelled 450 feet. The

blast stood as the longest home run in Busch Stadium history until Mark McGwire arrived.

1987 One of the worst multiple murders in St. Louis history took place. Two gunmen entered the National Supermarket at 4331 Natural Bridge after closing at 11 p.m. The robbers ordered seven workers to lie face down, and shot them in the head. Five people were killed.

September 5

1906 Bradbury Robinson of St. Louis University threw the first legal forward pass in football. This was the first season in which the forward pass was legal. The first pass in a practice game against Carroll College was incomplete and the Bills lost the ball. The next time, Robinson completed a 20-yarder for the first aerial touchdown.

1928 The dance marathon craze ended with a whimper here. City Health Commissioner Max Stoloff was preparing an order shutting down a marathon that had been running for four days, when the promoter shut it down. The three couples still standing split $750 of the $1,000 prize that that been offered. The promoters said they lost $2,000.

1929 Workers began clearing the area that would become the Lake of the Ozarks. About 30,000 acres of timber were cleared.

The entire town of Linn Creek, county seat of Camden County, was demolished. The lake flooded an area of 61,000 acres, with a shoreline of 1,300 miles.

1946 It was Joe Garagiola day at Sportsman's Park. Mayor Kaufmann presented the rookie Cards catcher with a new car. The Cardinals then went out and beat the Cubs, 10-1, to stay in first, two games ahead of Brooklyn.

2002 It was "Cedric the Entertainer" day in St. Louis. He appeared at the St. Louis premiere of the movie "Barbershop". Cedric Kyles is a former State Farm Insurance claims adjuster and a 1982 graduate of Berkeley High School.

September 6

1857 Lindenwood college in St. Charles opened. George Sibley and his wife, Mary, founded a school for young ladies at their estate, "Lindenwood." It was named for a large grove of linden trees. The Sibleys donated their property to the Presbyterian Church.

1896 City police were launching a crackdown on bicycle "scorching" and "wreckless wheeling" on the streets of St. Louis. A minister said bicycle riding, as he had seen it in Forest Park, endangered both health and morals. Police said they would charge any rider who injured a pedestrian with "felonious wounding."

1903 The inventor of wireless telegraphy, Guglielmo Marconi, was in St. Louis to meet with World's Fair officials on plans for a wireless station at the fair. A site was picked on a hill east of the Palace of Fine Arts for the station, expected to be one of the top attractions at the fair.

1996 In pregame ceremonies at Busch, the Cardinals retired the number nine worn by Enos Slaughter. Slaughter is best remembered for his mad dash from first to third on a single to win the 1946 World Series. He broke down and cried when he was traded to the Yankees in 1953.

1996 The heirs to the Wal-Mart fortune announced they were buying the St. Louis Blues and the Kiel Center. Bill and Nancy Laurie bought the team and the Kiel for $100 million from a consortium of St. Louis businessmen.

September 7

1749 According to church records, Rene Auguste Chouteau was born in New Orleans (other sources put the date of his birth as September 26, 1750). In December of 1763, he would accompany Pierre Laclede to choose a site for a trading post. In February of 1764, Laclede sent the young Chouteau to head a party of 30 men to begin construction on the site that would become the city of St. Louis.

1888 Bernard. F. Dickmann was born in St. Louis. He served as mayor of St. Louis from 1933 to 1941. Dickmann was a tireless campaigner for the Jefferson National Expansion Memorial. During his administration, strict regulations went into effect to rid St. Louis of its smoky air. The bridge constructed across the Mississippi at Poplar Street was named for Dickmann.

1982 The "Fabulous Fox" Theatre re opened with a presentation of the musical "Barnum." The theater was restored to its original grandeur under the guidance of Leon and Mary Strauss. The Fox opened in 1929, and had been vacant since 1978.

1993 Cardinals outfielder Mark Whiten slugged four home runs and drove in 12 in a single game. The blasts came in the second game of a doubleheader in Cincinnati. "Sunny" Jim Bottomley of the Cardinals was the last player to get 12 RBI's in one game, back in 1924. Bob Horner of the Braves was the last player to hit four home runs in a game, in 1986.

1998 Mark McGwire smashed his 61st home run of the season, tying the all-time single-season mark set by Roger Maris in 1961. The historic blast came in the first inning off Mike Morgan of the Cubs at Busch Stadium.

1866 Andrew Johnson became the first president to visit St. Louis. At the time, he was on his way to impeachment hearings in Washington, battling Congress and the radical Republicans because of his post-war reconstruction policies. Encouraged by the warm reception here, he made a fiery speech attacking his enemies. His words here would be used against him in his impeachment trial.

1898 Cardinal great Frankie Frisch was born. The "Fordham Flash" played for the Cardinals from 1927 until 1937, was a player-manager during the "Gas House Gang" years, 1933 until 1937, and managed the team in 1938. He died in 1973.

1963 KSD-TV announced that former fashion model Dianne White would take over the Sunday night weather forecasts. White became the first African-American on-air talent on St. Louis television. That same day, the station hired Mary Fran Luecke as their chief weather girl. She would later star on "Newhart."

1986 Mike Laga of the Cardinals became the first player to hit a ball out of Busch Stadium. Problem was, it was foul by about 150 feet. Nonetheless, it was an impressive feat. It is 130 feet from the roof of Busch Stadium to the field below. The ball was found in a flower bed in the employee parking lot.

1998 At 8:18 p.m. Mark McGwire lined the first pitch from Steve Trachsel 341 feet over the left field wall at Busch Stadium for his 62nd home run of the season. The record breaker was Big Mac's shortest home run of the year. Groundskeeper Tim Forneris retrieved the ball and presented it to Big Mac after the game.

September 9

1891 John Busch opened his new restaurant on Clayton Road. Originally known as The Woodlawn Grove, it had opened in 1860. Busch changed the name to "Busch's Grove." It is the oldest restaurant in the area operating in its original location.

1903 Union bootblacks here were threatening to strike. They were demanding ten cents per shine, up from five cents, and wanted the work day reduced to 13 hours from the current 16. The union said it was confident of victory, because St. Louisans would not stand for muddy shoes for very long.

1927 "Green Ones" leader Alphonse Palazolla was riddled with bullets outside a tombstone shop on "The Hill." A ricocheting bullet also killed a ten-year-old boy. Over the next three months, the war between the Cuckoo and the Green Ones Sicilian gangs would claim ten more lives. It got so bad that Archbishop John Glennon forbade the administering of last rites to dead gangsters.

The gang wars claimed about 60 lives in St. Louis between 1919 and 1932.

1977 After nearly 120 years, Falstaff beer was no longer being brewed in St. Louis. The company ended production at its plant at 1920 Shenandoah. Falstaff traces its origins to the Lemp Brewery, founded in 1858. The brewery took the image of Shakespeare's Sir John Falstaff, because Lemp felt it denoted the positive social aspects of drinking, instead of the negatives touted by prohibitionists.

1979 It was Lou Brock Day at Busch Stadium. Before the game, baseball's all-time base burglar was honored in ceremonies and showered with gifts. The Cardinals gave him a 33-foot yacht, and KMOX radio chipped in with a convertible.

September 10

1910 Captain Thomas S. Baldwin made the first airplane flight over the Mississippi. On his return trip, Captain Baldwin stunned the crowd lining the riverfront when he flew under the McKinley and the Eads Bridges at the breathtaking speed of 50 miles pe hour in his plane, "The Red Devil."

1935 A landmark day in St. Louis. Voters approved a $7.5 million bond issue for a riverfront memorial. There were rumors that the election was fixed, and an investigation by the *Post-Dispatch* seemed to support the theory. But the city refused to turn the ballots over to a grand jury. So, no one knows if the Arch was built on a foundation of stuffed ballot boxes!

1941 Phil the Gorilla arrived at the Ape House. Phil was named for the man who brought him to St. Louis, animal collector Phil Carroll. The Guinness Book of World Records estimated Phil's weight at 615 pounds, one of the largest gorillas on record. Phil was one of the zoo's top attractions. Schwarz Studios stuffed Phil after his death in December, 1958. He stands today in the Safari Shop near the Zoo's South Gate.

1974 As Jack Buck cried "He did it! One-oh-five for Lou Brock," Lou Brock broke Maury Will's single-season stolen base record. The record-breaker came off Dick Ruthven of the Phillies at Busch. The game was halted and hall-of-famer James "Cool Papa" Bell presented Lou with second base.

1991 The first riverboat casino in the St. Louis area opened. The Alton Belle was moored on the riverfront at Alton. It's hard to believe today, but "The Belle" charged $19.95 admission per person on nights and weekends.

1903 The World's Fair Company announced plans to lay pipes for the "distribution of coolness by ammonia gas" at the fair. The Globe said it was probably a good idea, but would not be surprised to find out that artifically-cooled buildings were unhealthy, "since we know by experience that everything nice is unhealthy."

1963 Nine Congress of Racial Equality leaders were arrested for contempt of court during the protests at Jefferson Bank and Trust. Among those arrested were Alderman William Clay, the Reverend Charles Perkins, and Norman Seay, Democratic Committeeman from the 26th Ward. The protests were a major turning point in the St. Louis civil rights movement.

1974 The Cardinals won a 4-3 decision over the Mets in 25 innings. It was the longest night game in major league history to that date, lasting seven hours and 13 minutes. Bake McBride opened the 25th with an infield single. He scored all the way from first on an errant throw. The longest game in major league history was a 26-inning affair between Brooklyn and Boston on May 1, 1920.

1999 The former site of Times Beach was re-dedicated as Route 66 State Park. The last residents moved out in 1986, after dioxin contamination was discovered. The buildings were leveled, and the site sealed off for 17 years. A controversial incinerator there burned dioxin from Times Beach and other sites in Missouri before it was dismantled and the site cleaned up.

2001 Early that morning, the big news was the arrival of Tiger Woods at Bellerive Country Club the day before. Woods put on an exhibition for thousands of fans as he prepared to play in the PGA American Express Championship. The news from New York broke shortly after 7:45 a.m., St. Louis time. Within an hour, air traffic was halted at Lambert Field and armed marshals patrolled the Eagleton Federal Courthouse. The Gateway Arch and the Old Courthouse were closed. Police Chief Joe Mokwa assured citizens that no terrorist threats had been received in St. Louis. By afternoon, most of the shopping malls were closed and blood donation centers were swamped. The PGA would call off the golf tournament.

September 12

1875 The former president of the Confederacy was in St. Louis on his way to speaking engagements in Fulton and Kansas City. St. Louisans who sided with the rebels "during the recent unpleasantness" were lining up to see Jefferson Davis at his hotel—the Southern.

1921 Following a plane crash at the Aviation Field in Forest Park in which a paying passenger was killed, Park Commissioner Frederich Pape ordered all planes at the field grounded. He said pilots had flagrantly violated his ban on excursion flights from the field.

1962 President John F. Kennedy was in St. Louis, for a visit to McDonnell Aircraft. He praised the company for its work in building the "Friendship Seven" capsule that had taken Alan Shephard into space a year earlier.

1980 South side dentist Dr. Glennon Engelman was convicted of the 1976 murder of Peter Halm. He would soon face trial for five more murders and would be sentenced to life several times over. It turned out that St. Louis' most notorious killer's crimes dated back to 1958. He claimed to have committed 23 murders. Engleman would marry off his ex-lovers and conspire with them to murder their husbands for the insurance money.

2001 On the day after, St. Louis struggled to return to normalcy. The Arch and Eagleton Courthouse re-opened, but the PGA concelled the World Golf Championship at Bellerive. Airport officials waited for word on when flights would resume, and blood donors faced waits of up to five hours due to the crowds. At 7:48 a.m. radio TV stations observed a moment of silence, followed by Sandi Patty's version of "The Star Spangled Banner."

September 13

1903 The World's Fair was narrowly assured of having the giant bird cage built in time for the fair. The deadline for opening bids had passed, with none of them coming in under the $15,000 limit. The mailman showed up with a bid from a St. Paul firm, and officials determined it had been mailed in time. The contract was awarded for $14,634.

1924 Farmers in O'Fallon and other outlying areas of St. Charles County celebrated the paving of a 26-mile stretch of the Booneslick Trail between St. Charles and Foristell. Before the road was opened, communities west of St. Peters were isolated from St. Charles by bad roads. The road later became U.S. 40, and eventually I-70.

1951 The Cardinals became the first modern era team to play two different teams on the same day at the same ball park. The Cards beat the Giants at Sportsman's Park, 6-4, in a make-up game from the previous night. Then, the Redbirds beat the Braves, 2-0, in a make-up game from earlier in the season.

1957 Trading closed for the last time at the Merchant's Exchange downtown. The building at 111 North Third was one of the city's architectural treasures. Samuel Tilden was nominated for president at the Democratic Convention there in 1876. The trading floor was described as the nation's single largest indoor space when it was built in 1875. The building came down to make room for I-70.

1993 The flood of 1993 officially came to an end at 6:15 p.m., as the Mississippi finally dipped below flood stage. The river had been over flood for 80 days, and for 44 days back in April, a total of 124 days.

September 14

1812 The birthday of Madison County, Illinois. Territorial Governor Ninian Edwards ordered the county carved out of St. Clair County and named after President James Madison. Thomas Kirkpatrick's log cabin served as the county seat, named "Edwardsville," after the governor.

1857 The St. Louis Fire Department was established. The paid department replaced the rowdy old volunteer companies. They raced each other to fires, sabotaged equipment, cut hoses, and even burned down a firehouse. A firefighter had been killed in a shootout between rival companies at a blaze in May, 1853. The volunteers did not go quietly. For a time they plagued the paid department by answering alarms and even resorting to violence.

1972 The city of Arnold was incorporated. Arnold is made up of five older towns: Wickes, Flamm City, Tenbrook, Maxville, Beck

183

and Old Town Arnold. George Arnold was a local land owner. The area around what is now Lemay Ferry and 141 was known as Maxville, after Max Stengel. He established the first business in the area in the 1870s. John Ten Brook donated the land for the Frisco Depot in 1902.

1989 Only 1,519 fans showed up for a game between the Cardinals and the Pirates at Busch. The game had been halted with no score after five innings the night before, and a day game was scheduled with virtually no notice. It was the smallest crowd in Busch Stadium history.

1992 John C. Vincent stunned St. Louis when he climbed to the top of the Arch and parachuted safely to the ground. The daredevil claimed he used suction cups to climb up. He was arrested as soon as his feet hit the ground.

September 15

1904 It was "St. Louis Day" at the World's Fair. Business was suspended in the city, and 358,000 people came to the fair, setting an attendance record. A record was also set for the largest number of people to board the streetcars in a single day.

1926 Unable to find the fogged-in landing field in Chicago, airmail pilot Charles Lindbergh jumped from his plane as it ran out of fuel over Ottawa, Illinois. "Lucky" Lindbergh parachuted to safety,

and the three sacks of mail from St. Louis were recovered safely and taken to Chicago by train.

1960 The birthday of UMSL. The first student was enrolled at what was then the University of Missouri, Normandy Residence, located at the former Normandy Country Club. It marked the beginning of the effort to establish a full-fledged campus here. Three years later to the day, the campus was dedicated.

1962 The *Globe-Democrat* reported that the folk music revival was sweeping Gaslight Square. One nightclub owner told a reporter that folk singers were playing in at least 1/2 of the bars in the area.

1969 Steve Carlton of the Cardinals set a major-league record as he fanned 19 Mets. Carlton struck out the side four times, and fanned at least one batter in every inning. But he lost the game by a score of 4-3!

September 16

1809 The first execution in St. Louis County took place. John Long, Jr. was hanged for the murder of his stepfather, John Gordon. Gordon once owned Taille de Noyer, the historic home that still stands in Florissant.   The county's last execution took place on June 30, 1933. James Kellar was hanged from the "Bridge of Sighs" at the Old County Courthouse for the murder of a Maplewood woman.

1907 Umpire William Evans was in serious condition after he was beaned on the head by a bottle thrown by a fan at Sportsman's Park the day before. The remorseful fan, one Hugo Dusenberg, confessed. He was charged with assault with intent to kill and fined $100. The crowd roughed Hugo up before police got to him.

1924 Cardinals first baseman "Sunny" Jim Bottomley went 6-6 and drove in 12 runs in a game at Brooklyn. The Cards won, 17-3. The 12 RBI's in a single game set a major league record that would stand for 69 years. Mark Whiten of the Cardinals broke it in 1993.

1952 The city of Clayton approved the construction of buildings more than five stories tall. By 1954, 16 new buildings had been authorized and six were under construction in the business district. By 1959, over $14 million worth of new construction was underway in Clayton.

1966 The first section of the Innerbelt Expressway opened. Then known as Missouri Route 725, it ran from Highway 40 all the way to Ladue Road! It made it to Page in 1970. It remained a dead end at Page until 1981.

September 17

1858 Dred Scott died of tuberculosis. After Scott lost his famous case, his owner gave him his freedom in May, 1857. He lived the rest of his days as a porter at Barnum's Hotel here.

1890 Emerson Electric was founded. Judge Wesley Emerson put up the money to help Alexander and Charles Meston open an electrical shop at 904 Olive. In 1892, the firm manufactured the first electric fans in America. Today, Emerson has 60 divisions in more than 150 countries, employing about 120,000 people.

1900 The first female professional team made its debut here. One thousand fans paid 50¢ each and were shocked to see the girls playing ball in trousers. They also found the team from Cincinnati could not play very well. The *Globe* called it "the most gigantic fraud and disgraceful exhibits ever given before a St. Louis audience."

1941 "The Man" played his first major league game. Stan Musial's first day in the majors was a good one, as he went 2-4 against Jim Tobin of the Boston Braves. Those were the first of his 3,630 career hits.

1980 James "Jimmy" Michaels was killed when a bomb ripped his car apart on I-55 in South St. Louis. David Leisure was put to death for his role in the bombing on September 1, 1999. The bombing marked the start of two years of bloody warfare between the Leisure and Michaels families over control of a labor union.

September 18

1883 The Browns were just one game out of first and club president Chris Von der Ahe was thankful there was no ladies day coming up. The Browns were 1-10 on ladies days. Von der Ahe said "the presence of the fair sex seems to demoralize the whole team instead of cheer them up."

1949 The new International Airport in Chicago was dedicated in honor of Lieutenant Edward "Butch" O'Hare of St. Louis. O'Hare won the medal of honor for single-handedly defending the carrier "Lexington" against seven Japanese bombers. He was shot down over Tarawa on November 27, 1943.

1958 Bill Bangert, the former mayor of Berkeley and owner of a road building firm was front page news. Bangert announced plans for a 100,000 seat domed stadium near what is now the I-270/70 interchange. He wanted the stadium to be the centerpiece of of an 840-acre sports complex to be known as the Village of Champ.

1968 Ray Washburn of the Cardinals pitched a no-hitter against the San Francisco Giants at Candlestick—just one day after Gaylord Perry threw a no-hitter against the Cardinals.

1981 Scullin Steel closed its doors. Founded in 1899, Scullin employed thousands during World War II. The factory site became the St. Louis Marketplace Shopping Center. The administration building still stands.

September 19

1864 General Sterling Price arrived in Missouri with 12,000 rebel troops to march on St. Louis. Halted by Union forces at Pilot Knob, Price's spies falsely informed him he was outnumbered at St. Louis. He turned towards Jefferson City, which his spies said was too heavily defended. He decided to move against Leavenworth, Kansas, but his defeat at Westport (near Kansas City) ended the Civil War in Missouri.

1883 A St. Louis barber was acquitted in what was considered to be a landmark case. Ignatz Scherringer was charged with violating the law banning unnecessary labor on Sunday. The jury took five minutes to decide that shaving was just as necessary on Sunday as any other day of the week.

1938 The radio station owned by the *St. Louis Star-Times* newspaper signed on the air. At the time, KXOK was at 1250-AM. It moved to the familiar 630 dial position in 1940.

1949 A $100 million plan for development of the Meramec River Basin for recreation was unveiled. Planners assumed that three dams recommended by army engineers would be built. They had already been approved by Congress. For the next 28 years, a battle would rage over the Meramec Basin.

1998 Helicopter traffic reporter Alan Barklage was fatally injured in the crash of his experimental helicopter at Parks Airport in Cahokia. Barklage reported traffic for KSDK-TV and KEZK-FM. He was famous for his on-air aerial rescues.

September 20

1904 The recently organized St. Louis County Telephone Company began stringing wires to connect the county seat of Clayton with Kirkwood and Webster Groves. The company said it would use automatic calling boxes to replace the "Hello Girls."

1916 Pigeons caused a major headache for residents of St. Charles. Sparks from a KATY train passing beneath the highway bridge set fire to pigeon's nests. The blaze consumed the entire wooden bridge deck. Ferries were pressed into service until the damage could be repaired.

1954 Educational Television came to St. Louis. KETC signed on at 9 p.m. The first broadcast was from McMillan Hall at Washington University. Following remarks by Arthur Holly

Compton, the station broadcast a play dramatizing the necessity for free speech. KETC became the fifth station in St. Louis, joining, KTVI, KSD, KWK (Channel Four) and WTVI (Channel 51) Channel Nine was the seventh educational station in the country.

1963 Pope John XXIII announced that the Old Cathedral had been elevated to the status of Basilica of St. Louis the King. The Old Cathedral at that time was one of only 17 churches in the United States to be designated as a basilica (now, the new cathedral has also been designated as a basilica, making St. Louis one of the few cities in the world with two of them).

2000 The Cardinals clinched the National League Central, with an 11-6 win over the Houston Astros. The Cardinals notched their second division title in five years. The Birds would sweep the Braves in the playoffs, only to fall to the Mets in the NLCS.

September 21

1934 Paul "Daffy " Dean threw a no-hitter in the second game of a doubleheader against Brooklyn. His brother "Dizzy" had thrown a one-hitter in the first game. After the game, Ol' Diz said "If I'd of known Paul wuz gonna throw a no-hitter I'da thrown one too."

1944 The Cardinals clinched their third pennant in a row with a 5-4 win over the Boston Braves. The Browns would clinch the American League flag on the final day of the season, setting up the "Streetcar Series."

1948 Benson Ford, vice president of the Ford Motor Company dedicated the new $12 million Lincoln-Mercury plant on Highway 66, near Lambert Municipal Airport. At that time, Hazelwood did not exist. The village was founded by residents concerned about plans by Florissant to annex the area that included the new plant.

1964 The Cardinals were still six-and-a-half games behind the Phillies with just 13 games to play. The Reds beat the Phillies that night, and the Phils would go on to drop the next ten games in a row.

1968 Topping out ceremonies were held for the Spanish Pavilion downtown. Mayor Cervantes led the effort to bring the pavilion here from the 1964 World's Fair as a cultural center. His fundraising corporation went bankrupt, and the pavilion sat vacant until developer Donald Breckenridge bought it. Today, the pavilion is the lobby of the downtown Marriott.

September 22

1842 Belleville attorney James Shields challenged Abraham Lincoln to a duel. The two men met on this date, but Lincoln's friends convinced the future president not to fight.

1961 The government announced it would build its new space flight facility in Houston. Twenty-two cities, including St. Louis, had been pushing to become the site of the proposed $60 million facility ("St. Louis, we have a problem" just doesn't have the same ring to it).

1964 Zoo officials unveiled plans for the proposed Charles H. Yalem Children's Zoo. It was named for the financier and philanthropist who donated $250,000 for the new zoo. Officials said it would include an animal nursery, and enable kids to get up close and personal with the animals.

1969 The "Paul is Dead" rumor reached the St. Louis area, as the Southern Illinois University newspaper printed an article reporting the various "clues." You remember these; the line "I buried Paul," supposedly at the end of "Strawberry Fields," the "signs of death" on the various album covers and so on.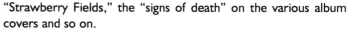

1989 The Chase Park-Plaza closed its doors. Built in 1922, the Chase Hotel became the center of nightlife in St. Louis after owner Sam Koplar combined it with the adjacent Park Plaza. Harry Fender broadcast on KMOX from the Chase, and who can forget "Wrestling at the Chase?" The hotel re-opened as an apartment complex in the summer of 1999.

September 23

1806 Lewis and Clark returned to St. Louis after their journey of discovery into the wilds of the Louisiana Purchase. They had traveled 1,700 miles in two years and four months. The people of the village of St. Louis lined the river bank and "Hizzard three cheers" as they landed.

1823 Jeremiah Connor died at the age of 50. Washington Avenue is his legacy. He laid out an area 80 feet wide through his land in 1818, and gave it to the city under the condition that the street be wider than all the others. The width of Washington Avenue was a factor in the location of the Eads Bridge some 50 years later.

1925 Nine business firms here announced plans to build the largest radio station in the country. The 50,000-watt station was to be built 16 miles outside of town to avoid drowning all the other stations out. It was expected to cost $100,000 and be on the air by Christmas (the "X" in KMOX stands for Christmas, 1925).

1929 Three-thousand people gathered for a banquet as part of the ceremonies marking the dedication of the Arena. Secretary of Agriculture Arthur Hyde and Governor Henry Caulfield spoke. The "almost perfect acoustics of the new structure were admirably demonstrated" by a 50-piece band and the singing of "The Masked Soprano." The Arena was built as the permanent home of the National Dairy Show. But the stock market crash bankrupted the promoters.

1967 The Blues played their very first game, an exhibition contest against Rochester of the American Hockey League. The Blues won, 3-2, with Terry Crisp scoring the first goal in Blues history. Jack Buck called the game on KMOX.

September 24

1805 Eberhard Anheuser was born in Bad Kruezbach, Germany. He took over the faltering Bavarian Brewery here in 1860, and renamed it A. Anheuser. He would later join forces with a brewery supplier who married his daughter—Adolphus Busch.

1864 Major James Morgan Utz was captured carrying contraband medical supplies to the Confederates west of the village of Manchester. Utz was a member of one of the first families to settle in what is now Hazelwood. His partner, Paul Fusz (yes, THAT Fusz family) was also arrested. Major Utz was hanged as a spy on December 26, 1864, just minutes before a pardon arrived from President Lincoln.

1926 The Cardinals clinched their first pennant with a 6-4 win over the Giants. The news set off a celebration here bigger than any seen since Armistice Day. Oddsmakers already had the Yankees as 6-5 favorites to take the series.

1988 The Cardinals' "Secret Weapon," Jose Oquendo, became the first player since 1918 to play all nine positions during a season, when he stepped in to catch the seventh inning during a 14-1 loss to the Mets.

1994 Many of the items in the shuttered Arena were auctioned off. Schmiezing's Sports Bar bought the 6,000-pound scoreboard. The dasher boards and glass panels sold for $6,000.

September 25

1864 Business was suspended here, and all men not drafted were put to work building defenses, as rebels under Sterling Price advanced towards St. Louis. His army was encamped near Pilot Knob, preparing to attack Fort Davidson. But resistance by outnumbered federals there convinced Price he could never take St. Louis.

1868 The eccentric Dr. Joseph Nash McDowell died. He founded the first medical college west of the Mississippi here. When his son and daughter died, he had their bodies placed in containers and suspended from the ceiling of a cave in Hannibal, to test the petrifactive qualities of water dripping from the ceiling. Some kids, among them a young Samuel Clemens, broke in. They saw the bodies and fled, ending up lost in the cave.

1949 The entire nation was intrigued by the repeated visits to St. Louis by Vice President Alben Barkley. He was here for a birthday visit with a St. Louis widow, Mrs. Carlton Hadley. Rumors were swirling that an engagement announcement was in the offing.

1986 The St. Louis Playboy Club closed its doors. The club at 3914 Lindell featured three levels, including a hanging "Playpen" that was used for private gatherings. The club would produce six "Playmates of the Month" and one "Playmate of the Year." The building is now a nightclub called "Kearbey's."

1989 St. Louis became a two-newspaper town again—briefly. The *St. Louis Sun*, a tabloid style paper, made its debut amid much fanfare. The paper folded in the spring of 1990.

September 26

1864 The city was in a near panic, Union General Rosecrans asked citizens of St. Louis who were exempt from military service, but capable of defending their homes, to organize under the mayor in the face of the invasion by rebels under Sterling Price. Five-thousand people responded.

1888 Poet T.S. Eliot was born in the family home at 2635 Locust. The family later moved to the home on Westminster Place which still stands today. Eliot would settle in England, though much of his work reflects his St. Louis youth. His grandfather, William Greenleaf Eliot, was one of the founders of Eliot Seminary, which became Washington University.

1949 The village of Hazelwood was organized. It was formed by residents intent on fighting an attempt by Florissant to annex the land that included the new Ford plant. The name Hazelwood comes from the country estate of Colonel Richard Graham. Senator Henry Clay, visiting in 1828, remarked that it reminded him of his estate back home, "Hazelwood."

1950 The first flight of the reborn Ozark Airlines left Lambert for Chicago—with one person on board. Ozark started during World War II with a couple of flights a day between Springfield, Kansas City and St. Louis. But the airline failed. This time, it took off. The familiar green planes were serving 67 cities in 25 states when TWA took it over in 1986.

1983 Bob Forsch became the only pitcher in Cardinal history to ever throw two no-hitters. He also became the 25th pitcher in major league history to do it. His second was a 3-0 win over Montreal. Only two runners reached base, and Forsch threw just 96 pitches.

September 27

1953 The St. Louis Browns played their last game here, before 3,174 die-hard fans. Jim Dyck flied to center at 3:44 p.m. for the final out. The Brownies naturally went out on a losing note, dropping the game to the White Sox, 2-1. They would open the 1954 season as the Baltimore Orioles.

1959 Seven months after the tornado, the *Globe* reported that the area around Boyle and Olive was bouncing back better than ever. The area now known as "Gaslight Square" was attracting a reputation as a hot night spot.

1968 Bob Gibson broke Grover Cleveland Alexander's season earned-run-average record. Gibson finished the season with an amazing 1.12 ERA. In baseball history 1968 became known as "the year of the pitcher."

1990 The city of East St. Louis hit rock bottom. A circuit court judge ordered the city to turn over the deed to city hall to Walter DeBow. DeBow won a lawsuit after he was beaten in the city jail.

1998 Mark McGwire blasted home runs 69 and 70 in the season finale at Busch Stadium. Number 69 came off Mike Thurman of the Expos in the third inning. Number 70 was a three-run shot off Carl Pavano in McGwire's last at bat of the season.

September 28

1902 Eleven automobiles took part in the first St. Louis automobile club endurance run, a 25-mile trip to Manchester Mills. A young boy was injured when he put a stick into the spokes of a moving auto. His father was quoted in the papers, "it's a purty thing for city folks to come out to the country and run down innocent children."

1912 Corporal Frank Scott was killed in a plane crash at College Park, Maryland. The pioneer airplane mechanic is believed to have been the first enlisted man to die in a plane crash. In 1917, the War Department named its new training base for aviation cadets in St. Clair County in honor of Scott. Scott Air Force Base is the only base to be named for an enlisted man.

1953 Six-year old Bobby Greenlease, the son of a wealthy Kansas City auto dealer, was kidnaped from his school and held for $600,000 ransom. His body was found on October 7th. Bonnie Brown Heady and Carl Austin Hall were captured in St. Louis and executed for the crime. What happened to half the ransom money was a mystery until 1982, when the FBI made public a confession by former city patrolman Elmer Dolan. He said Lieutenant Louis Shoulders and cab company president Joseph Costello had taken the money. Dolan and Shoulders were convicted of perjury in 1953.

1953 Voters here overwhelmingly approved a $1.5 million bond issue for clearance and development of an area bounded by 15th street, 18th, Market and Chestnut. The area was to be completely leveled to make room for a green-belt mall from Union Station to the Soldier's Memorial. Mayor Tucker hailed the vote as a mandate for an even larger slum clearance plan.

1996 It was "Ozzie Smith Day" at Busch Stadium. "The Wizard's" uniform number one was retired in emotional ceremonies before a sold-out crowd. Ozzie clashed with manager Tony LaRussa much of the season after he was forced to compete with Royce Clayton for the starting shortstop job.

September 29

1864 A detachment of Confederate cavalry raided the Cheltenham Post Office, near what is today Manchester and Sulphur. It was the closest any rebel forces would get to St. Louis. Outnumbered federals delayed the rebels at Pilot Knob long enough for reinforcements to rush to St. Louis. Price instead turned towards Jefferson City.

1892 The first Famous Store opened at Broadway and Morgan (now Delmar). David May and his partner had bought the clothing store for $150,000 at a fire sale. The firm merged with the William Barr Dry Goods Company in 1912.

1927 A tornado ripped through the southwestern part of the city. The twister struck near the city limits south of Manchester, tore across the Central West End, and crossed the Mississippi near the McKinley Bridge. By the time it was over, 86 people were dead, six square miles of the city were in ruins, and 1,500 people were hurt. Damage was estimated at over $10 million. Thousands were homeless.

1953 *The Post-Dispatch* reported that Chevrolet was planning to build a new fiberglass-body car here. Production of the Corvette would move to the St. Louis plant for the 1954 model year. Corvettes would exclusively be produced here until June, 1981.

1963 Stan Musial played his final game. On Stan Musial Day at old Busch Stadium, Stan got two hits, giving him a lifetime total of 3,630. Musial would move up to the front office after a career that saw him break or tie 17 major league and 30 National League hitting records.

1989 One of the city's most beloved figures, Gussie Busch, died at the age of 90. That night, a moment of silence was observed at the Cards-Cubs game at Busch, and the Cards players wore black armbands.

September 30

1864 The village of Kirkwood was the scene of much military activity. Two brigades of Union troops rushed in, ready to head off the invasion by Confederates under Sterling Price. Price was held off by outnumbered federals at Pilot Knob. When he learned of the reinforcements outside St. Louis, he abandoned his plans to march on the city, and the Battle of Kirkwood was never fought.

1900 A huge crowd gathered at the St. Louis Exposition to see how phonograph records were made. Until now, the process was a secret closely guarded by Thomas Edison. Since his patents were about to expire, Edison arranged the demonstration. The crowd watched a recording session by "world famous phonograph singer," Will Denny.

1927 The long process of cleaning up began after the devastating tornado. The bodies of five girls were found in the ruins of Central High School and the death toll was put at 86. Declining offers of aid from other cities, a citizen's relief committee and the Red Cross appealed for $500,000 to meet the immediate needs of the homeless. KMOX aired a plea for members of the St. Louis Naval Reserve to respond for help, and raised $20,000 to aid the victims.

1964 The 1964 pennant race came down to the wire. The Cardinals beat the Phillies 8-5. Then Cards fans tuned in to hear the Pirates down the Reds in a 16 inning game. The Cardinals were in first place. But the Birds would lose the next two to the Mets. The final day of the season found the Reds and Cards tied with the Phillies one game back.

OCTOBER

October 1

1812 Today is the birthday of St. Louis and St. Charles County. Governor William Clark signed an act dividing the Louisiana Territory into the districts of St. Charles, St. Louis, Ste. Genevieve, Cape Girardeau and New Madrid. The act also called for the election of Missouri's first representative legislature and delegate to Congress.

1926 The first talking motion pictures were shown in St. Louis. Those first "talkies" were shown at the Capitol Theatre. They included a short selection of music, plus John Barrymore in "Don Juan."

1930 The "TWA" brand name was born. Transcontinental Air Transport merged with Western Air Express, creating Transcontinental and Western Airlines. The name was officially changed to Trans World Airlines in 1950.

1944 The city was assured of the only All-St. Louis World Series ever. The Browns clinched the pennant with a 5-2 win over the Yankees. A crowd of 37,815 packed Sportsman's Park— the first sellout of a Browns game in 20 years. Oscar Grimes flied out to George McGuinn for the final out.

1963 Mark David McGwire was born in Pomona, California. Big Mac was a member of the 1984 U.S. Olympic Baseball team. In 1987, he won the American League Rookie of the Year honors and set a rookie record with 49 home runs. McGwire became a Cardinal on July 31, 1997, in a trade that sent pitcher T.J. Mathews, Eric Ludwick and Blake Stein to the Oakland A's. McGwire shattered the single season record for home runs in 1998.

October 2

1864 After turning away from St. Louis, rebels under Sterling Price rode into Pacific. They burned the bridges and much of the town. Guerilla leader William Quantrill and Jesse James accompanied Price. Legend says when the rebels destroyed a Union gunpowder plant at "Salt Petre Cave," James became familiar with the hideout we now know as Meramec Caverns.

1960 The Giants beat the football Cardinals 35-14, in their debut at old Busch Stadium. A crowd of 26,089 paid to see the game. It marked the first NFL game played in St. Louis in 26 years.

1969 Fairview Heights was incorporated as a city. The area was known as Prairie Ridge until about 1900, when the Fairbrother Realty Company began promoting lots in "Fairview." In the mid-1960s, voters were asked to choose between Fairview Heights, Lincoln Heights or Prairie Ridge as the name of their community.

1977 Bob Gassoff's number three became the first number to be retired by the Blues. Gassoff was killed in a motorcycle accident on May 29, 1977.

1986 A group of local investors led by Michael Shanahan signed a deal to buy the Blues from Harry Ornest for $19 million. An aldermanic committee recommended that the city buy the Arena for $15 million through its Land Clearance for Redevelopment Authority.

October 3

1926 For the first time ever, the Cardinals won a World Series game. They beat the Yankees 6-2, in game two of the series at Yankee Stadium. Grover Cleveland Alexander got the win. Billy Southworth became the first Cardinal to ever hit a World Series home run.

1960 Huge crowds met Democratic presidential candidate John F. Kennedy during a campaign swing across Southern Illinois. Kennedy made 14 speeches on a day that took him to Alton, Granite City, Venice, National City, East St. Louis, Belleville, Scott Air Force Base and Carbondale. Five thousand people heard Kennedy speak in the Belleville Square.

1962 It was a big day for motorists. An important link in the "Circumferential Highway" opened to traffic. The section completed I-270 between the Mark Twain Expressway and Bellefontaine. It carried the designation "By-Pass U.S. 66" until 1965.

1999 Mark McGwire won the home run title for the second season in a row. McGwire hit his 65th home run of the season in the first inning of a game at Busch Stadium. Sammy Sosa of the Cubs finished the season with 63. McGwire also moved into tenth place on the all-time home run list.

1999 The new Family Arena in St. Charles opened with a concert by John Cougar Mellencamp. The biggest complaint on opening night concerned the long lines of traffic getting in and out of the arena.

October 4

1906 The statue of St. Louis on Art Hill was dedicated. The statue became the symbol of the city, eclipsed only when the Arch was built in 1965. More than 7,000 people took part in the parade to mark the occasion. The statue was a bronze cast from a plaster-of-Paris original at the world's fair by Charles Niehaus.

1911 Walter Brookins carried the first air mail in the city of St. Louis, and only the second in the United States. He flew the mail from Kinloch Field to Fairgrounds Park at a top speed of 60 miles per hour.

1944 The first all-St. Louis World Series opened. The Cardinals beat the Browns 2-1 at Sportsman's Park. Denny Galehouse got the win and George McQuinn homered in the fourth. The Brownies seemed to be the sentimental favorite as Mayor Aloys Kaufmann proclaimed it to be "Baseball Week in St. Louis." The "Streetcar Series" was played with no days off.

1964 The Cardinals capped one of the most exciting pennant chases ever, clinching their first pennant since 1946 with an 11-5 win over the Mets at Busch while the Phillies beat the Reds 10-0. Tim McCarver caught a pop  foul off the bat of Ed Kranepool for the final out. The Cardinals had been six-and-a-half games behind the Phillies in late September, with just 12 games to play. They went into the final day of the season tied with the Reds for first.

2001 Mark McGwire slugged a home run off of Rocky Coppinger in Milwaukee. It would turn out to be the last of his career. McGwire had missed virtually all of the second half of the season, due to his recurring knee injury. In November, McGwire would announce his retirement in a fax to ESPN. His 583 career home runs puts Big Mac fifth on the all-time list.

October 5

1782 Nobody knows for sure exactly when Florissant was founded. But on this date, Francois Dunegant received a tract of land from the Spanish to establish a government house and organize a village along Coldwater Creek. The Spanish called the village San Fernando, but the locals called it by the French name, "Florissant." The French had declared the area "Un vale Fluerissant" or "Valley of the Flowers."

1916 Ten people died, including seven firemen, in a fire at the Christian Brothers College at Kingshighway and Easton (now Dr. King). The other casualties were two of the brothers and the school watchman. The city bought the site of the college and turned it into Sherman Park.

1926 In the first World Series game ever played in St. Louis, the Cardinals won game three of the 1926 series, 4-0. Jesse "Pop" Haines held the Yankees to just five hits, and added a home run of his own. The first two games had been played at Yankee Stadium.

1942 The Cardinals won game five, and took the 1942 World Series from the Yankees, four games to one. The Redbirds of

1942 were 13 games out of first in August, but tied the Dodgers, and beat them in a playoff to make it to the series.

1953 Carl Austin Hall spent the night at the Coral Courts Motel in the company of Sandra O' Day, described by police as "a woman of easy virtue." The next day, Hall was arrested for the kidnapping and murder of Bobby Greenlease. Half of the $600,000 ransom was never found, prompting rumors that the money was stashed in the walls at the Coral Courts. No money was found when the Coral Courts were demolished.

October 6

1918 As a deadly flu epidemic swept across the country, the city health commissioner asked Mayor Kiel to close all schools, churches, theaters and saloons in an attempt to halt the spread of the disease. The flu arrived here anyway, and killed at least 1,700 people. The toll was lower in St. Louis than in many cities, because City Health Commissioner Max Starkloff convinced the mayor to issue the order.

1951 The Browns announced that Dizzy Dean was returning to St. Louis—as a broadcaster. He signed a deal with Falstaff to do the Browns radio broadcasts. His colorful mangling of the English language on-air would rankle St. Louis grammar teachers, who tried to have him fired.

1953 Lieutenant Louis Shoulders and officer Elmer Dolan arrested Carl Austin Hall and Bonnie Heady for the kidnapping of Bobby Greenlease. Half of the $600,000 ransom was recovered from Hall's apartment on Arsenal. Shoulders and Dolan claimed they brought the two suitcases containing the money to the station. Witnesses said they didn't see the officers bring the money in, but the suitcases were at the station later that night. The other half of the ransom was never found.

1967 Mayor Cervantes was in Washington, D.C., testifying before the National Advisory Commission on Civil Disorders. President Johnson created the commission, to find the causes of the rioting that had swept the major cities of the country—but not St. Louis. The mayor credited the calm here to his administration's recognition of the problems of the poor and to good Negro leadership.

1991 The Missouri Department of Natural Resources dedicated the Scott Joplin State Historic Site in St. Louis. Joplin and his bride, Belle Haden, lived in the home at 2658-A Morgan (now Delmar) in 1902. Eight of Joplin's best known compositions, including "The Entertainer" were published that year.

October 7

1794 The town of Bridgeton was laid out as "Villa a Robert" by the Spanish commander, Francois Dunegant of San Fernando

(Florissant). The French had known the settlement already in place as "Marais des Liard." The name means "cottonwood swamp" (or perhaps, "under the runway").

1878 Tony Faust's Restaurant became the first building in St. Louis to be lit by electricity. The machinery was purchased in Paris, where it was reported many buildings—and even some streets, were lit by electricity.

1905 The first major automobile factory in St. Louis opened. Officers of the Dorris Motor Car Company leased a plant at 1219 North Vandeventer. The plant later moved to 4100 Laclede. They expected to begin production within a month. At one time, St. Louis was the second-largest producer of automobiles in the nation.

1909 Glenn Curtis made the first airplane flight in St. Louis. The first flight lasted only a few seconds. But huge crowds would turn out to watch his flights at Forest Park throughout the Centennial Week celebrations. The crowd on Art Hill that day also witnessed a flight by three dirigibles.

1954 The St. Louis Housing Authority announced that the first of the 20 high-rise buildings at the Captain Wendell Pruitt Homes were ready for occupancy. Executive Director John O'Toole said the buildings were "more liveable, with more individuality." Within a few years, the Pruitt-Igoe project was devastated by crime, vandalism and disrepair. Three buildings were imploded in 1972. Demolition work began on the rest of the most notorious housing project in the U.S. a year later.

October 8

1830 John Howdershell and Julius Utz were among a group of commissioners named to mark out a road "from Jump's Bridge on the Missouri Bottom on the St. Charles Road by way of Owen's Station (Bridgeton) to Barry's Tavern" (at the present day Goodfellow and Dr. King). The road was named Natural Bridge, after a stone arch over a small creek near what is now Salisbury Street.

1878 The first Veiled Prophet ball and parade was held in St. Louis. Merchant Charles Slayback dreamed up the Veiled Prophet. He saw the event as a way to drum up business during October fair week and build support for the Agricultural and Mechanical Exposition.

1910 The International Air Meet got underway at Kinloch Air Field. At the historic meet, Theodore Roosevelt became the first president to ride in an airplane. Arch Hoxsey set a cross-country record by winging it all the way from Springfield, Illinois. Alfred LeBlanc set the American speed record at 68 miles per hour.

1925 Ground was broken for the studios and transmitter for "The Voice of St. Louis" Corporation's new radio station near Geyer and Manchester. The station was tentatively assigned the call sign "KVSL." The corporation wanted "KMO." It turned out those call letters were already assigned, so an "X" was tacked on the end.

1982 The *Post-Dispatch* reported that FBI files had unlocked the secret behind the missing Greenlease ransom. The files showed that patrolman Elmer Dolan and Lieutenant Louis Shoulders admitted that they brought the money to career criminal and Ace Cab Company owner Jerry Costello. Costello sold the money to some of his mob connections, and they "laundered" the $300,000.

October 9

1909 Mayor Frederick Kriesman dedicated Fairgrounds Park to "the children of St. Louis." The area served as the site of the St. Louis fair nearly every year between 1856 and 1902. No fairs were held during the Civil War, when the site became Benton Barracks.

1928 Babe Ruth blasted three home runs in game four of the World Series at Sportsman's Park. One of the blasts cleared the right field pavilion and flew out of the park. The ball shattered the plate glass window of an auto dealership across the street. The next day, "The Babe" came to Wells Chevrolet to pose for pictures. The Yankees won game four, sweeping the Redbirds in the series.

1934 The "Gashouse Gang" Cardinals clinched the 1934 World Series with an 11-0 win over Detroit. Joe Medwick slid hard into the Tiger third baseman. When he returned to the field, angry Detroit fans pelted him with debris. The commissioner ordered him removed from the game for his own safety.

1944 The Cardinals won "The Streetcar Series," defeating the Browns, four games to two. The Brownies hit just .138 against the powerhouse pitching staff of the Cardinals, led by Mort Cooper, Max Lanier and Ted Wilkes.

1969 Harry Caray was fired as the the voice of the Cardinals. Rumors were sweeping the city that Harry was having an affair with Susan Busch, the wife of August Busch III. As a parting shot to the brewery that day, Harry hoisted a can of Schlitz for the TV cameras.

October 10

1700 A French missionary, Father Gravier, noted in his journal, "discovered the river Mirameguoua, where the very rich lead mine is situated, 12 or 13 leagues from its mouth." Today we just refer to that river as the Meramec (it's an Indian word, meaning "catfish").

1913 Adolphus Busch, who had made Anheuser-Busch the largest brewery in the world, died at his castle on the Rhine. He was buried after a 20-mile funeral procession from One Busch Place to Bellefontaine Cemetery. The entire route was lined with St. Louisans paying their respects. The mayor ordered all business halted for five minutes during the funeral. Even the streetcars stopped.

1926 The Cardinals won their first world championship, defeating the Yankees, four games to three. Grover Cleveland Alexander came out of the bullpen to fan Tony Lazzeri with the bases loaded in the late innings, saving game seven at Yankee Stadium. St. Louis erupted in a wild celebration as radios told of the final out.

1931 The Cardinals clinched the world championship, beating the Philadelphia Athletics, 4-3. "The Wild Horse of the Osage," Pepper Martin, was the hero for the Redbirds. He batted .500, ran wild on the bases, and made a spectacular catch in the final game.

1939 Mayor Bernard Dickmann wielded a silver wrecking bar, prying out a brick from a building facing the Old Cathedral. The ceremony marked the start of demolition work on the riverfront for the proposed memorial. Thirty-seven blocks were cleared. But World War II and wrangling over the elevated railroad tracks on the riverfront delayed actual construction work until 1959.

October 11

1910 Former president Theodore Roosevelt became the first president to ride in an airplane. He went aloft at the International Air Meet held at Kinloch Field. Upon landing, he described the experience with one word, "bully."

1964 The Cardinals were trailing two games to one in the World Series, and had fallen behind in game four. Ken Boyer turned the series around with one swing at bat. His grand slam off Al Downing of the Yankees, gave the Redbirds a 4-3 win, and evened the series.

1967 The Blues played their very first regular season game, tying Minnesota, 2-2, at the Arena. Arthur Godfrey, Anna Maria Alberghetti and Guy Lombardo's Royal Canadians Orchestra all took part in the pregame festivities. Larry Keenan scored the first Blues goal, at 3:22 of the first period. The Blues went all the way to the finals in their first season, but were swept by the mighty Montreal Canadiens.

1991 Red Foxx died of a heart attack while filming an episode of the TV series, "The Royal Family." Born Elroy John Sanford in St. Louis in 1922, he is best remembered for his role in TV's "Sanford and Son."

1992 President George Bush met candidates Bill Clinton and Ross Perot in the first presidential debate of the 1992 campaign. The debate was held in St. Louis at Washington University.

October 12

1861 James B. Eads launched his first ironclad warship at Carondelet. Eads had a contract from the government for seven ships like the "St. Louis," to be built in just 64 days. Because of bureaucratic entanglements, it took 100 days—still an impressive achievement. The "St. Louis" was the first ironclad in the world to engage a naval force.

1877 Ralph Clayton deeded 102 and 1/2 acres of his land to St. Louis County, newly separated from the city. The land was to be used for a new courthouse, provided that the county seat be named after Clayton.

1964 Martin Luther King made his final appearance in St. Louis. Speaking at the Jefferson Hotel, King said religious bodies must take the lead in booting out racial prejudice in their own congregations and institutions.

1967 The Cardinals clinched the 1967 world championship, defeating the Boston Red Sox, four games to three. Lou Brock led the Birds, batting .414 in the series and swiping seven bases. Bob Gibson got three of the four victories.

1972 Mercantile Trust Company announced plans for a $150 million redevelopment project downtown. The heart of the six-block project was to be a 35-story office tower. At that time, it would be the tallest building in St. Louis.

October 13

1809 St. Charles was incorporated as a village under the laws of the territory. Nathan Boone was named to make a new survey of the village. When Louis Blanchette settled on what is now Main Street, he called the village that sprang up around his post "Les Petites Cotes" or "Village of the Little Hills." The Spanish named it San Carlos. That was anglicized to St. Charles when the Americans took over.

1834 A road was planned and laid out from the Village of Carondelet to "LeMais" ferry on the Meramec River. For some reason, over the years, the name was corrupted to become Lemay Ferry.

1882 Death came to the *Post-Dispatch*. Managing Editor J.W. Cockrell killed prominent attorney Alonzo Slayback. The dispute started over an editorial critical of Slayback's partner, a candidate for Congress. Cockrell said Slayback came into his office and pulled a gun.  After the killing, a mob tried to break down the door at the *Post* Building with a battering ram. A grand jury refused to indict Cockerill.

1954 Channel Four broadcast a color television program for the first time. At that time, the station was known as KWK TV. There were only a few hundred sets in the area capable of seeing the color broadcast of the CBS "Best of Broadway" presentation of "The Man Who Came to Dinner."

1985 This is where it all started to go downhill. Cardinal outfielder Vince Coleman was run over by "The Killer Tarp" at Busch Stadium prior to the start of a playoff game. The Cardinals beat the Dodgers that night, 12-2. They would go on to the World Series, but their offense was no match for the Royals without Coleman.

October 14

1906 What is probably the first professional stock car race in St. Louis took place at the old fairgrounds (now Fairgrounds Park). The ten-mile race was won by a Packard. In the five-mile race, the great Barney Oldfield averaged nearly 60 miles per hour to take the win. Oldfield set a record in the two-mile race.

1923 In the first NFL game ever played in St. Louis, the St. Louis All-Stars lost to the Hammond, Indiana, Pros by a score of 6-0. A crowd of 719 fans saw the game at Sportsman's Park. The All-Stars lasted just one season.

1936 President Roosevelt came to St. Louis to dedicate the Soldier's Memorial downtown. A crowd of 75,000 people jammed Memorial Plaza for the ceremonies. Today, a museum inside the memorial houses a collection of military artifacts.

1985 "Go crazy folks! Go crazy!" Ozzie Smith's dramatic home run in with one out in the bottom of the ninth gave the Cardinals a 3-2 win over the Dodgers in game five of the National League playoffs. The home run off Tom Niedenfuer was just the 14th of Ozzie's career, and his first ever batting lefthanded.

1987 Jose Oquendo belted a surprise home run as the Cardinals clinched the National League pennant with a win over the Giants. It was only the third home run of his career for the "Secret Weapon." The Cardinals won game seven, 6-0.

October 15

1852 The seventh and final debate between Abraham Lincoln and Stephen Douglas was held in Alton. The Republican Lincoln and Democratic Douglas were battling for a seat in the U.S. Senate. Douglas would win this election.

1899 Twenty-two-year old Miss Frankie Baker, a regular in the Tenderloin District of St. Louis, was arrested for the murder of 17-year old Albert Britt. A song called "Frankie and Albert" was written about the murder. It was eventually changed to "Frankie and Johnny." When a movie was made based on the song, Baker sued. She lost, as the court ruled it was considered a folk song.

1928 Today is the birthday of Highway 40. On this date, the St. Louis County Planning Association announced a new state and county road program, including a plan for a highway from Wentzville to St. Louis. Highway 40 was opened from Wentzville to Lindbergh in 1938, but residents kept it a dead end at Brentwood Boulevard until the 1950s.

1946 The Cardinals won the World Series, taking the seventh and deciding game from the Boston Red Sox. Enos "Country" Slaughter was the Redbird hero. He made a mad dash from first to home on Harry Walker's double in the eighth inning, sliding in just ahead of the throw from shortsop Johnny Pesky. Third base coach Mike Gonzalez had frantically signaled for Slaughter to hold at third.

1964 The Cardinals clinched their first world championship in 18 years, as they beat the Yankees in the seventh game at old Busch Stadium. Bob Gibson got the win for the Birds. Lou Brock home-red as the Cardinals scored three runs in the fifth inning. The next day, Cards manager Johnny Keane stunned fans when he stepped down as manager to become skipper of the Yankees. The Yanks fired Yogi Berra a few days later.

October 16

1900 Cardinal President Frank Robison ripped his team for their mediocre finish after the owners lavished $30,000 on "supposed baseball stars." He blamed a fifth place Redbird finish on "late hours, general debauchery and incessant gambling." He warned next year's salaries would be based on this year's performance.

1981 George Faheen died when a bomb ripped apart his car at the Mansion House Garage. He was the nephew of Jimmy Michaels Sr., killed by a car bomb in 1980. He was also the cousin of Jimmy Michaels Jr., accused of the revenge car bombing that maimed reputed mob enforcer Paul Leisure. Leisure associate Michael Kornhardt was charged with the Faheen bombing, but he was shot to death in July, 1982.

1985 The Cardinals clinched the 1985 National League pennant in dramatic fashion. Jack Clark homered off Tom Niedenfuer of the Dodgers in the ninth inning to give the Cardinals the win, and set up the "I-70 Series" between the Cardinals and the Kansas City Royals.

1986 A special Chuck Berry concert was held at the Fox Theatre. The show, organized by Keith Richards, was filmed for the documentary "Hail, Hail Rock and Roll." Eric Clapton, Linda Ronstadt, Julian Lennon and others joined Chuck on stage to celebrate his 60th birthday.

2000 Missouri Governor Mel Carnahan, his son Randy, and top aide Chris Sifford died when their small plane crashed in Jefferson County. Pilot Randy Carnahan reported a problem with the plane's attitude indicator minutes before the crash in foggy and wet weather. Carnahan was in the midst of a bitter campaign for the U.S. Senate with incumbent John Ashcroft. Carnahan won the election posthumously, and his wife, Jean was appointed to serve in his place.

October 17

1803 President Thomas Jefferson sent the Louisiana Purchase to Congress for approval. Critics were blasting Jefferson for the biggest land deal in history. Many said he was exceeding his authority, and the deal was unconstitutional. Lewis and Clark were already planning an expedition to explore the vast territory.

1974 Professional basketball returned to St. Louis as the "Spirits" of the ABA lost to Memphis. A crowd of 5,400 showed up at the Arena for the first game. The Spirits would only last two seasons before the ABA merged with the NBA. But the team included memorable characters such as Marvin Barnes and Fly Williams. The team's rookie announcer on KMOX was a fellow by the name of Bob Costas.

1980 Former Big Red kicker Steve Little was left paralyzed from the shoulders down when he lost control of his sports car and hit a sign on I-270. Just a few hours earlier, Little learned he was being cut from the team.

1996 Donovan Osborne was rocked and the Cardinals were pounded by the Atlanta Braves, 15-0, in the seventh game of the National League playoffs. The game was the last one for Ozzie Smith. In his final at bat, "The Wizard" pinch hit for Andy Benes in the sixth inning. He fouled out to Jermaine Dye on the first pitch, but received a standing ovation from the Atlanta crowd.

2000 Vice President Al Gore and Texas Governor George W. Bush met in the final presidential debate of the 2000 campaign at Washington University. Before the debate, the candidates observed a moment of silence in memory of Missouri Governor Mel Carnahan. They then traded barbs on health care, taxes and government spending.

October 18

1847 Boatmen's Bank opened for business. George K. Budd, who had served as the city's first school superintendent and comptroller, founded Boatmen's. He conceived the idea of a bank for individuals and small depositors. At the time, banks were for the wealthy. Boatmen's merged with NationsBank in January, 1997. Bank of America swallowed up NationsBank in 1998.

1926 Rock and Roll legend Chuck Berry was born in St. Louis. His family lived on Goode Street, which is one reason why Chuck's autobiographical song is called "Johnny B. Goode." Goode Street is now known as Annie Malone Drive. Berry worked at the Fisher Body Plant and trained as a hairdresser at the Poro Beauty School before scoring his first hit with "Maybelline" in 1955. In 1986, Berry was among the first performers to be inducted into the Rock and Roll Hall of Fame.

1958 The Missouri Highway Department approved the controversial route for the proposed I-44. The plan called for a 14-mile route between the Third Street Expressway and US 66 at Sylvan Beach on the Meramec River in St. Louis County. The proposed route would run parallel to Lafayette, then follow the Frisco tracks through Shrewsbury and Webster Groves.

1958 KMOX became the first station to broadcast complete baseball games from outside of the continental United States. Joe Garagiola was behind the mike for broadcasts of Cardinal games during a goodwill tour of Japan.

1972 Mayor Cervantes abandoned his plan to turn the River des Peres into a "green belt." Residents derided the $14 million plan as the "River des Peres Yacht Club." Cervantes envisioned inflatable dams at Lansdowne and Morganford to provide an area for boating and a marina.

October 19

1907 The Grant's Cabin Association announced that August A. Busch had agreed to place Grant's Cabin in a park he had created on the farm. The cabin was currently residing in Forest Park. It had been moved there from its original site on the Dent estate as an exhibit for the world's fair.

1955 *The Globe-Democrat* reported on the new Military Personnel Records Center on Page. Colonel David Arp, the commander of the center, said the building was constructed in such a way that water used to fight any fire would not soak the vital records. A 1973 general alarm fire at the Records Center would destroy thousands of records.

1964 The National Park Service rejected the latest section added to the Arch, because of wrinkles on the skin. Construction was halted for a month while the problem was solved. Engineers agreed to pour reinforcing concrete higher up than first planned.

1983 The Sverdrup Corporation announced plans for a 370-acre retail, office and industrial center south of Interstate I-70 east of the Missouri River. The plans called for the total investment at "Riverport" to approach $500 million within ten years.

1990 The motion picture "White Palace" opened nationally. James Spader plays a widowed 27-year old yuppie. He falls for a 43-year old waitress at a St. Louis hamburger joint, played by Susan Sarandon. The film features many St. Louis locations, including the "White Palace" at 18th and Olive, Dogtown, Duff's Restaurant, the Hi-Pointe Cinema and the Arch grounds. It also featured Jason Alexander, Cathy Bates and Eileen Brennan.

October 20

1897 *The Globe-Democrat* reported that St. Louis would soon have its first horseless vehicles. Steel magnate Harry Scullin had ordered an electric "runabout buggy." Doctor E.V. Dittllinger had become the first American to order a gasoline powered vehicle for private use. It was made in Germany at a cost of $1,200 and could do 12 miles an hour.

1962 St. Louis was preparing for a visit from President John Kennedy. Just three hours before the scheduled appearance at Westroads Shopping Center, word came that Kennedy couldn't make it because he had a respiratory infection. No one was told the real reason. Kennedy was rushing back to Washington to face the news that Soviet missile sites had been discovered in Cuba.

1964 Red Schoendienst was named manager of the Cardinals. He replaced Johnny Keane, who had quit three days earlier to take the job as manager of the Yankees. Keane was sacked early in 1966, after the Yankees finished last in 1965. He died about a year later.

1982 Bruce Sutter blew a third strike past Gorman Thomas of the Milwaukee Brewers, and the Cardinals were the champions of the world. The final score in game seven was 6-3. Darrell Porter and Bruce Sutter were the heroes as the Redbirds won their first world championship since 1967.

1982 The Environmental Protection Agency released a list of 15 sites that could be contaminated with dioxin. The list included "various streets in Times Beach." The EPA had been investigating mysterious animal deaths in Jefferson County since 1974. The investigation found a possible link with the chemical, found in waste oil sprayed by Russell Bliss to keep dust down in the 1970s.

October 21

1785 Henry Miller Shreve was born in New Jersey. In 1827, he left his St. Louis steamboat business. He invented, the "snag boat" that helped clear the Mississippi of submerged logs that wrecked steamboats. He helped clear the Red River, making it navigable to the city that bears his name—Shreveport, Louisiana.

1839 The cornerstone was laid for the new courthouse downtown. The building we now know as the "Old Courthouse" included this original structure in one of its four wings. The entire structure was not finished until 1862. The first two trials in the Dred Scott case were held there. The last public auction of slaves in St. Louis took place on the courthouse steps on January 1, 1861.

1955 Elvis Presley made his first concert appearance in St. Louis. At the time, he had yet to have a national hit, so he was relegated to opening act status for Roy Acuff at the Missouri Theatre.

1972 Chuck Berry scored the only number one hit of his amazing career. Berry had originally released the song as "My Tambourine" in 1958. But it was a live version of the childish wee-wee joke ditty re-named "My-Ding-A-Ling" that mortified rock and roll purists when it became Berry's first chart topper.

1994 Frank Sinatra made his final concert appearance in St. Louis. A crowd of 15,000 people saw the concert at the new Kiel Center.

October 22

1876 This may be one of the most important dates in St. Louis history. In what seemed like a good move at the time, St. Louis City and County were officially separated. The city boundaries were fixed permanently. The "Great Divorce" is now blamed for many of the city's problems, as the population spread far beyond the city limits. In 1876, city residents were tired of paying for services in rural St. Louis County.

1877 Commissioners appointed by the County Court reported their choice for a site for the courthouse of St. Louis County, separated from the city the year before. The commissioners chose a 100-acre tract donated by Ralph Clayton, to be joined with four acres donated by Martin Hanley. The choice was subject to approval by the voters.

1970 A former Washington University student became the first person in the nation to be convicted under the 1968 Civil Disobedience Act. Howard Mechanic was convicted for tossing a cherry bomb during the burning of the ROTC building in May 1970. He got five years, but spent 30 years on the run living under an assumed name. In February, 2000, his past caught up with him when he ran for city council in Arizona.

1981 The Cardinals traded relief pitcher Bob Sykes to the Yankees for a 23-year old minor league prospect. The deal that brought Willie McGee to St. Louis didn't get much attention at the time.

1985 The Cardinals were heavy favorites as the "I-70" World

Series opened in Kansas City. John Tudor got the win and Todd Worell notched the save, as the Cardinals took game one, 3-1. The Cards would jump out to a 3-1 lead in the series, before things took an ugly turn.

October 23

1826 The army officially changed the name of its post south of St. Louis from Camp Adams to Jefferson Barracks. Jefferson Barracks was established as a military post to replace Fort Bellefontaine, on the Missouri River north of St. Louis. Many of the greatest names in military history, including five presidents, spent part of their service at Jefferson Barracks before it closed in 1946.

1941 A group called the "Campaigners of Americanism" filed a petition to change the name of Lindbergh Boulevard back to the original Denny Road. The group said Lindbergh's name had become "repugnant" to many St. Louisans because of his isolationist activities.

1980 Four employees of Pope's Cafeteria in Des Peres were found murdered at the restaurant. Three more were critically wounded. Maurice Byrd was convicted of killing James Wood, Carolyn Turner, Edna Ince and Judy Cazaco. Byrd was executed in August, 1991.

1992 Gunmen robbed a Brinks Armored Car guard of about $900,000 in the basement at the United Missouri Bank in the Equitable Building. The largest cash armed robbery in city history remains unsolved.

1995 The Cardinals announced that Tony LaRussa would take over as manager. In his first NL season, LaRussa would guide the Cardinals to the 1996 Central Division title. LaRussa would be named Major League Manager of the Year.

October 24

1905 The *Globe-Democrat* reported that the Ferris wheel was the only remnant of the 1904 World's Fair awaiting demolition. The Chicago Company that had the contract to remove the buildings from Forest Park offered to give the wheel to anyone who would remove it. They got no takers, and eventually used dynamite to bring it down.

1947 Actor Kevin Kline was born in St. Louis. A 1965 graduate of St. Louis Priory School, Kline won a best supporting actor Oscar for "A Fish Called Wanda" in 1989. He is also known for his roles in "The Big Chill," "Dave," and "The Ice Storm."

1949 One-hundred-twenty-eight tax payers signed a petition proposing the incorporation of the village of Town and Country.

The boundaries of the proposed village were Bopp Road on the east, the Daniel Boone Parkway or the south, Des Peres Road on the west and Spring Drive on the north.

1960 Stan Musial was named as "Comeback Player of the Year." He was hitting .235 in June, and many thought his career was over. Over the last three months of the season, Stan hit .292, and finished with a .275 average.

1962 As the Cuban Missile Crisis escalated, federal agencies in St. Louis received instructions to renew their plans for evacuating the city in the event of a nuclear attack. The local civil defense office reported it was receiving 60 to 70 calls a day about what to do if the bombs fell.

October 25

1987 The Cardinals injury-riddled offense was no match for the Minnesota Twins. The Cards dropped game seven of the 1987 World Series in the MetroDome. The final was 4-2. In the series, the Cardinals won every game played at Busch, but the Twins won the games in the dome.

1993 Actor Vincent Price died at the age of 82. Price was born in St. Louis on December 27, 1911. A graduate of St. Louis Country Day School, he was famous for his sinister portray- al of villains in many classic horror films, and his "rap" on Michael Jackson's "Thriller."

1995 St. Louis was in shock, after Anheuser Busch announced it was selling the St. Louis Cardinals. The brewery had bought the team back in 1953. In December, a group of investors led by Country Day friends and classmates, William DeWitt, Andrew Bauer and Frederick Hanser bought the Birds for $150 million.

1997 One of St. Louis' most off-beat attractions opened its doors. The City Museum was the brainchild of Gail and Bob Cassilly, who brought an eclectic mix of hands-on exhibits and art work for the young and old to the former International Shoe Warehouse Building at 15th and Lucas.

1999 As a group of protesters looked on, the first home was demolished to make room for the controversial WIW plan to expand Lambert Field. The plan called for the demolition of 2,000 homes and businesses in Bridgeton.

October 26

1834 The "new" St. Louis cathedral was consecrated. Today, we know that building as the "old" cathedral. The night before, someone jammed some cannons that were to have been used in the ceremony. Some enraged Frenchmen thought it was the work of the Presbyterians. They wanted to turn the cannons on the Presbyterian Church, but cooler heads prevailed.

1925 Almost the entire town of Fenton and a big crowd from St. Louis County turned out for the dedication of a new highway bridge over the Meramec. The bottle of pre-prohibition champagne put aside for the christening turned up missing before the ceremony.

1985 One of the darkest days in Cardinal history. The Redbirds took a 1-0 lead over the Kansas City Royals into the bottom of the ninth in game six of the "I-70" Series. Umpire Don Denkinger called Jorge Orta safe at first on a grounder, though TV replays showed Orta was out. A passed ball and a dropped pop up allowed pinch hitter Dane Iorg to drive home the winning run. Denkinger deserves his share of the blame, but the Cardinals did bat a measly .185 during the series.

1986 The familiar green and white planes of Ozark Airlines began disappearing, as TWA acquired the airline for $224 million. Carl Icahn's TWA now controlled 75% of the gates at Lambert Field.

1993 Hopes for an NFL franchise in St. Louis appeared to be fading. The NFL awarded an expansion franchise to Charlotte, and announced it would hold off on announcing a second one until November. The day before, Jerry Clinton had stepped down as head of the partnership trying to bring a team here. Columbia businessman Stan Kroenke had stepped forward to head up a new group. But on November 30th, the second franchise was awarded to Jacksonville.

October 27

1842 As the plaque in the lobby at One Memorial Drive attests, "Abraham Lincoln slept here." Abe and his family spent the night in St. Louis on their way to Washington, D.C., where Lincoln was to be sworn in as a Congressman. At that time, Scott's Hotel stood on the site at Third and Market.

1914 Barnes Hospital was dedicated. The will of businessman Robert Barnes left $100,000 for construction and a $900,000 endowment for the hospital when he died in April, 1892. Trustees postponed construction and invested the money until there were enough funds to build one of the most modern hospitals in the world.

1965 The legs of the Arch were jacked apart in preparation for the fitting of the final section the following day. Ironworkers were back on the job. The union ended a work stoppage after receiving assurances from the National Park Service and Pittsburgh-Des Moine that the site was safe.

1965 Mayor Alfonso Cervantes signed an agreement accepting the Spanish Pavilion from the New York World's Fair. He moved it to St. Louis for a cultural center. But the foundation that raised the money went bankrupt. "Cervante's Folly" sat vacant until developer Donald Breckenridge bought it. Today, the pavilion is the lobby of the downtown Marriott.

1985 Joaquin Andujar blew his stack, and the Royals humiliated the Cardinals in game seven of the "I-70" World Series. The seventh game was set up by Don Denkinger's bungled call and several Cardinal miscues in game six.

October 28

1922 WCK, The "Grand-Leader" radio station, broadcast the first radio sports in St. Louis. Listeners heard bulletins on the football game between St. Louis University and the University of Missouri. Mizzou won, 9-0.

1928 The Banner Buggy Company of St. Louis, once the leading manufacturer of of horse-drawn carriages in the nation, went out of business. The company was a casualty of the automotive age. Orders had fallen from 100,000 in 1908 to just 50 in 1928.

1965 A landmark day in St. Louis history, as the Gateway Arch was completed. The heat caused the south leg to sag a bit, threatening the placement of the final section. But the fire department called in three pumpers to spray water to cool the steel down. As thousands watched, the 142nd and final piece was lifted into place. The Arch revitalized the downtown area. It has become a symbol of the city, known throughout the world.

1968 Bob Gibson of the Cardinals was named the National League Cy Young Award winner for 1968. The unanimous choice for the top pitcher's award had won 22 games and set an ERA mark of 1.12.

1971 James LeRoy Cochran surrendered to the FBI in Kentucky, ending a massive six-day manhunt. He abducted eight people in ten states, after shooting it out with police during a bank robbery here. He fled through Northwest High School, holding 14 students at gunpoint and threatening to kill the football coach. He also abducted a Jefferson County family.

October 29

1864 Six Confederate prisoners held at the Gratiot Street prison were executed near Lafayette Square. The executions were in retaliation for the murder of Union Major James Wilkinson and six of his men by Confederate guerillas. A crowd of 3,000 watched the executions.

1869 Joseph Folk was born in Brownsville, Tennessee. As St. Louis Circuit Attorney, he exposed the corrupt alliance between government and big business that led to the sensational "boodle" trials. The investigation won national attention, and got Folk elected as the youngest governor in Missouri history in 1904. St. Louis never forgave him for going after the city's most prominent citizens, and always voted against Folk.

1929 The stock market collapsed, falling 11.6% after a 13% drop the day before. Unemployment in St. Louis would hit 9.8% by the end of the year. By 1931, the rate was 24%. It peaked at 30% in 1933, when 100,000 people here were out of work.

1977 The first issue of the *Riverfront Times* was published. The alternative news weekly didn't emerge as a serious journalistic force until about 1980. It has remained an important voice in the community, especially since the demise of the *Globe-Democrat*. Then there's the other side of the coin — the racy personals and phone-sex line ads.

1986 St. Louis became a one-newspaper town, as the financially troubled *Globe-Democrat* published its final issue. The *Globe*'s fate was sealed when a court refused to hear a friendly suit that would have cleared the way for bonds to be issued to keep the paper going.

October 30

1877 Irma Rombauer was born. The St. Louis widow risked her own money to publish "The Joy of Cooking" in 1931. The book became the most successful cookbook in American History.

1900 The entire University of Missouri football team resigned, "rather than disgrace the university by continual failure." Players were upset over a restriction that only full time students with an average of 75 or higher were eligible to play football.

1946 Vincent C. Schoemehl, Jr. was born. Only 34 years old when elected, he was the youngest mayor in St. Louis history. He served as mayor from 1981 until 1993 making him one of only three mayors to hold the office for three terms. Known for his "Ready, Fire, Aim" approach, he was the object of both praise and controvesy. After a failed campaign for the Democratic gubernatorial nomination, he decided not to seek a fourth mayoral term.

1990 Plans were unveiled for an $85 million sports arena to be built on the site of Kiel Auditorium. Some of the top business leaders in the area formed a partnership to develop the 18,000 seat facility.

2001 The Illinois Department of Transportation closed the 90-year old McKinley Bridge, declaring it unsafe to carry traffic. St. Louis now has fewer lanes crossing the Mississippi than it did when the Poplar Street Bridge opened in 1967.

October 31

1904 St. Louisan Ray Knabenshue made what is believed to have been the first controlled directional flight. He attached a small motor to his balloon and rose above a crowd of thousands in Forest Park. Knabenshue took 37 minutes to cover the seven-mile course.

1921 William Egan, a powerful figure in Democratic city politics, was shot to death as he stood in the doorway of a saloon on 14th Street. His dying words were "I don't know who shot me, and I wouldn't say if I did. I'm a good sport." Within days, "Egan's Rats" and the Hogan Gang was involved in a bloody war for control of the St. Louis underworld. At least 30 hoods would die over two years.

1926 The great Harry Houdini died at the age of 52. In St. Louis, he is best remembered for a 1922 stunt. He escaped from the best straitjacket in the homicide department's wardrobe—while suspended from the 5th floor of city hall.

1978 The last train pulled out of Union Station, once one of the busiest in the world. Amtrak's Number 22, bound for Chicago, ended 84 years of service to the grand old station. Amtrak moved operations to the forlorn "Amshak" east of the station. Union Station deteriorated, a haven for the homeless, until redeveloped in 1985. Today, it is the second biggest tourist attraction in the area.

1999 A St. Louis landmark closed its doors forever. The Parkmoor Restaurant at Clayton Road and Big Bend opened in 1930. It was the first restaurant in the area to offer curb service. At one time, there were five Parkmoor locations.

November 1

1855 Disaster struck as Missourians celebrated the completion of the Pacific Railroad to Jefferson City. A special inaugural train carrying dignitaries plunged into the Gasconade River as a bridge gave way. Thirty-four people died and 100 were injured. The mayor of St. Louis was seriously hurt and the president of the City Council was killed.

1892 The Lemp family brewery was incorporated as the William J. Lemp Brewing Company. Adam Lemp had brewed the first Lager beer in St. Louis in 1842. By the turn of the century, Lemp was producing 500,000 barrels per year, and employed 1,000 people. Its flagship brand was Falstaff, intro- duced in 1903. The Lemps are best remembered for the four suicides in the family, three of which occurred in the mansion at 3322 DeMenil.

1915 In Webster Groves, the cornerstone was laid for one of the first women's Catholic colleges west of Mississippi. Loretto College was staffed by eight sisters of Loretto and attended by five students. The name was changed to Webster College in 1924 and to Webster University in 1983.

1930 The Octagon Building in University City was dedicated as city hall by Governor Henry Caulfield. The 250-million candlepower searchlight on top of the building was re-lit. The founder of University City, Edward Garner Lewis, built the landmark to be the headquarters of his publishing empire.

1965 City police said Gaslight Square was one of the safest areas in St. Louis. Business owners were complaining that publicity over crime was hurting their business. They blamed crowds of teenagers jamming the sidewalks in front of the "Whiskey-a-Go-Go."

November 2

1734 Daniel Boone was born in Buck's County, Pennsylvania. He came to Missouri in 1799. The Spanish governor granted him 1,000 arpents of land for bringing 50 families to what is now St. Charles County. Boone died in 1820 at his son's home, and left specific orders that he was to be buried at Dutzow. But 25 years later, Frankfort, Kentucky, led a successful effort to have the remains moved there.

1829 Bishop Rosati revived a failed college that Bishop DuBourg had first opened in 1818. It had been closed since 1827. Rosati brought Jesuits from the seminary at Florissant to teach at the school, which was chartered as St. Louis University in 1832.

1948 Missouri's Harry S Truman upset Thomas Dewey in the presidential election. He had been trailing in the polls and in the early returns, prompting the *Chicago Tribune* to run the headline "DEWEY DEFEATS TRUMAN." The famous photo of Truman holding the paper was taken as his train pulled into Union Station here the next morning.

1971 Amid protests both pro and con, the musical "Hair" opened at the American Theatre. The Board of Aldermen had passed an anti-obscenity ordinance aimed at stopping the show. But a court order prevented the city from using it. Plainclothes policemen were on hand anyway, to make sure the show didn't violate the ordinance. There were no arrests.

1978 Cornell Haynes Jr. was born in Texas. His father was in the Air Force, so the family moved quite a bit, ending up in St. Louis. Haynes moved with his mother to University City when he was in his teens, and formed a group called "The St. Lunatics." As "Nelly," he scored a huge hit with his 2000 CD, "Country Grammar."

November 3

1762 Under the Secret Treaty of Fountainbleau, France ceded the territory of Louisiana to Spain, in return for Spain's agreement to British Peace terms. The news did not make it to St. Louis until September, 1764. Wary of the reaction from locals, the Spanish didn't take over until March, 1766.

1870 A huge crowd cheered as a caisson was launched to be sunk on the East St. Louis side of the Mississippi. It would mark the start of work on the east pier of the Eads Bridge. James B. Eads told the crowd the caisson would probably rest at the bottom of the river for all time.

1926 St. Louis-to-Chicago airmail pilot Charles "Lucky" Lindbergh survived his fourth parachute jump. He bailed out when his plane ran out of gas over Bloomington, Illinois, and landed atop a barbed wire fence. After searching for several hours, he managed to find the mail.

1967 Camille Henry became the first Blues player to ever score a "Hat Trick," or three goals in a game. The first Blues hat trick came against the Red Wings in Detroit.

1968 Harry Caray, radio voice of the Cardinals, was hit by a car as he crossed a rain slickened street here. He broke his shoulder, fractured both legs, and suffered cuts and bruises. The driver got a ticket for not having a license. Harry got one for crossing the street in the middle of the block.

November 4

1901 Adolphus Busch, chairman of the World's Fair Committee on Foreign Relations, returned from a six-month tour of Europe. He declared the fair would have to be postponed for a year past the planned April, 1903, opening day to give nations more time to prepare their exhibits. David R. Francis, president of the fair, insisted that it would open on time.

1907 The School Board unveiled plans for a $750,000 high school on Union between Kensington and Fairmount. The building would hold 1,600 students, making it the third largest high school in the nation. The new school would be named for pioneering St. Louis School Superintendent Louis Soldan.

1962 Mayor Tucker appointed a citizen's committee to design a new city flag in time for the 1964 bicentennial. The city would choose a design by Professor Emeritus Theodore Sizer, Pursuivant of Arms at Yale University. The design called for a red field, with blue wavy lines outlined in white, representing the rivers. The intersection of the rivers is covered by a blue fleur-de-lis in a gold circle, representing the founding of the city by the French.

1979 Militant Iranian students seized the U.S. embassy in Tehran. They took 52 American hostages, including Marine Sergeant Rocky Sickmann of Krakow, Missouri. The hostages were released on January 20, 1981. Sickmann now works as a training specialist for Anheuser-Busch.

2002 Blues great Bernie Federko was introduced into the NHL Hall of Fame. Federko played for the Blues for 13 seasons. He racked up 1,130 points in 1,000 NHL games.

November 5

1904 The *Globe* reported that the tribe of pygmies living in the International Village at the fair wanted to buy an airship. After seeing one at the fair, they were convinced an airship would make them great elephant hunters. They asked the official in charge of the village to negotiate for them, promising him the first three elephant tusks they would bag from the air.

1955 The St. Louis Hawks made their NBA regular season debut. The Hawks defeated the Minneapolis Lakers 101-89 before a crowd of over 7,000. Frank Selvy and Bob Petit scored 21 points each.

1971 Former Cardinal third baseman and outfielder Mike Shannon was named as Jack Buck's partner on the Redbird broadcasts. Shannon's playing career had ended in 1970, when he learned he suffered from a kidney ailment during spring training.

1971 Federal highway officials were stunned by an offer from residents of "The Hill" neighborhood in South St. Louis. The citizens were offering to pay for an overpass across the new I-44 to keep their community from being cut in two. They had raised $50,000 during the Hill Day festivities (they eventually got the overpass).

1981 Federal authorities said that over $36 million in securities were missing from the Stix and Company Brokerage firm. The firm was declared to be insolvent. Vice President Thomas Brimberry quickly emerged as the central figure in the investigation.

November 6

1860 Abraham Lincoln was elected president. The Illinois lawyer failed to win a majority of the popular vote. But he carried 18 states, with 180 of 303 electoral votes. Stephen Douglas carried Missouri. Lincoln carried only St. Louis and Gasconade Counties.

1925 The new $1.35 million Union Market on Broadway was dedicated. It was the first project completed under the $87 million 1922 bond issue. Because of the bond issue, downtown St. Louis was undergoing a facelift like never before. The biggest project was the levelling of the tawdry saloons and brothels along Market Street to widen the street and create Memorial Plaza.

1951 The heaviest snowfall here since 1912 dumped a foot of the white stuff on the city. Traffic was paralyzed, schools and industry were shut down. The storm still stands as the largest November snowfall in city history.

1971 A five-alarm fire destroyed the Riviera Club at 4460 Delmar. Performers such as Ella Fitzgerald, Nat King Cole and Duke Ellington had played there. At the time, it was home to the powerful Democratic organization headed by Jordan Chambers. Chambers was known as "The Negro Mayor of St. Louis."

1989 Sixteen-year old Tina Isa was stabbed to death by her father while her mother held her arms at their South St. Louis apartment. An FBI surveillance tape captured her screams and her father saying "die my daughter, die." The Isas were Palestinian immigrants, under surveillance for alleged terrorist activities. The parents were upset that their daughter had been seeing a black boy and embracing American ways. The Isas were sentenced to death.

November 7

1805 The Lewis and Clark Expedition sighted the Pacific, at the mouth of the Columbia River in present-day Oregon. William Clark wrote in his journal "Ocian in view! O! the joy!" They had journeyed over 4,000 miles in 18 months, exploring and mapping the unknown Louisiana Territory.

1837 Elijah P. Lovejoy, publisher of the "Observer," was killed by a mob in Alton. He had been forced to move his paper there after mobs in St. Louis, angered by his anti-  slavery stance, threatened him and destroyed his presses. Lovejoy became a martyr for abolitionists, and is remembered today as a defender of freedom of the press.

1951 Richard M. Nixon was in St. Louis. The Republican Senator from California decried the lack of high morals in government today, saying restoring them was the biggest task in U.S. history. Nixon said "We have had corruption before in our history, but never have we seen such corruption defended and endorsed by those in high places."

1968 An unbelievable night for Red Berenson of the Blues. Red scored six goals in one game against the Flyers at the Spectrum in Philadelphia. It still stands as the greatest single-game performance ever by a Blues player.

2000 It was an emotional election night in St. Louis. Missouri voters chose the late Governor Mel Carnahan over incumbent John Ashcroft in the Senate race. Carnahan's wife, Jean, would be appointed to serve in his place. A judge ordered the polls to stay open late in St. Louis, ruling that long lines were denying some people the right to vote. The Republicans went to court to get the polls closed, saying the whole thing was a Democratic plot.

November 8

1861 President Abraham Lincoln removed John C. Fremont as Commander of the Department of the West, headquartered in St. Louis. Fremont put St. Louis under martial law and freed the slaves of Missouri without consulting the president. Fearful of angering the border states, Lincoln had the order rescinded.

1868 *The Missouri Democrat* reported that the landmark which gave St. Louis the nickname "Mound City" was being destroyed. The Big Mound had been bounded by Broadway, Second, Mound and Brooklyn Streets. Its owners used it as fill for a railroad bed, destroying an untold number of Indian artifacts. Today, a plaque marks the site.

1932 St. Louis breweries were getting their plants in shape to produce "real" beer and hotels and restaurants were advertising for waiters with experience in serving alcohol. Franklin Roosevelt was expected to win the election that day. He was expected to repeal prohibition soon after he was inaugurated.

1934 NHL hockey came to St. Louis, as the St. Louis Eagles opened the season with a 3-1 loss to the Chicago Blackhawks.

The Eagles only lasted one season. But the Flyers of the AHL did very well, until the demise of the league in 1958. The Flyers often drew bigger crowds than the baseball Browns.

1945 The first post-war automobiles to reach St. Louis were awarded to 13 veterans in a ceremony at Forest Park. The Ford dealers of St. Louis, East St. Louis and St. Louis County presented the cars. The U.S. Employment Service predicted that there would be 55,000 jobless in St. Louis by 1946. There were just 2,000 in May. The increase was blamed on the end of war plant work and returning servicemen.

November 9

1809 St. Louis was incorporated as a town by the Court of Common Pleas of the Indiana Territory. The petition had been filed by 80 of the 101 taxable inhabitants on July 5, 1808. By 1809, the population was estimated at 1,000. When the Missouri Territory was organized in 1812, St. Louis was made the capitol.

1935 The greatest Cardinal pitcher of all-time was born. Bob Gibson became a basketball star at Creighton, and even played for the Harlem Globetrotters before the Cardinals brought him up in 1959. His greatest season came in 1968, when he won 22 games and set a record low earned run average of 1.12.

1967 After seven years of planning and construction, the Poplar Street Bridge opened with little fanfare. The barricades were removed at 12 noon. Traffic was very light on the first day, but officials said that would change once motorists became accustomed to the maze of on and off ramps. The bridge carried U.S. 66 from 1967 to 1977.

1968 St. Louis was shaken by a 5.5 earthquake. Damage was minimal, and only one person was seriously hurt. A guide told shaken tourists that the Arch "sways all the time" in order to avoid panic at the top. The quake was centered 120 miles southwest of St. Louis and was felt in 23 states.

1998 A nationwide manhunt was launched for the man police believed was the "Southside Rapist." Jefferson County authorities said Dennis Rabbitt was responsible for two attacks. A few days later, St. Louis Police charged him with 11 rapes. He would eventually be sentenced to 16 life sentences for attacks on 14 women over nearly a decade.

November 10

1907 Jane Froman was born in University City. One of the top female singers of her day, she was seriously injured in a plane crash while on a USO tour in 1943. Susan Heyward starred in the Hollywood version of Froman's life, "With a Song in My Heart" in 1952.

1908 Farmers around Manchester warned that they had organized a vigilance committee to punish "automobile scorchers." They warned they would stretch chains across the Manchester Road to snag any vehicle whose driver tried to get away.

1910 The McKinley Bridge officially opened. The bridge is not named for President William McKinley. It was for Congressman William McKinley, then president of the Illinois Traction Company, later the Terminal Railroad Association. The bridge carried U.S. 66 traffic from 1926 until 1932. It closed to auto traffic in 2001.

1930 The Moon Motor Company of St. Louis closed its doors. Moon cars had been made in St. Louis since 1905. The company had hoped production of the Ruxton model would stimulate sales. But the shrewd promoter of the Ruxton gained control of the company, after the old owners barricaded themselves inside the building. The subsequent legal battle depleted the firm's treasury.

1971 Joe Torre of the Cardinals was named the National League Most Valuable Player. His .363 average, 230 hits and 137 runs batted in led the league. Torre played three more seasons for the Cardinals before he was traded to the Mets. He began his managerial career with Atlanta in 1982, returning to manage the Cards from 1990 to 1995.

1870 Disaster struck the St. Charles railroad bridge for the first time. Nineteen construction workers were killed when a lifting hoist broke. The bridge opened on May 29, 1871, the longest of its type in the US. Five people would die when a span gave way as a train crossed in November, 1879. A similar accident killed an engineer in 1881. The current structure opened in October, 1936.

1918 Factory whistles here blew at 2:30 a.m. upon the news from Europe that World War One was over. By three in the morning, the streets were filled with people celebrating. Mayor Henry Kiel declared it a public holiday. Most business had been suspended anyway, in an effort to halt the flu epidemic. One-thousand-57 St. Louisans died in World War One.

1932 The cornerstone was laid for the new Municipal Auditorium. It was dedicated in April, 1934, and later named for former Mayor Henry Kiel. His construction firm built the auditorium. The convention hall was torn down in 1992 to make room for the new Kiel Center.

1934 The St. Louis Gunners of the National Professional Football League played their first game. A crowd of 13,678 saw the Gunners defeat the Pittsburgh Pirates 6-0 at Sportsmen's Park. The NFL had disbanded the Cincinnati Reds franchise, and brought in the Gunners to play out the Reds schedule. The Gunners disbanded in May, 1935.

2001 Mark McGwire announced his retirement, in the form of a fax to ESPN. Cards management was upset that they found out on television. McGwire had batted just .187 during an injury plagued 2001 season. 2001 also saw his single-season home run record eclipsed by Barry Bonds. Big Mac's 583 career home runs ranks him fifth on the all-time list.

November 12

1928 "Ripley's Believe it or Not" says the first aerial bombing on U.S. soil took place in Southern Illinois. Members of the Shelton gang dropped bombs from an old Curtiss Jenny over the Shady Rest hideout of the Charley Birger Gang. Most of the dynamite bombs were duds, and no one was hurt.

1946 Albert Bond Lambert died at the age of 70. The aviation pioneer was the son of the man who invented Listerine. He developed a flying field near Bridgeton at his own expense, and offered it to the city at his cost. One of the financial backers of Charles Lindbergh's flight, Lambert was also the first Olympic athlete from St. Louis. He took part in both of golf's only Olympic outings, in 1900 and here in 1904.

1947 The city of Crestwood was incorporated by a county court. The residents of the Crestwood Subdivision wanted to avoid annexation by the adjacent town of Oakland. The subdivision was built in 1925, and took its name from a large oak tree at the "crest" of a hill on Diversey Drive.

1995 The Trans World Dome made its debut. A crowd of 65,598 watched as the Rams beat the Carolina Panthers 28-17. Some painting and electrical work remained to be done on the $280 million facility. Fans said the sound system needed some work too.

2001 Albert Pujols was the unanimous choice as the National League Rookie of the Year. Pujols had set a National League rookie record with 130 RBI's. He also batted .329 and slugged 37 home runs.

November 13

1921 St. Charles Rock Road was opened as a modern concrete highway from Wellston to the Highway Bridge at St. Charles. It was the first complete concrete highway in St. Louis County. The project cost $600,000. The original route of The Rock Road west of Natural Bridge ran along what is now Boenker Lane.

1934 The first penalty shot ever scored in the National Hockey League occurred in St. Louis. Ralph Bowman of the St. Louis Eagles scored on his shot against the Montreal Maroons. The

Eagles only spent one season in St. Louis. Previously, they were the Ottawa Senators, the first team to win Lord Stanley's Cup.

1968 Bob Gibson was named as the National League Most Valuable Player, capping an unprecedented sweep of the MVP and Cy Young Awards. On this date in 1979, Keith Hernandez of the Cardinals was named National League Co-MVP. He shared the award with Willie Stargell. It was the first time ever that the National League selected two MVPs.

1983 A Corvette driven by August Busch the Fourth careened off an Arizona road and overturned. Michele Frederick of Tucson was killed. Busch walked away and returned to his townhouse. Key evidence in the case was obliterated, and Busch was never charged.

1986 Calgary Flames rookie Brett Hull scored his first National Hockey League goal. Hull was the Blues top star from 1987 until 1998. He signed with the Dallas Stars in July, 1998. He joined the Detroit Red Wings in 2001.

November 14

1836 William Carr Lane announced he was building an "addition." (What we would call a "subdivision" today) He named the streets in his addition after his sons and daughters. That's why we have Sidney, Victor and Anne Streets today. Lane was the first mayor of St. Louis, and was re-elected seven times.

1870 Mayor Nathan Cole predicted a period of rapid growth for St. Louis. He said "The smoke will roll heavenward from her furnaces, mills, machine shops and factories—and shall cover like a silver sheen her hills and valleys far and near."

1922 The St. Louis Board of Education announced a new high school would be built on the site of the old Cardinal Baseball Field at Vandeventer and Natural Bridge. It would be named after a famous St. Louis physician, William Beaumont.

1936 The new Jewel Box in Forest Park opened. It's official name is the St. Louis Floral Conservatory. It proved to be so popular that electric lights were installed and the hours extended few months after the opening. William Becker, an engineer with the City's Board of Public Service, designed the deco architectural treasure. The 50-foot-tall vertical walls are made up of 15,000 square-feet of glass.

1961 Federal officials okayed the plans and location for a new free bridge across the Mississippi at Poplar Street. State highway officials were predicting it could be finished within four years. Labor problems would delay the opening of the bridge until 1967.

November 15

1827 The County Court appointed commissioners to view the route of the state road from St. Louis to St. Charles. The commissioners determined there really was none, and recommended four routes. One of the routes followed an Indian trail that would become St. Charles Rock Road.

1877 A measure was introduced in the City Council to tear down city-owned Lucas Market and make 12th Street a grand boulevard between Market and Washington (which is why the street is so wide today). Opponents denounced the plan as a disaster for merchants who owned stalls in the market.

1906 City schools were closed for the first time because of pollution. The schools were equipped only for daytime use. Officials feared they would remain closed for several days because of a dense smoke pall that covered the city.

1915 The Riverfront Docks and Plaza Association proposed an arch on the St. Louis riverfront. Their plan called for a stone arch resembling the Arc D'Triomphe in Paris, topped with a statue of St. Louis. The group also called for a plaza on Market between the riverfront and 12th Street.

1964 The football Cardinals and the New York Giants played a game that went down in history as "The Mud Bowl." A torrential rain had turned old Busch Stadium into a sea of mud, obliterating the field markings and making for spectacular tackles and miscues. It ended in a 10-10 tie.

November 16

1818 The birthday of St. Louis University. The forerunner of SLU, St. Louis Academy, was founded on this date by Bishop William DuBourg in a private home. It closed in 1827. But Bishop Rosati reorganized the school in 1829. He brought in Jesuits from Florissant to teach. In 1832, the school received its charter from the state. It was renamed St. Louis University, the oldest college west of the Mississippi.

1873 "The Father of the Blues," W.C. Handy, was born in Florence, Alabama. He came to St. Louis in 1893, trying to earn a living as a musician in the saloons and pool halls along Targee Street. Those hard times were the inspiration for his signature song, "St. Louis Blues." Today, the St. Louis Blues hockey team plays at Savvis Center, which stands on the site of Targee Street.

1887 St. Louisans were called upon to vote on ending the teaching of German in the public grade schools. The *Globe* said "the language of Goethe, Schiller and Hegel can be served up afterward at the high school level. The language of Milton, Bacon,

Scott, Byron, McCaulay and Dickens ought to be sufficient for the regular bill of fare."

1965 The strut placed between the legs of the Arch to stabilize it during construction was removed and the memorial stood on its own. Only the creeper cranes still marred the lines of the Arch. The cranes stayed up until March, 1966.

1975 Mel Gray of the Big Red made the famous "phantom catch." The referee initially ruled the pass was incomplete, but then reversed the decision. The Cardinals went on to beat the Redskins in overtime, 20-17. To this day, Washington fans insist he never made the catch.

November 17

1791 One of the most beloved men in the history of St. Louis was born in Louisville. John O'Fallon served as first president of the Bank of St. Louis, and was a great philanthropist. He donated the land for the first city waterworks, the first Methodist Church, and O'Fallon Park.

1951 The Missouri State Highway Commission approved a master plan for expressway development in St. Louis City and County. The plan called for construction of 163 miles of expressways, to be known as the Mark Twain (I-70), the Ozark, (U.S. 66, now I-44) and the Daniel Boone (U.S. 40, now I-64). Construction on the first stretch, I-70 in St. Charles, would begin in 1956.

1953 KSD-TV announced plans to bring color television to St. Louis by the first of the year. General Manager George Burbach said the station hoped to broadcast the Rose Parade in color. He admitted that there were probably only about a half-dozen color sets in St. Louis.

1955 Representatives from 2/3 of the 96 municipalities in St. Louis County met to urge adoption of a uniform 30 miles per hour speed limit. They called the current hodge-podge of speed limits "chaotic." They cited the example of Natural Bridge, where the speed limits ranged from 20 to 45 miles per hour.

1965 St. Louisans heard their first airborne radio traffic report. Police Captain Don Miller reported from the KSD traffic copter. Robert Hyland soon wooed Miller over to KMOX.

November 18

1852 Today is the feast day of St. Rose Phillipine Duchesne. Mother Duchesne died at the convent she founded at St. Charles on this date in 1852. She came here with four other nuns in 1818 to establish a seminary and school for girls, the first in the United States founded by the Society of the Sacred Heart. The brick convent school building, erected in 1835, still stands today. Mother

Duchesne became one of the pioneer educators in the Western U.S. She was canonized in 1988.

1949 Vice President Alben Barkley married a St. Louis widow, the former Mrs. Carlton Hadley, at St. John's Methodist Church. The vice president's many trips to St. Louis had made headlines before the engagement was announced in October.

1953 Four St. Louisans had the dubious distinction of being the first speeders here to be nabbed by radar. The radar unit weighed 40 pounds and was packed in the trunk of a  police car on the side of the road. The drivers pleaded guilty to exceeding the 40 mile per hour limit on the Express Highway (U.S. 40) and paid a total of $150 in fines.

1971 The church bells rang out at St. Ambrose on "The Hill" in celebration. The State Highway Department announced that the residents had won their long battle to keep their neighborhood from being cut in two by the new I-44. The Highway Department agreed to build an overpass at Edwards Avenue.

1993 Nine-year old Angie Housman disappeared from her bus stop in St. Ann. Nine days later, her body was found in St. Charles County. The Housman case is one of a few area child murders that have not been solved. Those include: Donna Jean Mezo, 16, who disappeared while visiting relatives in Belleville in 1992, Arlin Henderson, 11, who disappeared while riding his bike in Lincoln County in 1991 and Scott Allen Kleeschulte, age 9. Kleeschulte was last seen near his St. Charles home during a terrible thunderstorm in 1988.

November 19

1904 A huge fire destroyed one of the finest buildings at the World's Fair, two weeks before it was to close. The Missouri Building burned quickly, but most of the treasures inside were saved. U.S. Marines rushed in to save the bell that Missourians had bought with their donations for the battleship "Missouri."

1953 A Kansas City jury sentenced Carl Austin Hall and Bonnie Brown Heady to death for the kidnapping and murder of six-year old Bobby Greenlease. Justice moved swiftly in 1953. They were sent to the gas chamber on December 18th. Heady was the first woman executed in Missouri since 1834.

1981 The Rolling Stones came to the Checkerdome in support of their new album, "Tattoo You." A crowd of 17,050 saw the first concert here by the Stones since 1978. Back then, Mick and the boys had played the 3500-seat Kiel Opera House.

1988 The great Dan Kelly broadcast his final Blues hockey game on KMOX. He died of cancer on February 10, 1989. Kelly was the voice of the Blues for 21 seasons. He was named to the

Hockey Hall of Fame as a broadcaster in 1989.

1998 Mark McGwire finished second behind Sammy Sosa in the National League MVP balloting. McGwire had hit a record 70 home runs in 1998, while Sosa finished the season with 66. But Sosa won the MVP balloting 438-272.

November 20

1861 The fabled Pony Express made its last run from St. Joseph. Although steeped in romantic western lore, the Pony Express never made a profit. The coming of the telegraph rendered the service obsolete.

1885 The man who served as the first mayor of East St. Louis was killed. John Bowman was a progressive and honest mayor. He continued to speak out against the corruption that flourished after he left office. Witnesses identified two police officers as the killers. But the witnesses disappeared before the trial.

1901 Police here were dismissing reports that the notorious "Hole in the Wall" gang was about to begin operations in St. Louis. A train robber arrested here was a former member of the gang. But police said Butch Cassidy and the Sundance Kid, the leaders of the gang, had fled the country.

1908 The *Globe-Democrat* reported that automobilists were upset at the way Clayton Road had been oiled in the county. The road was oiled in both directions to keep dust down. Usually, only one side at a time would be oiled. Drivers were convinced it was a scheme to keep them from speeding.

1920 Lester Benson broadcast the Harding-Cox election returns over his experimental radio station at the Benwood Radio Company here. Benson was the first man to broadcast from a moving car. He would put the station that became WIL on the air in April, 1922.

November 21

1795 Doctor William Beaumont was born in Connecticut. As an army surgeon in 1822, he conducted his famous experiments on the digestive tract by observing Alexis St. Martin. St. Martin was a trapper who had been shot, and still had a hole in his stomach. Beaumont was transferred to Jefferson Barracks, and later became head of surgery at St. Louis University's Medical School. His estate was where you find Beaumont Street today.

1891 Ten representatives from small local unions representing 286 people met at Stolley's Dance Hall on Biddle Street. They formed the National Brotherhood of Electrical Workers Union, now the International Brotherhood of Electrical Workers.

1895 The conductor of the Washington University Glee Club was forced to resign after the faculty criticized a song he had written. The song ended with the words, "If you want a kiss, why take it." The university felt it unseemly to sing of "human passion."

1920 Stanley Frank Musial was born in Donora, Pennsylvania. He joined the Cardinals in 1941, and was a three-time MVP. "The Man's" stats include 3,630 hits, 475 home runs and a .331 career batting average. He retired in 1963, and was inducted into the Baseball Hall of Fame in 1969.

1963 Plans for Walt Disney to help design an attraction on the riverfront hit a snag. Disney envisioned a family oriented entertainment district for "Riverfront Square." He wanted the area to be alcohol-free. But city officials said the project would not go through without beer. Their objection eventually killed the plan.

November 22

1729 Pierre Laclede Liguest was born in Bedous, near the French Pyrenees. He would come to New Orleans and form a company to trade with the savages of the Mississippi. In 1763, he led an expedition up river to choose a site for a trading post. The following year, he sent young August Chouteau to oversee construction on the site that would become the city of St. Louis.

1944 The motion picture "Meet Me in St. Louis" made its world

premiere here. Judy Garland starred in the story of the Smith family, who lived at 5135 Kensington Avenue on the eve of the 1904 World's Fair. The movie includes classic songs such as "The Trolley Song" and "Have Yourself a Merry Little Christmas." It was nominated for four Academy Awards, including best song for "The Trolley Song."

1963 "Cleopatra" was playing at the Fox. Phyliss Diller was appearing at the Crystal Palace in Gaslight Square. The big news in St. Louis that morning was a train collision in North St. Louis the day before that left several persons injured. Seven civil rights demonstrators had been arrested during a protest that tied up downtown traffic. Famous-Barr announced it had selected a site at Lindbergh and the Rock Road for a $10 million shopping center. An item on page four of the Globe-Democrat mentioned that President Kennedy was in Dallas.

1963 It was a rainy day in St. Louis when the news broke from Dallas. A crowd of 200 people gathered in the TV department at Stix, Baer and Fuller. The Board of Education Radio Station, KSLH, passed the news onto the public schools. Principals were told to give the details over their public address systems, but classes continued. Phyliss Diller cancelled her performance at Gaslight Square. The Chase Club at Chase-Park Plaza Hotel was closed. Most of the other establishments remained open, but the crowds were subdued.

1980 Kenneth M. Swyers of Overland slid down the north leg of the Arch to his death. He had parachuted to the top of the Arch as a publicity stunt. But the wind caught his chute, and sent him down the side.

November 23

1900 City officials compiled a lengthy list of improvements needed before the world's fair. Among the beautification, park improvements and sewer projects was a proposal to tame the pesky River des Peres. The plan would enclose it as a sewer through the park. Officials agreed it would be costly, but said it would be an insult to visitors if it were not done.

1926 It was reported that the bloody bootleggers war here appeared to have come to an end. So far, 15 had been killed and 20 wounded in the war between the Italian and "Cuckoo" gangs. Informants said Italian gangsters from New York had come in and forced rival gang members to agree to stay out of each others territory.

1926 A corporation representing several civic and business interests was granted a license to operate a radio station by the Commerce Department. The "Voice of St. Louis" group applied for the call letters "KMO." But those call letters were already assigned, so they tacked an "X" onto the end.

1934 Dizzy Dean demanded $25,000 to pitch for the Cardinals in 1935. Owner Sam Breadon was offering $15,000 to Dizzy and $7500 to brother Paul. In 1934, Dizzy won 30 games, while Paul won 19.

1963 A day after President Kennedy was assassinated in Dallas, the dedication of the newly-widened Manchester Road in Ellisville was postponed. Also cancelled were two St. Louis Symphony Programs featuring Captain Kangaroo. The Washington University game with Washington and Lee was postponed. Authorities said a planned mass polio vaccine would go on as scheduled, since the vaccine was perishable.

November 24

1868 Composer and pianist Scott Joplin was born in East Texas. He came to St. Louis in 1890 to play in the saloons that lined Market Street. He moved to Sedalia in 1896, but returned to St. Louis in 1901. Joplin combined classical musical styles with African-American rhythm, leading the development of the music we know as "Ragtime." He lived at 2658 Morgan, now Delmar.

1904 At the World's Fair, thousands took advantage of the Thanksgiving holiday. A feast was prepared for the Indians at the Indian School. The Igorottes and other tribes at the Philippine

Village enjoyed a turkey banquet (the Igorottes were more accustomed to feasting on dog during special occasions).

1911 Joe Medwick was born in New Jersey. One of the most legendary members of the Cardinals "Gas House Gang" of 1934, he is best remembered for being removed from game seven of the World Series for his own safety. Angry Tiger fans pelted Medwick with debris after he slid hard into the third basemen.

1923 A ten-mile segment of the planned transcontinental "Victory Highway" was completed west of St. Charles. For the first time, a decent paved road linked St. Charles and St. Peters.

1963 Thirty-thousand-people, their ranks swelled by those paying tribute to President John F. Kennedy, marched from the Soldier's Memorial to the Old Courthouse for racial justice. Mayor Tucker declared that Monday, November 25th, would be a day of mourning in St. Louis. All busses and streetcars would halt for one minute at 11 a.m., the hour of the president's funeral.

November 25

1820 Governor Alexander McNair signed a bill making St. Charles the capital of Missouri upon admission to the union. The building at 206 North Main would serve as the capitol until 1826, when the seat of government was moved to Jefferson City.

1844 Carry Amelia Moore Nation was born in Kentucky. She settled in Cass County, Missouri, in 1855. Her husband died of alcoholism, leaving her with an infant son, and a burning hatred of booze. She began smashing saloons in Kansas. In 1901, she tried to smash up a saloon on Market Street in St. Louis, but police stopped her. She also came here in 1904, denouncing the world's fair as a tool of the devil.

1947 Sam Breadon sold the Cardinals to Postmaster Robert Hannegan and Fred Saigh. For $4 million, the new owners got the club, 16 minor league franchises, and the lease on Sportsman's Park.

1959 City officials announced that the landmark Grand Avenue viaduct over the Mill Creek Railyards would be torn down. It was replaced with a generic looking six-lane structure. The end of the viaduct also spelled doom for the Grand Avenue streetcars.

1963 At the hour of President Kennedy's funeral in Washington D.C, the city and county of St. Louis came to a standstill. Busses and streetcars were halted for one minute in tribute. Public and parochial schools were closed. The major department stores closed until after the funeral.

November 26

1898 A Missouri Historical Society committee proposed a celebration be held among the states of the Louisiana Purchase to commemorate the centennial of the purchase in 1903. The proposal was forwarded to Missouri Governor Lon V. Stephens, recommending that delegates from the states meet in St. Louis to decide where to hold the festivities.

1904 President Theodore Roosevelt visited the World's Fair. He walked through the exhibits, pausing only for lunch, and invited the Apache Chief Geronimo to Washington. The president thwarted plans for an elaborate welcome when his train arrived several hours early. It parked inside the grounds until embarrassed fair officials could get there.

1921 A group of parents formed a committee to organize a "Country Day" school for their daughters. Mrs. George Gellhorn and Ernest Stix urged the committee to form a co-ed school. Land was purchased a year later on Price Road at the railroad right-of-way. The school would be named after naturalist John Burroughs.

1939 Anna Mae Bullock was born in Nutbush, Tennessee. She moved to St. Louis at age 16, and was a student at Sumner High School when she met Ike Turner. She soon began perform- ing with his "Kings of Rythym," and rose to fame as Tina Turner.

1962 The Missouri Highway Department announced construction was underway on the first section of the proposed interstate highway loop around St. Louis. The first section of I-244, between 44 and Manchester, would take two years and cost $14 million. The 4.7 mile roadway would eliminate a terrible bottleneck on Kirkwood Road in the Kirkwood business district.

November 27

1922 Promising Cards outfielder Austin McHenry died of a brain tumor at the age of 27. He stayed at his post until midway through the 1922 season, and still managed to hit .303. He was taken out of a game and sent to the doctor by Branch Rickey after he misjudged two fly balls. It was then he learned he had a fatal tumor.

1928 The St. Louis Flyers of the American Association played the first professional league hockey game here. The Flyers beat defending champs Minnesota, 3-2. Forty-five-hundred fans saw the game at the Winter Garden.

1982 In an article in the *Globe*, nurses at St. John's Mercy Medical Center said they had noticed a marked increase in births nine months after the February blizzard. The babies began arriving on schedule between October 23rd and November 14th.

1984 KMOX personality Jack Carney died of a heart attack at the age of 52. In the late '50s, he was a top deejay at WIL known for his zany stunts. He took a job at WABC in New York in 1960, only to walk away a year later because he was disgusted with "teeny bopper" radio. Robert Hyland lured him to KMOX in 1971.

1985 Vince Coleman of the Cardinals became only the fourth player in major league history to be unanimously elected as Rookie of the Year (the others were Frank Robinson, Orlando Cepeda and Willie McCovey).

November 28

1861 Missouri was admitted to the Confederacy, as the Congress of the Confederate States recognized the actions of the pro-southern government headed by ousted governor Claiborne Jackson in Neosho. The rebel legislation was roundly ignored in the North.

1906 A pre-dawn fire at the Salvation Army Hotel at Ninth and Market left ten people dead and 14 injured. The high toll was blamed on the fact that the doors were locked after the hotel's 250 beds were filled. Dozens jumped to safety into nets held by firemen.

1931 The President of Union Electric promised development of hotels and resorts "on a grand scale" at the newly created Lake of the Ozarks. Louis Egan pledged that UE would make the lake "the finest and best-known playland in the Middle West."

1939 The St. Louis area suffered through "Black Tuesday," the worst smoke pall in city history. The air was black. Everything was covered in soot. Even electric lights could not cut the gloom. Black Tuesday spurred city fathers to take action to tackle the smoke problem that had made St. Louis one of the dirtiest cities in the nation.

1964 The Big Red used the 12th pick in the NFL draft to select quarterback Joe Namath of Alabama. But the Cardinals lost a bidding war to the New York Jets. Namath signed a three-year-deal for an unheard of $427,000. St. Louis fans complained that the Big Red owners, the Bidwell family, were cheap.

November 29

1808 Robert A. Barnes was born in Washington, D.C. He made a fortune as a merchant in St. Louis. Barnes left the bulk of his estate for the establishment of his dream—a Methodist Episcopal hospital that would care for patients regardless of creed. By 1914, his $940,000 estate had grown to $2 million, and Barnes Hospital was established.

1901 The birthday of Monsanto. John F. Queeny, a moonlighting purchasing agent for the Meyer Brothers Drug Company, started the Monsanto Chemical Works with $1,500 of his own money and another $30,000 he borrowed. The company was named for his wife, Olga Melendez Monsanto Queeny.

1904 Mayor Rolla Wells announced that the final day of the fair, December 1st, would be declared David Francis Day. It would be a civic holiday, with the schools closed to give everyone a chance to see the fair for the last time. It was also announced that the grounds would be open the following Sunday, to give St. Louisans a chance to watch the demolition. Admission would be 25 cents.

1972 Workmen began tearing down the old Biedermen's Store at 8th and Dr. Martin Luther King Drive. It marked the first demolition work to make room for the new convention center.

1982 The *Globe* quoted an industry source as saying that the HBE Corporation was planning a world class hotel downtown. The hotel would be built on the site of the Pierce Building, at Fourth and Chestnut. The source said plans for the "Adams Mark" hotel would be announced in December.

1835 Samuel Langhorn Clemens was born in Florida, Missouri. He spent quite a bit of time in St. Louis as a young steamboat pilot. It was during that period that he picked up a steamboater's term for the depth of the water and adapted it as his pen name—"Mark Twain."

1837 St. Louis Chamber of Commerce President Edward Terry presided over a sumptuous banquet at the National Hotel (now the site of KMOX and KMOV). Eighty prominent St. Louisans with New England backgrounds attended to recall the eastern "Thanksgiving" custom. Thanksgiving did not become a national event until Abraham Lincoln's edict some 25 years later.

1920 Actress Virginia Mayo was born in St. Louis as Virginia Jones. She sang at the Muny Opera before Samuel Goldwyn signed her to an acting contract. Mayo appeared in dozens of pictures, including "White Heat" and "The Best Years of Our Lives."

1957 Vladimir Golschmann announced he would retire at the end of the season. Golschmann had conducted the St. Louis Symphony Orchestra for the past 27 years. His leadership was credited with making the orchestra one of the finest in the nation.

1982 Residents looked on as technicians in "moon suits" began taking soil samples in Times Beach. The town was listed as one of 41 sites in Missouri possibly contaminated by dioxin. The streets were sprayed with dioxin-contaminated waste oil to keep the dust down in the summer of 1972.

DECEMBER

December 1

1904 The greatest period in St. Louis history came to an end, as the World's Fair closed. A crowd of 100,000 watched as David Francis, president of the exposition, said "farewell to all thy splendor," and threw the switch. The band played "Auld Lang Syne" as the lights went down. More than 20 million people had seen the fair.

1958 "Phil the Gorilla," one of the largest gorillas on record and a beloved resident of the St. Louis Zoo since 1941, died of ulcerative colitis. Zoo employees took Phil to the city scales in a truck. The truck was weighed with Phil, then without him. They calculated Phil's weight at 776 pounds. Schwarz Studios stuffed Phil, and he stands today in the Safari Shop near the South Gate of the Zoo.

1972 Only one theater now remained open in the once thriving Grand Avenue theater district. The Leow's Mid-City closed its doors, leaving only the Fox Theatre open in the area. The Leow's opened in 1925 as the Shubert Rialto. It served as the home of the American Theatre from 1950 to 1961.

1979 The new I-70 bridge into St. Charles opened. The new bridge was built next to one that opened in 1958, and had been clogged with traffic from the start. Both bridges were then named after Louis Blanchette, the first settler of St. Charles. The westbound span is the old one.

1993 Parents in the St. Louis area were terrified that a serial killer might be preying on young children. Just 12 days after Angie Housman was found murdered, the body of ten-year old Cassidy Senter was found in an alley in North St. Louis. Thomas Brooks would be charged with killing Cassidy in February, 1994.

December 2

1904 Arsonists saved workers the trouble of tearing down "Ancient Rome" and four other major exhibits on "The Pike" at the World's Fair. Numerous priceless antiques and art objects were lost in the general-alarm fire that swept the amusement area.

1913 Mayor Henry Kiel signed an ordinance setting aside 1,300 acres in Forest Park for a zoo. The zoo actually dates back to the 1890s, when the parks department began keeping a small collection of mostly domestic animals in the park. George Dieckmann began pushing for a zoo in 1911. It was through his efforts that the collection had expanded to include bear cubs, a llama, and a camel by 1912.

1924 Officials were once again calling for something to be done about the smoke that choked St. Louis. The poor visibility was blamed for two deaths. A driver hit the railing of the Free Bridge (now MacArthur) and was thrown into the river. Thieves took advantage of the gloom to commit 616 holdups.

1948 Stan Musial was named as the National League Most Valuable Player. Musial led the league with a .365 average and 131 RBI's. His 39 home runs put him just one behind league leaders Johnny Mize and Ralph Kiner.

1966 The Board of Aldermen passed a measure naming the under construction Poplar Street Bridge in honor of Bernard Dickmann. Dickmann was the mayor of St. Louis from 1933 until 1941. He was instrumental in obtaining funds for the riverfront memorial.

December 3

1901 The American League transferred the Milwaukee franchise to the St. Louis Browns. St. Louis would become "first in beer, first in shoes, and last in the American League." The only exception was in 1944, when the Browns managed to win the pennant

only to lose to the Cardinals in the World Series.

1918 The terrible flu epidemic reached its peak in St. Louis. That day alone, 1,467 new cases were reported. Seventeen-hundred people died in St. Louis. The toll would have been much higher if the city health commissioner had not ordered the schools and business closed early in the outbreak.

1930 The St. Louis County Court voted to rename Denny Road in honor of Charles Lindbergh. Officials hoped to have the Lindbergh Boulevard signs up in time for the opening of an improved section of the road. Lindbergh would soon be a 20-foot-wide concrete strip between the St. Charles Rock Road and Lemay Ferry.

1967 The riverboat restaurant "River Queen" suddenly sank on the riverfront. No one was injured, but officials were mystified as to the cause. The River Queen was one of the last "Texas-Deck" stern-wheelers left on the river.

1990 This was the day we were supposed to have been hit with a major earthquake along the New Madrid Fault. That was according to Dr. Iben Browning, a New Mexico climatologist. His prediction prompted a barrage of media coverage. Throughout southern Illinois and Missouri, schools cancelled classes, and police and fire departments stood on alert.

December 4

1877 Voters in St. Louis County voted to accept a donation of 100 hundred acres of land from Ralph Clayton and the family of Martin Hanley for the new county seat. The city and county had recently separated. The value of the land was put at $300 per acre. That land is now prime Clayton real estate.

1896 Raymond Tucker was born in St. Louis. Tucker first rose to prominence when Mayor Dickmann appointed him to solve the city's smoke problem in 1933. Tucker served three terms as mayor, from 1953 to 1965. He was largely responsible for the revitalization program for downtown, and bond issues that built the planetarium and the major interstates in the city.

1904 Frank "Buster" Wortman was born in St. Louis. He led the Capone Gang interests in St. Louis and southern Illinois. During the '40s and '50s, Wortman and his associates  controlled the nightclubs, taverns, gambling, a racing news service and a trucking line. He lived in a home near Collinsville, surrounded by a moat.

1979 A group calling themselves the Coalition of Parents Against Rock Concerts called for a ban on concerts "in which the drug culture is promoted" at the Checkerdome. Eleven fans attending a concert by "The Who" in Cincinnati had been trampled to death a day earlier. Local promoters said it could never happen here, because all seats were reserved.

1982 The rampaging Meramec River flooded the streets of Times Beach. On December 23rd, the federal government would tell residents displaced by the flood not to come back. The town had been contaminated by dioxin in waste oil sprayed on the streets back in the 1970s. Times Beach was removed from the maps. After a massive cleanup, Route 66 State Park occupies the site today.

December 5

1927 Seven people were killed, ten injured, in a fire at the Buckingham Hotel at Kingshighway and West Pine. There were more than 100 guests in the hotel at the time. Among them were 32 students from the Central Institute for the Deaf. All of the kids got out safely. The owners of the hotel were later charged with murder for hiring an arsonist so they could collect insurance money.

1933 Repeal of prohibition became a certainty, as Utah became the 35th state to ratify the 21st amendment. August A. Busch said "happy days will be here again—and soon." He added "this is going to be a free country." In Missouri, hard liquor was still unavailable, as the legislature had yet to repeal the state dry laws.

1948 Robert Moore, the son of a Portland Place doctor, was arrested for speeding. By 1950, the exploits of "Hot Rod Moore" were front page news. The Republican candidate for county prosecuting attorney ran on a platform of putting Moore in jail. Moore eventually served four months in prison.

1999 The Rams clinched the NFC West Title with a 34-21 win over the Carolina Panthers. It marked the team's first NFC West Title since 1985.

2000 The "Admiral" was moved from it's berth near the Eads Bridge, home for 60 years. The owners of the "President Casino on the Admiral" said the move north to Laclede's Landing would increase revenue and provide protection from wayward barges. Over 70 gamblers were injured when a runaway barge struck the casino in 1998.

December 6

1862 Claiborne Fox Jackson died at the age of 56. As governor at the start of the Civil War, he tried to lead Missouri into the Confederacy. When that failed, he took the state militia to fight against the Union, and set up a rebel government in Neosho. His forces were driven from the state in 1861.

1865 A huge ball marked the opening of the Southern Hotel here, described as the finest west of the Mississippi. The six-story building covered the entire block from Walnut to Elm, between Fourth and Fifth where the Stadium East garage stands today. On April 11, 1877, it was the scene of one of the most tragic fires in St. Louis history. At least 21 people were killed.

1875 Aviation pioneer Albert Bond Lambert was born. Lambert developed an interest in aviation while working for his father's company, the makers of Listerine. He formed the Aero Club of St. Louis, established an air mail route, and developed an airfield at his own expense. He sold the field, now worth millions, to the city at his own cost in 1928.

1900 Agnes Moorehead was born in Clinton, Massachusetts. She moved to St. Louis as a child, spent four seasons as a dancer at the Muny Opera, and debuted as a radio singer on KMOX. She was nominated for five academy awards, but is best remembered for her work on TV's "Bewitched."

1948 Workmen began demolishing the historic National Hotel, formerly Scotts, at Third and Market. Among those who stayed there at one time: Abraham Lincoln, Robert E. Lee, Jefferson Davis, and Zachary Taylor. Today, KMOV-TV and KMOX radio occupy the site.

December 7

1922 Three-hundred barrels of pre-prohibition whiskey disappeared from the Jack Daniels Distillery on Duncan Avenue. The whiskey, valued at nearly $2 million, had been stored there by the U.S. government.  The thieves siphoned the whiskey through a hose that ran into another building. About 25 prominent St. Louisans would be charged with conspiracy in the case. The charges against a congressman, a state senator and the operator of Jack Daniels were eventually dismissed.

1941 Governor Donnelly and St. Louis Mayor Dee Becker wasted no time in reacting to the news from Hawaii. Sixty-five-thousand soldiers on leave from Fort Leonard Wood, Scott Field and Jefferson Barracks were told to report for duty immediately. Detachments from Jefferson Barracks rushed to guard the bridges and the 12 largest private industrial plants. Mayor Becker said "St. Louis is ready to take up its share of the burden." He said the city would immediately begin to set up agencies to accelerate production, promote civil defense and prevent sabotage.

1941 There were about 140 St. Louisans at Pearl Harbor. Most were members of a naval reserve unit called to active duty in 1940. They served mostly on the destroyers "Schley," "Allen" and "Chew," all World War I vintage four-stackers. Twelve St. Louisans died aboard the battleship "Arizona."

1941 Lieutenant George A. Whiteman of Sedalia became the first American airman killed in World War II. He was hit as he tried to take off to battle the Japanese pilots hitting Pearl Harbor. Whiteman Air Force Base outside Sedalia is named after him.

1958 The *Globe-Democrat* reported that city leaders were discussing the possibility of a new stadium on the St. Louis riverfront. August A. Busch Jr., the chairman of Civic Progress, said he was 100% in favor of the idea.

December 8

1698 The Reverend Francois Ste. Cosme and two other missionary priests celebrated mass on the banks of the Mississippi at Cahokia. Five months later, they established Holy Family Church. Mass has been celebrated regularly at Cahokia longer than any place in the United States. The first church burned in 1783. But the one built on the same foundation in 1799 still stands today.

1904 Plans to save "The Pike" and make it a permanent amusement park were abandoned in the face of opposition by officials at Washington University. Concessionaires reluctantly agreed to remove everything at the World's Fair amusement area within 60 days as originally agreed.

1941 Nervous guards at Jefferson Barracks opened fire on a milk truck that failed to obey a command to halt at four in the morning. No one was hurt. Police rounded up 22 Germans and one Italian alien deemed "dangerous to the welfare of the city." Six-hundred men swarmed the Army, Navy, Marine Corps and Coast Guard recruiting stations in the Federal Building.

1945 St. Louis officials were on their way to London with a bid for St. Louis to become the "World Capitol." They were headed for the meeting of the United Nations Preparatory Committee with a proposal to headquarter the U.N. at the site of the old T.N.T. plant at Weldon Spring.

1977 The Cardinals traded pitcher Al Hrabosky to the Royals for Mark Littel and Buck Martinez. The "Mad Hungarian" whipped Cardinal fans into a frenzy with his Fu Manchu mustache and stalking routine behind the mound. Hrabosky clashed with new manager Vern Rapp, who had banned facial hair.

December 9

1852 The first trains ever to run west of the Mississippi began operations along five miles of completed track on the Pacific Railroad. The rails ended at Cheltenham, in what is now southwest St. Louis. They reached Kirkwood in May, 1853 and Jefferson City in 1855.

1922 John Elroy Sanford was born in St. Louis. He was called "Red" because of his complexion and adopted the name of baseball player Jimmie Foxx. He became famous as Redd Foxx.

1958 Charles L. Farris, executive director of the Land Clearance for Redevelopment Authority, unveiled plans for a $30 million sports stadium downtown. After Anheuser-Busch gave the first $5 million towards construction in 1959, the decision was made to name it Civic Center Busch Memorial Stadium.

1980 St. Louis stations KADI and KWK-FM were airing tributes to the murdered John Lennon. Record stores reported they had sold out of Lennon's latest album, "Double Fantasy." The manager of Wuxtry Records in University City closed his store in memory of Lennon.

1982 The Cardinals sent Ken Reitz and Leon Durham to the Cubs for reliever Bruce Sutter. A day earlier, Whitey Herzog had traded Terry Kennedy, Steve Swisher, Mike Phillips, John Littlefield, John Urrea, Kim Seaman and Al Olmstead to the Padres. In return, the Birds picked up Rollie Fingers, Bob Shirley and Gene Tenace.

December 10

1873 Construction superintendent Theodore Cooper became the first person to cross the Eads Bridge. In a hurry to cross, he had workmen throw narrow planks across the two remaining gaps, one 12 feet wide, the other 24 feet across. As the stunned workmen watched, he nonchalantly crossed, 90 feet above the river.

1895 St. Louis was selected as the site of the 1896 Republican National Convention, to be held in June. Within days of the announcement, every hotel in the city was booked solid. City officials called for owners of boarding houses and homeowners with extra rooms to make them available.

1908 The St. Louis Police Department received the first electric patrol car. The "speed buggy" was manufactured by Studebaker, cost $3,000, and was capable of hitting 60 miles per hour.

1931 A huge crowd turned out for a performance by Duke Ellington and his orchestra at the Hotel Coronado. The $2 admission charge was donated to unemployment relief. The "Globe" said the audience was treated to "the bluest melodies that have been heard in St. Louis in years."

1933 A crowd of 4,000 cheered as the cornerstone was laid for the new Homer G. Phillips Hospital for the Colored. The $2.2 million facility at St. Ferdinand and Whittier opened in 1937. The hospital was named for the St. Louis attorney who crusaded for its construction before he was murdered. "Homer G" closed amid much controversy in 1979.

1904 The *Post-Dispatch* reported that St. Louis was in danger of losing the giant bird cage constructed as part of the U.S. Government exhibit at the World's Fair. The Smithsonian Institute wanted the cage for the zoological gardens in Washington, D.C. The city ended up purchasing the cage for $3,500.

1925 The Department of Commerce assigned the call letters "KMOX" to the station sought by a group of civic and business leaders. Kirkwood Mayor R.L. Jacobsmeyer said the calls stood for "Kirkwood, Missouri's Christmas Gift to the World." The first transmitter was located in Kirkwood, and KMOX would begin broadcasting on December 24, 1925.

1948 The first "Steak and Shake" restaurant in St. Louis opened at 6622 Highway 66. It was the 26th restaurant in the chain founded in 1934 by A.H. Belt in Bloomington, Illinois. The chain planned to open six more restaurants in St. Louis.

1954 The first locally-originated color television show here aired over KSD-TV, Channel Five. The show was a 15-minute documentary on St. Louis produced for the Chamber of Commerce.

1980 The Veiled Prophet organization announced plans for the first "V.P. Fair." It was to be held on the Gateway Arch grounds July 3rd through the 5th. Fair General Chairman Robert Hermann promised the biggest fireworks display ever seen in St. Louis, along with big name entertainment and spectacular air shows.

December 12

1839 A last-minute truce averted a war between Missouri and Iowa. The border dispute began when the Clark County sheriff tried to collect taxes along the disputed state line. He was thrown in jail by Iowa authorities. Both Missouri and Iowa called out the militia. But "The Honey War" was settled before there was any fighting.

1878 The first issue of the *St. Louis Post* and *Dispatch* hit the streets, just days after Joseph Pulitzer bought the bankrupt *Dispatch* at an auction. The first issue had a circulation of 987 and was distributed by wheelbarrow. The name was shortened to the *Post-Dispatch* in February, 1879.

1944 A crowd jammed the Old Courthouse rotunda to honor black aviator Wendell Pruitt of St. Louis. Pruitt won the Distinguished Flying Cross for shooting down three German planes, destroying 70 on the ground and helping sink an enemy destroyer. Four months later, he was killed while training pilots

for the "Tuskegee Airmen." In 1955, the city would name its gleaming new public housing project after Pruitt.

1972 Football great Larry Wilson announced his retirement. Wilson was a member of the original Cardinals, and was inducted into the Hall of Fame in 1978. He helped popularize the safety blitz and set a team record with 52 interceptions during his 13-year career.

1980 The Cardinals made one of their least memorable deals. They traded Rolllie Fingers, Ted Simmons and Pete Vuckovich to the Brewers. In return, the Birds got Larry Sorenson, Sixto Lezcano, and minor leaguers David Green and David LaPoint. Fingers would win the Cy Young in 1981. Vuckovich won it the following year.

December 13

1837 The newly-created Board of Education advertised for teachers for a public school to be established in St. Louis. The ad called for four males, to be paid $900 per year. Four females would also be hired, at $500 annually.

1926 The first major auto manufacturer in St. Louis announced it was closing. Officials with the Dorris Motor Car Company said they could no longer compete with the financial giants now prevalent in the auto industry. The plant at 4100 Laclede still stands today. The building is on the National Registry of Historic Places, and houses the Center for Emerging Technologies.

1973 A spokesman for a dealers association said President Richard Nixon's fuel association order would close 300 gas stations within a month. He predicted 1,200 people would lose their jobs, and prices would soon hit 50¢ per gallon.

1986 A group of local investors led by Michael Shanahan purchased the Blues from Harry Ornest. The deal ended nearly a decade of turmoil and financial instability for the team. The group hired John "Jack" Quinn as president, and the Blues went on to win the Norris Division title.

1987 The football Cardinals played their last game at Busch Stadium. They beat the Giants 27-24 before 29,623 die-hard fans. The highlight of the game came when Vai Sikahema returned a punt 76 yards for a touchdown.

December 14

1822 The Missouri General Assembly authorized a commission to select a site for a courthouse. They would choose a site offered by John Lucas and Auguste Chouteau on Fourth Street. At the time, the public whipping post occupied the site where the Old Courthouse now stands.

1980 Five thousand people gathered in Forest Park for a tribute to John Lennon. They observed ten minutes of silence at 1:00 p.m. That was the same hour millions of fans around the world paused in prayer as requested by Lennon's widow, Yoko Ono.

1982 Gary and Donna Decker were abducted from the parking lot of a North County store while Christmas shopping for their four-year old son. Their bodies were found the next day in a field in East St. Louis. Donna Decker had been raped. Walter Harvey Jr. was sentenced to life for the crime after eight years of trials and appeals.

1982 The H.B.E. Corporation announced plans for a 600-room "world class hotel" downtown. The Adam's Mark of St. Louis would be built on the site of the old Planter's Hotel and Pierce Building on Chestnut between Fourth Street and Memorial Drive.

1992 Blues superstar Brett Hull fired a puck into a net on the site to symbolically begin demolition work on the Old Kiel Auditorium and parking garage to make room for the new Kiel Center. The Kiel Center opened just 22 months later on October 14, 1994. In August, 2000, the naming rights were sold to Savvis Communications.

December 15

1919 The city of Brentwood was incorporated. The incorporation was a hurried attempt by residents to avoid being annexed by Maplewood. The incorporation papers were filed about 24 hours before the election on the proposed annexation.

1945 The Rams won their first NFL title, defeating the Washington Redskins. At that time, they were the Cleveland Rams, playing their eighth and final season there before moving to Los Angeles in 1946.

1964 Anheuser-Busch became the first brewery ever to produce 10 million barrels of beer in a single year. AB began as a brewery founded by a man named Schneider in 1852. Soap manufacturer Eberhard Anheuser took over when the brewery failed. His son-in-law, Adolphus Busch, joined the brewery in 1865.

1974 The Big Red clinched St. Louis' first NFL division title with a 26-14 win over the New York Giants at Busch. Jim Hart was named NFC Offensive Player of the Year and Terry Metcalf was picked as runner-up. The Cardinals would lose their first playoff game to Minnesota on December 21st.

1991 The Eads Bridge was closed to vehicle traffic. Bi-State said it should re-open by July, 1992, when the Metro Link Station was completed. But the bridge deck was too badly deteriorated, and it has been closed ever since.

1811 The great New Madrid earthquake rocked nearly half of the continent. The Mississippi flowed backward, islands appeared and disappeared, and Reelfoot Lake was formed by a change in the river's course. The quake was clearly felt in St. Louis. But there were few deaths because the area was sparsely populated. Hundreds of aftershocks rattled the area all winter long, and another massive quake struck in February.

1899 It was beginning to sink in that St. Louis would host a World's Fair. The planning committee chairman, former governor David Francis, reported he had received a bid of $1 million dollars for the concessions and amusements at the fair. He also said the city had nearly reached its goal of raising $5 million dollars for the fair by popular subscription.

1905 The Board of the St. Louis Fine Art Museum announced an effect to try to obtain the Fine Arts Building from World's Fair. The Board said it would turn the building into one of the finest art centers in the world.

1932 The Missouri Supreme Court ruled that the Old Courthouse was the property of the city. J.B.C. Lucas and Auguste Chouteau had donated the site in 1822, with the stipulation that it be forever used as a courthouse. Their heirs sued after the last courts in the building moved out in 1930.

1993 A Buick rolled off the assembly line at the General Motors Plant in Wentzville, the last automobile produced in St. Louis. St. Louis was once the second largest manufacturer of automobiles in the country. The GM plant began producing mini-vans in 1995. Chrysler and Ford had already converted their plants to mini-van or truck production.

December 17

1949 Brown's president Bill Dewitt announced the Brownies would try a new approach next spring. The club had hired a New York psychiatrist to work with the team. He would work with the players to try to teach them to relax, overcome tension and their "defeatist" attitude.

1953 Educational television was seen here for the first time, but only by a few people. KETC broadcast on a closed circuit to two groups of school administrators and members of the commission on educational television. Commission members said they hoped to have the station on the air by March, 1954.

1958 The body of James Bullock, a 27-year old college student was found in front of the Art Museum. His wife's ex-husband, Dr. Glennon Engelman, became the focus of the investigation but was not charged. Over the next 20 years, the "South Side Dentist" would kill at least seven more times. Engleman arranged to marry off his ex-lovers, kill their husbands, and split the insurance money with the widows.

1979 The "Admiral" left for a New Orleans dry-dock for repairs to its hull. The repairs were expected to take just a few weeks, but it turned out the Admiral had made her last cruise. By 1981, it appeared the Admiral would never return to St. Louis and was doomed to the scrap heap.

1992 A great day for commuters. The new "Discovery Bridge" carrying Highway 370 across the Missouri north of St. Charles was opened. It replaced the old 115 Bridge. Almost immediately, the daily backups headed for the Blanchette Bridge on Highway 70 began to ease.

December 18

1865 Mayor James Thomas approved the present house numbering system in St. Louis. North and south blocks were numbered from Market. East and west streets were numbered from the wharf. Each block represented 100 numbers.

1916 Ruth Elizabeth Grable was born in St. Louis. Her mother brought her to Hollywood in 1929. She launched her career with small parts for Goldwyn. It was when Daryl Zanuck signed her in 1941 that "Betty" Grable's career took off. She seldom returned to St. Louis, making her final appearance at the Muny in 1971.

1936 The Eugene Field home at 634 South Broadway, opened as a children's museum. The home was once part of a row of 12. It was barely saved from the wrecking ball by two St. Louis businessmen.

1953 A few minutes after midnight, Carl Austin Hall and Bonnie Heady were put to death in the Jefferson City gas chamber for the kidnapping and murder of Bobby Greenlease, the son of a wealthy Kansas City auto dealer. Heady was the first woman put to death in Missouri since 1834. That same day, a grand jury investigating the missing $300,000 of the ransom money indicted suspended St. Louis patrolman Elmer Dolan for perjury. Half the ransom disappeared when the kidnappers were captured in St. Louis.

1955 The Municipal Judges Association of Greater St. Louis ordered a study of the relationship between "lewd and scurrilous comic books and similar literature" to violent crime in the area. The judges said some offenses committed by juveniles were inspired by comics.

December 19

1934 A federal commission appointed by President Roosevelt, Congress and the Jefferson Memorial Association, began meeting at the Jefferson Hotel in St. Louis. They began to make plans for a riverfront memorial to honor the pioneers and commemorate the Louisiana Purchase.

1972 I-44 was opened to traffic between I-55 and Laclede Station. I-44 was now completed across Missouri, rendering Route 66 obsolete. Officials were predicting a bottleneck at I-55, because only one exit was complete. I-55 was still under construction south of 44.

1973 The smallest crowd ever to see a Blues game at the Arena braved a foot of snow to watch the Blues beat the L.A. Kings, 3-1. Only 4,115 fans made it in. Fans were allowed to sit in the empty seats, and concessions were on the house. The snowstorm was the worst in St. Louis since 1890.

1984 Demolition work was underway on the old Channel Two tower at 5915 Berthold. The top half of the St. Louis landmark was sheared off in the 1959 tornado. The bottom half then served as a base for microwave and other antennas. Those were now being moved to the top of Deaconess Hospital.

1996 The Blues fired Mike Keenan as coach and general manager. His tenure in St. Louis had been marked with controversy, including trades that sent many of the top players away. It was also marked by a feud with Brett Hull.

December 20

1003 The United States formally took possession of the Louisiana Territory at New Orleans, completing the biggest real estate deal in U.S. history. The Louisiana Purchase doubled the size of the U.S., at a cost of about $20 per square mile. President Jefferson came under fire for the deal. Some said he had exceeded his authority and the territory was too large to be governed effectively.

1812 Sacagewea died. As a young Shoshone Indian woman in 1804, she accompanied Lewis and Clark on their journey into the unknown Indian lands of the west. Travelling with her two-month old baby boy strapped to her back, her services as an interpreter were vital to the expedition.

1901 Formal ground breaking ceremonies were held for the World's Fair. There was five inches of snow on the ground, and the bitter cold forced the postponement of the huge parade planned to mark the occasion. A bonfire was kept burning to thaw the ground.

1926 The world champion Cardinals stunned the city with the announcement that they had traded the great Rogers Hornsby to the Giants for Frankie Frisch and Jimmy Ring. Hornsby had been in a dispute with management over his contract. The St. Louis

Chamber of Commerce asked Commissioner Kenesaw Landis to prevent the trade, but Landis would not intervene.

1935 Mayor Bernard Dickmann arrived in Washington to ask for the first federal money for the Jefferson National Expansion Memorial. The Attorney General said federal law wouldn't permit such an expenditure. But Dickmann gently reminded President Roosevelt that he needed to carry Missouri to win the next election. St. Louis had the money the next day.

December 21

1847 The first telegraph message was sent to St. Louis. A message from Louisville was sent to the offices of the *Missouri Republican* via the newly-opened East St. Louis telegraph office. The messages were sent across the river, allowing the paper to boast that it could publish the news from the East Coast almost to the moment the paper was published.

1959 Zoo officials were searching for the popular chimpanzee, "Mr. Moke." He had been kidnapped. A $1,000 cashier's check was left behind in his cage. It turned out that Mr. Moke's former owner had taken him to Florida to perform in motion pictures. He turned up a few months later.

1973 One of the worst traffic tie ups in city history. Because of a blizzard two days earlier, many highways were still narrowed to one or two lanes when St. Louisans returned to work. The crush of shoppers trying to take care of Christmas shopping put off due to the weather added to the mess.

1974 The "Cardiac Cardinals" came up short in their drive to the Super Bowl. They lost the first game of the playoffs to the Minnesota Vikings, 30-14. It was the first playoff game ever for a St. Louis NFL team.

1981 Guardian Angels founder Curtis Sliwa and his fiancee announced they would spend their honeymoon in the Vaughn Housing Projects to focus attention on the conditions there. They told the media they were asking for "rat traps and roach spray" as wedding presents.

December 22

1861 Thirteen-hundred Confederate prisoners arrived in St. Louis, packed into a 36-car train. They were marched into a gloomy building at Eighth and Gratiot, a former medical college converted into a prison. Conditions were harsh, but typical of the prisons on both sides during the Civil War.

1945 The busiest day in Union Station history. The station was jammed with servicemen returning home. Incoming trains ran four to eight hours late. The railroads tried to give preference to military personnel. But many soldiers and civilians were left behind when the trains pulled out crammed to the aisles.

1995 A group headed by William DeWitt, Frederick Hanser and Andrew Bauer announced they were purchasing the Cardinals from Anheuser-Busch for $150 million. The brewery shocked the city in October when it announced the Cardinals were for sale.

1996 Brett Hull became the 24th player in NHL history to score 500 goals, notching a hat trick in a game here against the Los Angeles Kings. Brett and his father Bobby became the first father and son to join the 500-goal club.

1996 The Rams announced they were firing coach Rich Brooks after his second season behind the bench. Dick Vermeil would be hired to take over the coaching duties.

December 23

1809 The city's first police ordinance was passed. No formal force was established, but each male citizen was required to serve, or provide a substitute. An actual police force was established in December, 1839.

1946 Real estate promoter Cyrus Willmore announced he would donate 70 acres of land to the city for a park. The land ran along the River des Peres, east of Jamieson. The northern end joined Willmore's new "St. Louis Hills" subdivision.

1949 Mayor Darst announced that the city had picked a 40-block site for a combined privately financed slum clearance project and a federally subsidized low-cost housing project. Twelve-thousand units would be built on the site bounded by 18th and Cole, Cass and Jefferson, a site that would become notorious as the Pruitt-Igoe housing project.

1959 A federal grand jury indicted Chuck Berry on a charge of transporting a minor across state lines for immoral purposes. A 14-year old girl said Berry brought her from El Paso, Texas to work as a hat check girl in his tavern. Berry was sentenced to three years after a second trial.

1982 The Centers for Disease Control and the Missouri Division of Health recommended that the town of Times Beach be evacuated. Just two months ago, residents learned the town could be contaminated with deadly dioxin, contained in waste oil sprayed to keep the dust down on the streets years ago. A devastating flood along the Meramec River came just days after residents learned of the contamination.

December 24

1774 Work began on the first church in St. Louis. The small log church was built on the same site where the Old Cathedral stands today. Father Valentin blessed the first church bell on Christmas Eve in front of the assembled inhabitants of the village.

1872 The coldest Christmas Eve on record in St. Louis. The temperature dipped to -17° below. That's also the coldest date on record here during the month of December.

1892 William Danforth opened a small feed store near the riverfront. In January, 1894, he would incorporate as the Robinson-Danforth Company. After the 1896 tornado wiped out the store, he put up a new building on Gratiot. In 1902, the name of the company was changed to Ralston-Purina.

1925 At 7 p.m., "The Voice of St. Louis Station," KMOX radio, signed on the air with a word from announcer Nate Caldwell. That was followed by a performance of the national anthem and "Hail to the Chief" by the Little Symphony Orchestra and an address by Mayor Miller. At the time, the station broadcast from studios in the Mayfair Hotel at 1070 on the dial.

1988 A Shell Oil Pipeline under the Gasconade River ruptured, sending oil pouring into what had been a crystal-clear Ozark stream. The cleanup came under fire when the workers soiled bags and coveralls were found buried along the river. The Anheuser-Busch brewery in St. Louis was shut down for a time after oil was detected in its water.

1895 Inside Bill Curtis' saloon at 14th and Morgan (now Delmar), Billy Lyons grabbed the lucky hat belonging to Lee Shelton, known as "Stack Lee." Shelton shot him. The incident became the basis for the folk song "Stagger Lee," a number one hit for Lloyd Price in 1959.

1913 The whitest Christmas on record in St. Louis. Nine-point-five inches of snow fell on Christmas Eve and Christmas Day.

1927 "The Jazz Singer," the first full-length talking picture, had its St. Louis premiere. The film at the Grand Central Theatre wowed a capacity invitation-only audience.

1941 A disaster shocked the city on Christmas. A city bus smashed into a fuel tank at Ninth and Allen in South St. Louis. The bus burst into flames, trapping the passengers inside. Most of the victims were returning from midnight mass at St. Vincent's. Ten people died and 22 were injured.

1983 The coldest Christmas Day ever recorded in St. Louis. The temperature hit -13°. Eight people had died since the cold snap had begun eight days earlier. December, 1983, would go down in the record books as the coldest in St. Louis history. The average temperature for the month was 20.8°.

1864 Major James Morgan Utz was hanged as a rebel spy. His uncle, County Judge Frederick Hyatt had gone to Washington to secure a pardon from President Lincoln. But he arrived just moments after the hanging. The Utz home still stands in Hazelwood, but is in danger of being demolished to make room for a subdivision.

1931 The first professional hockey game was played at the Arena. The St. Louis Flyers tied the Chicago Shamrocks, 1-1, in overtime. Shrimp McPherson of the Flyers scored the first goal in the Arena (he would become the equipment manager for the Blues in their first season).

1932 The Arena was the site of the only recorded professional hockey game played on natural ice. The Arena investors couldn't pay the electric bill. So, the management of the St. Louis Flyers opened the doors and windows so the ice would freeze.

1954 Osborne Earl Smith was born in Mobile, Alabama. The Cardinals acquired "The Wizard" from San Diego for Garry Templeton on February 11, 1982. Ozzie retired in 1996 after a season in all-star form. Ozzie was a 13-time gold glove winner and boasted a lifetime fielding percentage of .978. He was named to the Hall of Fame in 2002.

1972 Former President Harry S Truman died at the age of 88. Truman is the only native Missourian to become president. The former haberdasher from Independence was thrust into the office upon the death of President Roosevelt in 1945. Truman was elected in his own right in 1948.

December 27

1906 A group of citizens headed by E.G. Lewis announced they had founded the University City Trust Company. The company planned to create a "model city" in the newly-created municipality. It was charged with making plans for parks, boulevards and residential districts.

1908 The Marquis and Count de Lafayette of Paris were suing the city of St. Louis. They demanded the city turn over Carondelet Park and the site of the Southern Hotel. They traced ownership to a woman in their family who had married a St. Louis man. The suit said the money was needed to "keep up the dignity and position which the family name demands."

1926 Charles Lindbergh came to his employer with a proposal. He asked William B. Robertson for help in financing his attempt at the first solo Trans-Atlantic flight. Lindbergh had already secured the backing of aviation booster Albert Bond Lambert.

1931 The first church services were held in the "Hooverville" shantytown that covered the riverfront beneath the Free Bridge (now the MacArthur). Residents built the "Full Gospel Mission" with packing crates and lumber fished out of the river.

1983 Walther Nothies, better known as Walter Scott, disappeared from his St. Charles County home. His body was later found at the bottom of a well. Scott sang lead on the Bob Kuban hit, "The Cheater" in 1965. James Howard Williams Senior was convicted of the murder. Scott's former wife received five years in prison after a plea bargain.

December 28

1832 St. Louis University received its charter. St. Louis University was the first university west of the Mississippi. It was founded in 1818 by Bishop DuBourg as the St. Louis Academy and expanded into St. Louis College in 1820. The Jesuits took over in 1828.

1874 The town of Fenton was officially incorporated. It was a move by citizens to try to bring some order to the town, which had a rough reputation. The town was founded by William Long, an Englishman. He named the town after his mother, who he claimed was a descendant of the Earl of Fenton. According to the petition for incorporation, Fenton had "35 legal voters, 40 to 50 women and about 90 children, with fair prospects for an increase in the latter."

1957 Boston Pops Conductor Arthur Fiedler in St. Louis said rock and roll was a passing phase. He was here for a benefit with the St. Louis Symphony. Fiedler said a nation that survived the Charleston and the Black Bottom would survive rock and roll.

1972 Harry S Truman was buried in a simple ceremony in the garden outside his office at the Truman Library in Independence. One of the first arrivals for the funeral was Missouri Senator Stuart Symington. He had just flown from Washington, D.C., where he attended the funeral of his wife.

1988 Charlotte Peters died at the age of 76. Known as the "First Lady of St. Louis Television," she hosted "The Charlotte Peters Show" in the '50s and '60s.

December 29

1865 August Busch, Sr. was born. He took over the brewery upon the death of Adolphus Busch in 1913. August and his sons, Adolphus III and August, Jr., kept the business afloat dur- ing Prohibition. The brewery made yeast, corn and syrups for the baking industry. In intense pain due to illness, August Busch Sr. shot himself in 1934.

1913 The city of Richmond Heights was incorporated. At the time, the population was about 500. The city got its start because

of a wandering quail hunter. Frederick Nelson, a wealthy realtor, strayed onto part of the old Spanish land grants while hunting. He was so impressed, he promised to live there one day.

1922 Depressed over the closure of the Lemp Brewery, William Lemp Jr. killed himself at the mansion, just as his father had done back in 1904. In 1929, his brother Charles would become the third Lemp to kill themselves at the mansion. A sister, Elsa Lemp, shot herself at her Hortense Place home in 1920.

1950 The city of Ballwin was incorporated. The population stood at about 750. John Ball, who moved to the area in 1800, founded the community. In 1826, the state established a road between St. Louis and the new capitol at Jefferson City. The road ran through Ball's land. He laid out a town he called "Ballshow," but the name was later changed to Ballwin.

1958 The portion of the Mark Twain Expressway (now I-70), from Bircher to Florissant Road was opened to traffic. This stretch is now the most accident-prone in the state, and is currently being replaced. The segment between Bircher and downtown would be completed in 1961.

December 30

1904 Prince Pu-Lin, China's Imperial High Commissioner to the fair, donated the lavish Chinese pavilion to fair president David R.

Francis. The donation was made with the condition that it remain intact. Francis said he was so astonished by the gift, he wasn't sure what he would do with it. No one knows exactly what happened, but parts of the pavilion ended up in private homes in St. Louis.

1944 The minesweeper "U.S.S. Inaugural" was launched at Winslow, Washington. It earned two battle stars in the Pacific. St. Louisans Eugene Slay and Robert O'Brien brought it here as a tourist attraction. It sank during the flood of 1993 and remains in the river south of the MacArthur bridge.

1949 Famous-Barr announced that construction would begin soon on a $25 million store at Kingshighway and City Route 66. The "Southtown" Famous would be the second outlying Famous store, and the third in the St. Louis area.

1964 Some say this was the day Gaslight Square began to die. The area was shaken by the murder of Mrs. John Heller. She was shot during an attempted robbery. Area tavern  owners and nightclub operators said it was an isolated incident. But publicity over subsequent crimes and teenagers hanging around the "Go-Go" joints ended the glory days of Gaslight Square.

1974 The Blues traded fan-favorite Red Berenson to Detroit for tough-guy Phil Roberto and a draft pick. Berenson still holds the Blues record for goals in a single game. He scored six in one night in Philadelphia in 1968.

December 31

1814 *The Missouri Gazette* carried a notice of the first theatrical performance to be held in St. Louis. A group of young men had formed a "dramatic corps." They were planning to present "The School for Authors" and "Budget of Blunders" at the courthouse on January 6th.

1907 St. Louis celebrated one of the quietest New Years eve's ever. Governor Joseph Folk barred merry-making, cowbells and horn blowing. Police were strictly enforcing the order.

1996 Demolition work began on a St. Louis landmark, the 10-story International Fur Exchange Building at Fourth and Market. The neighboring Thomas Jefferson and American Zinc Buildings were also slated to come down. All three were saved, and the Fur Exchange is now the home of the Drury Inn.

1997 Millionare-adventurer Steve Fossett took off from Busch Stadium in his balloon the "Solo Spirit." Fossett's attempt at the first solo around-the-world flight ended in a Russian wheatfield a few days later. He did establish a distance record.

1999 The St. Louis area braced for the worst in case the "Y2K" bug caused havoc. Ninety percent of the city police officers were on duty, along with 24 extra firefighters and six additional ambulances. TWA cut its schedule by one-third, and hospitals brought in extra workers.

SELECTED BIBLIOGRAPHY

Amsler, Kevin. *Final Resting Place*. St. Louis: Virginia Publishing, 1997

Bartley, Mary. *St. Louis Lost*. St. Louis: Virginia Publishing, 1994

Broeg, Bob. *The 100 Greatest Moments in St. Louis Sports*. St. Louis: Missouri Historical Society Press, 2000

Burnett, Betty. *St. Louis at War*. St. Louis: Patrice Press, 1987

Charlton, James. *The Baseball Chronology*. New York: Macmillan Publishing, 1991

Chinn, Sandra Hardy. *At Your Service KMOX and Bob Hardy: Pioneers of Talk Radio*. St. Louis: Virginia Publishing, 1997

Christenson, Lawrence O, Foley, William E, Kremer, Gary R, and Winn, Kenneth H. *The Dictionary of Missouri Biography*. Columbia, MO: University of Missouri Press, 1999.

Couch, Ernie. *Missouri Trivia*. Nashville, TN: Rutledge Hill Press, 1992

Curtis, Skip. *The Route 66 Tour Book*. Lake St. Louis: Curtis Enterprises, 1994

Dahl, June Wilkerson. *A History of Kirkwood, Missouri*. Kirkwood Historical Society, 1965

Dickson, Terry. *Clayton - A History*. Von Hoffman Press, 1976

Dickson, Terry "The Story of the Arch" in *Cherry Diamond*. St. Louis: Missouri Athletic Club, 1964

Eisenbath, Mike. *The Cardinals Encyclopedia*. Philadelphia: Temple University Press, 1999

Everson, Linda. *St. Louis Rams Facts and Trivia*. South Bend, IN: E.B. Houchin, 1995

Faherty, William Barnaby, S.J. *St. Louis - A Concise History*. St. Louis: Masonry Institute of St. Louis, 1989

Fox, Tim. *Where We Live*. St. Louis: Missouri Historical Society Press, 1995

Graham, Shellee. *Tales From the Coral Court*. St. Louis: Virginia Publishing, 2000

Grant, H. Roger, Hofsommer Don L. and Overby, Osmund. *St. Louis Union Station*. St Louis: St. Louis Mercantile Library Association, 1994

Hannon, Robert E. *St. Louis: Its Neighborhoods and Neighbors, Landmarks and Milestones*. St. Louis: St. Louis Regional Commerce and Growth Association, 1986

Harris, NiNi. *Legacy Of Lions, a History of University City*. University City: University City Historical Society, 1981

Hazelwood Historical Commission. *The City of Hazelwood*. Jostens Publishing, 1992.

Hernon, Peter and Ganey, Terry. *Under The Influence, the Unauthorized Story of the Anheuser-Busch Dynasty*. New York: Simon and Schuster, 1991

Horgan, James J. *City of Flight*. St. Louis: Patrice Press, 1984

Jackson, Patti Smith. *St. Louis Arena Memories*. St. Charles: GHB Publishers, 2000

Jenson, Billie Snell in *Lousiana Purchase Exposition*. St. Louis: Missouri Historical Society, 1979

Kirschten, Ernest. *Catfish and Crystal*. Garden City, NY: Doubleday, 1960

Leptich, John and Baranowski, Dave. *This Date In St. Louis Cardinal History*. New York: Stein and Day, 1983

Linzee, David. *St. Louis Crimes and Mysteries*. St. Louis: Palmerston and Reed, 2001

Loughlin, Caroline and Anderson, Catherine. *Forest Park*. St. Louis: Junior League of St. Louis and University of Missouri Press. 1986

Magnan, William B. and Marcella C. *The Streets of St. Louis*. St. Louis: Virginia Publishing, 1996

Miksicek, Barbara; McElreath, David and Pollihan, Stephen. *In The Line of Duty*. St. Louis: Metropolitan Police Department, 1991

Nunes, Bill. *Southern Illinois An Illustrated History*. Glen Carbon, IL: Bill Nunes, 2001

Potter, McClure. *Missouri: Its Geography History and Government*. Chicago: Laidlaw Publishers, 1940

Powell, Jim. "Route 66 Timeline" in *Show Me Route 66 Magazine*, Fall 2001.

Priddy, Bob. *Across Our Wide Missouri* (3 Volumes) Independence, MO: Herald House/Independence Press, 1982

Primm, James Neal. *Lion of the Valley*. Boulder, CO: Pruett Publishing, 1981

Steele, Tim. *The Cardinals Chronology*. St. Louis: Palmerston and Reed Publishing, 2001

Scharf, John Thomas. *History of St. Louis City and County*. Philadelphia: Louis Everts and Co. 1883

Stadler, Frances Hurd. *St. Louis Day By Day*. St. Louis: Patrice Press, 1989

Stage, William. *Mound City Chronicles*. St. Louis: Hartman Publishing, 1991

Start. Clarissa. Webster Groves. City of Webster Groves, 1975

St. Louis Globe Democrat

St. Louis Post Dispatch

St. Louis Republic

St. Louis Star-Times

St. Louis Walk of Fame. St. Louis Walk of Fame - 75 Great St.Louisans. 1998

Unknown. *The History of St. Charles County, Missouri*. Reprint with Introduction By Paul Hollrah. St. Charles: Patria, 1997

Wacker, Steven P. *Lemp-the Haunting History*. St. Louis: Lemp Preservation Society, 1988

Wayman. Norbury L. *St. Louis Union Station And Its Railroads*. St. Louis: The Evelyn E. Newman Group, 1987.

Whitburn, Joel. *The Billboard Book of Top 40 Hits*. New York: Billboard Publications, 1987

Winter, William C. *The Civil War In St Louis*. St. Louis: Missouri Historical Society Press, 1994

Works Progress Administration. *Missouri The WPA Guide to the Show Me State*. Jefferson City, Missouri State Highway Department, 1941

Wright, John A. *Discovering African-American St. Louis: A Guide to Historic Sites*. St. Louis: Missouri Historical Society Press, 1994

About the Author

Joe Sonderman grew up and still lives in Hazelwood with wife Lorraine, and daughters Cathy and Kim. He began his radio career at KCFV, the Florissant Valley Community College radio station. Joe worked as DJ and music director for KHTR and KLOU (103.3 FM) before coming to Metro Networks. Since 1995, he has served as traffic reporter on KMOX (1120 AM), and, occasionally for KTVI as well. He currently manages Metro Networks operators at the new MO-DOT Traffic Information Center in Chesterfield.

Joe is a passionate Route 66 enthusiast and collector. His website "greetingsfrom66.com" is dedicated to postcards and photos from the "Mother Road." You'll often find him cruising 66 in his other pride and joy, a 1957 Chevrolet.

About the Publisher

Stellar Press is a St. Louis-based publishing firm that specializes in titles about St. Louis or written by St. Louisans. Recent titles published by Stellar Press include: *St. Louis Flavors - The Loop*, by Jim Hunstein, a Loop history and cookbook featuring recipes from Loop restaurants and merchants; *Mrs. Wistrom's ABC - What I Learned Raising Three All-Americans*, by Kathy Wistrom (mother of St. Louis Ram defensive end Grant Wistrom) in which Mrs. Wistrom instructively and humorously comments on life raising three great football players; and, *The Tooth Fairy Palace*, by St. Louis television news anchor Randi Naughton and her Daughter Allex Oelkers, a children's book about losing baby teeth which also raises funds for the St. Louis Children's Hospital.

Stellar Press also manages the titles published under the imprint of Palmerston & Reed Publishing where readers can find titles such as: *Infamous St. Louis Crimes & Mysteries* by David Linzee; *How 'Bout Them Rams - The Guide To Rams Football History* by Jim Hunstein; *The Cardinals Chronology* by Tim Steele; and, *Pushcarts & Stalls - The Soulard Market History Cookbook* by Suzanne Corbett.

In addition to its publishing activities, Stellar Press also owns and operates **BooksOnStLouis.com**, an on-line bookstore which sells Stellar Press titles and many other titles about St. Louis or authored by St. Louisans.

Stellar Press

BooksOnStLouis.com

Contact us at:
634 North Grand Boulevard, Suite 10C
St. Louis, Missouri 63103
stellarpress@swbell.net
Telephone or Fax: 877-572-8835 (toll free)
www.StellarPress.com

ORDER YOUR COPY OF THESE TITLES FROM STELLAR PRESS

Title	Price	Quantity	Total
St. Louis 365 by **Joe Sonderman** - Intriguing events from each day of the year in St. Louis history.	$17.95		
Infamous St. Louis Crimes & Mysteries by **David Linzee** - The true story behind some of St. Louis most notorious crimes and mysterious events.	$19.95		
St. Louis Flavors - The Loop by **Jim Hunstein** - A history of the development of the Delmar Loop and recipes from Loop restaurants and merchants.	$16.95		
Mrs. Wistrom's ABCs by **Kathy Sasse Wistrom** - How Kathy and Ron Wistrom raised three All-American football players, including St. Louis Ram Grant Wistrom.	$16.95		
How 'Bout Them Rams by **Jim Hunstein** - The fan's guide to the history of Rams football.	$19.95		
Completed order form, including shipping information and send with check, money order, or provide credit card information below, to: **STELLAR PRESS** 634 N. GRAND BLVD., STE. 10-C ST. LOUIS, MO 63103	**Sub-total Amount of Order**		
	Tax (If Missouri Resident) at 7.616 %		
	Shipping & Handling ($6 first book; $2 each additional)		
	TOTAL AMOUNT DUE		

Credit Card Type: Visa   MC   AmEx

Card Number: _____

Exp. Date: _____   Name on Card: _____

Signature: _____

Ship To: _____

Street: _____

City: _____ St: ____ Zip: _____